Competitive Leadership

Twelve Principles
for Success

Competitive Leadership

Twelve Principles for Success

BRIAN BILLICK

JAMES A. PETERSON, PH.D.

TRIUMPH
BOOKS
CHICAGO

This book is available in quantity at special discounts for your group or organization. For further information, contact:

Triumph Books
601 South LaSalle Street
Suite 500
Chicago, Illinois 60605
(312) 939-3330
Fax (312) 663-3557

Printed in the United States of America

ISBN 1-892049-50-3

Interior design by Patricia Frey

Selections from *The Ten Commandments of Goal Setting*, copyright © 1999 GoalsGuy Learning Systems, Inc., used with permission on pp. 80–81 of this book.

To my mother, Mildred, and my father, Donald, from whom all blessings flowed.
—B. B.

To Wesley F. "Bo" Gill and John T. Sullivan, two close friends and colleagues who passed away this year. Your friendship inspired me to be a better person.
—J. P.

contents

foreword

During the 2000–2001 NFL playoffs, it came to light that Brian Billick's Super Bowl practice schedule had been in place since training camp. I never understood why his meticulous preparation was mistaken for overconfidence. Not too many coaches find themselves *suddenly* preparing for the Super Bowl in January. Those that get there planned for it. Super Bowls, like gourmet meals, don't just happen.

Brian Billick didn't merely win a Super Bowl in his second season as a head coach; he *led* his Ravens to the championship. He earned the respect of his players and willed them to believe they were good enough to win. Consequently, they became a reflection of their leader: passionate, relentless, and supremely confident. The man has a presence: you can't miss that six-foot, five-inch frame on the field. The man can communicate. As early as training camp last year, he invoked the famous "greed is good" speech from the movie *Wall Street* in relating to and motivating players, many of whom already were making an ungodly amount of money. And no one is immune from his barbs. Keenly aware of the media's portrayal of him, he opened his remarks the day after winning the Super Bowl by announcing, "If you thought I was arrogant before, whoa . . . Wait until you get a load of me now." He's about as subtle as a Ray Lewis hit. You see how the Ravens take on their head coach's personality.

Brian is considered a protégé of Hall of Fame coach and three-time Super Bowl champion Bill Walsh. But he's bringing the Walsh philosophy, and coaching in general, into the 21st century. Rather than crack a whip, he wields a computer pointer. Instead of talking just *X*'s and *O*'s, he discusses schematics and parameters. The chalkboard is being replaced by weekly game-plan e-mails. One day he hopes to substitute the voluminous playbook for a CD-Rom. He even envisions virtual reality training for quarterbacks or linebackers like the military uses flight simulators for pilots. He is not doing all this just because he enjoys computers and technology. Brian has figured out how information and planning integrate with leadership.

I've known Brian since he broke into the NFL from the collegiate ranks in 1992. I've been in his team meetings and felt the energy he evoked while breaking down a blitz or explaining why community service was mandatory. I've watched numerous practices and listened in when he was miked for sound. Even when he was a position coach and coordinator, I'd never observed an assistant control the tempo of practice with the success and authority that he did. I've sat in his office the day before games (as long as I didn't run over into his precious and rejuvenating nap time) and been taught why the x receiver running a skinny post could exploit some form of man-free or three-deep coverage. (However, if the defense rolled its coverage to the weak side, there would be a chance of getting a first down if the z receiver ran a 5 route.) I've secretly worried he'd make me take one of his night-before-the-game quizzes to make sure I really understood . . . But I did learn; he took the time to teach me.

He's so loquacious that some of his players have said in jest that they need to check *Webster's* after getting home from practice. I've asked him to pontificate on subjects ranging from "Why hasn't your team scored an offensive touchdown in five games?" to "How does a middle class white guy from Redlands, California relate to a young black superstar who hails from the swamps of Florida?"

Brian's immediate answer to this question was . . . silence. For as successful a strategist as he is, as compelling a motivator, as riveting a speaker, above all, this 21st-century coach is a thinker. He has pondered long and hard about the delicate issue of how to relate to players—"men," he calls them, and he treats them as such. That is one reason why he has imposed no curfew during his tenure as head coach—he trusts and expects players to behave a certain way and to be accountable for their actions. But he remains cognizant that his players may have a different world view than he does, and he strives to keep that perspective. He appears to have struck a balance between not being too judgmental and maintaining a reasonable set of rules. It's a philosophy that works in a locker room or a boardroom.

It's ironic that Brian's name is often misspelled as "Brain" Billick, since he breaks the stereotype of the football coach who has complete tunnel vision toward his job. (There's a famous story of the legendary Don Shula being introduced to "Don Johnson from *Miami Vice*" and Shula complimenting him about the security in a particular Miami neighborhood.) Brian, on the other hand, is conversant on nearly any topic, but says he has no time for hobbies, that all his free time is devoted to his family. When he mentioned he was writing a book, I wondered how he had the time. But it was his forethought that led him to start collecting ideas for this book years ago, not as a reaction to a championship.

Competitive Leadership is not just the diary of a season but rather the merger of several dynamic concepts that make his message relevant beyond sports: look at it as brawn meets brain, organization meets passion, and Nietzsche finally meets Nitschke.

But there's something you need to know about the author before you delve into *Competitive Leadership*. Brian Billick is not perfect. He cannot cook.

However, his wife Kim is as adept in the kitchen as Brian is in a game-plan session; so the husband took hundreds of his wife's recipes and inputted them into a laptop computer for easier access in the kitchen. Yes, there is a computer in the Billick kitchen. Gourmet meals, like Super Bowls, don't just happen.

—Andrea Kremer
ESPN Field Correspondent
Los Angeles
March 2001

preface

No one likes to start a book with a disclaimer, but in this instance, I feel that one is appropriate. This book is not a chronology about the incredible sequence of events that culminated in the Baltimore Ravens winning the world championship following the 2000 season. Frankly, more competent writers exist who could provide a far more entertaining perspective on those circumstances than I could. Nor is this publication a biography of my coaching career up to and through the heady days of the 2001 Super Bowl. (This book may have a limited enough appeal as it is.)

Rather, this book is about leadership—a topic that I have been interested in for as long as I can remember. Throughout my professional career, it is the single topic that has intrigued me most. As such, I have attempted to study the behavior, thought processes, and insights of successful individuals in all walks of life, including business people, educators, military leaders, politicians, and, of course, coaches . . . especially coaches. If a book has been published about a coach, I own it—particularly if it was written *by* a coach.

Most coaches are individuals who, when they were younger, were the ones who at the end of the contest, with the game on the line, said, "Give me the ball." Unfortunately, like myself, most of these would-be coaches did not have the physical skills to play at a professional level. Nevertheless, we were willing to step to the forefront and say, "Follow me." We were the ones who got the game together, chose up sides, and set the rules. Truth be known, it was usually our ball to begin with.

The dictionary defines "to lead" as: to guide in direction, course, action, or opinion (i.e., the intrinsic responsibilities of coaches at all competitive levels). It is this behavioral aspect that has intrigued me and has captivated my interest the most over the years. It is also the attribute that people are ultimately most interested in and are drawn to whenever the concept of success is discussed.

I have wanted to be a coach for most of my adult life. I can't really tell you exactly why I love this game and precisely why I enjoy coaching so much, but I do. When I first got into coaching, a veteran coach told me, "If you can do without this profession, do so. You and your family will be much happier." Obviously, I can't do without it because I can't imagine doing anything else professionally.

I actually began this book two years before I had the opportunity to become the head coach of the Baltimore Ravens. In 1997, the legendary coach Bill Walsh asked me to collaborate with him on a book about the process of running a professional football team. During the previous ten years, I had worked under Denny Green as an assistant coach both at Stanford University and with the Minnesota Vikings. Denny had worked with Bill and had gone on to apply his personal touches to Bill's "system" very successfully as a head coach.

No book of this detail or magnitude had ever been written about developing and operating a successful NFL team, and I was honored to be asked to be a part of it. Bill had given me my first real opportunity to work in the NFL as his assistant director of public relations with the 49ers—a position I found very appealing because of the opportunity to work with Bill and the chance to apply my formal education in journalism to a field that I loved.

As the book, titled *Finding the Winning Edge,* came together, I found the process exhilarating, as well as enlightening. I had been adhering to and advocating many of the basic principles that we were outlining in the book, having already put them into practical application with Denny Green both at Stanford and in the NFL. Having to explain these principles clearly and concisely in print enabled me to view them with even greater clarity and definition and further verified the essential nature of these concepts as integral components of successful leadership.

About this time, I decided to begin documenting my observations on the events attendant to what I hoped would be my ascension to a head coaching position in the NFL. I undertook this endeavor for the clarity and definition of the principles and elements involved in the process (similar to what had occurred when I was helping to write *Finding the Winning Edge*), rather than some precognition of the success that I would be afforded as the head coach of the world champion Baltimore Ravens.

When positive things are written about me, and even my harshest critics have had to at least occasionally pen some positive statements (particularly on a Super Bowl–winning year), it is their comments about my ability to lead that hearten me the most. My personal and professional interest in and admiration for the dynamics of successful leadership continues unabated to this day.

The renowned novelist James A. Michener once wrote, "It is the moral obligation of every individual to put themselves through the process of chronicling their existence, regardless of the perceived value of their lives." I personally know this to be true because I have benefited greatly from my studies and reading of those who have taken the time to follow "the process" and present their observations and opinions. Moreover, I have found that in attempting to live up to Michener's "moral obligation," at least partially by writing this book, I have gained immeasurably by putting myself through the simplicity of the process.

The observations and concepts presented in this book are not intended to be perceived as either right or wrong. They simply are my insights into what constitutes the essence of successful leadership. Use them as you will. If you find them helpful, then writing this book will have been well worth the time and effort involved.

acknowledgments

To try and give proper attribution in this book for every idea, phrase, and concept that has been "borrowed" from some other source would be impossible. We are nothing if not an amalgam of the collective experiences of those we have worked with and learned from. I can honestly say that I have never worked with a single coach from whom I did not learn at least one thing. I would never begin to submit the principles and ideas presented in this work as being original. Instead, they are a collection of concepts and observations that I have used in a practical application as I progressed through my career. The only way I know to repay those who have aided me in my development as a coach and as a person is to do a good job with the responsibilities given to me and to help those I'm in a position to help.

—B. B.

A number of individuals have helped make this book possible. The efforts of Rachel Adams, Shannon Koprowski, and Doug Wenger contributed immensely in this regard. Finally, the guidance and assistance of everyone at Triumph Books were invaluable—particularly, Mitch Rogatz, publisher; Blythe Smith, managing editor; Kris Anstrats, production manager; Patricia Frey, designer; and Tom Bast, editorial director.

—J. P.

chapter 1

UNDERSTANDING THE ESSENCE OF LEADERSHIP

"Leadership: The art of getting someone else to do something you want done because he wants to do it."

—Dwight D. Eisenhower
34th president of the United States

At one time, leadership was considered simply a position of authority. Over time, that viewpoint has changed considerably. The new paradigm of leadership implies that leadership involves a position of responsibility—responsibility for setting the vision of an organization; responsibility for putting into place a process whereby the vision can be achieved; responsibility for motivating and inspiring others in the pursuit of greater goals than they themselves might have believed possible; responsibility for establishing a value system and an institutional culture that reflects the organization's vision and the strategic plan for achieving that vision; and finally, responsibility for providing both momentum and urgency for achieving the organization's goals.

What, then, is a precise definition of the term "leadership"? In reality, no irrefutable definition of leadership exists, despite the fact that countless volumes have been written on the topic. Frankly, there are almost as many definitions put forth concerning the subject as there are individuals willing to share their opinion on the matter.

Personally, my professional experiences and observations have led me to believe that leadership might best be defined as the ability to influence the behavior and actions of others to achieve an intended purpose. As such, being a successful leader requires the presence of several specific traits and qualities (many of which are discussed in subsequent chapters of this book).

For those individuals looking to better understand the concept of leadership, however, a dilemma arises: no single, itemized recipe for leadership exists. Not only do leaders come in a variety of sizes, genders, ethnicities, personalities, and backgrounds, the mix of the traits and qualities required to lead successfully in a given situation tends to vary from situation to situation and individual to individual.

For a while, the emergence of "quantitative managerialism" (an approach that mostly involved the reduction of all tasks to bureaucratic routine) seemed to be the norm for the appropriate focus of leadership. "Quantitative managerialism" is based on the belief (however valid or erroneous) that quantifiable routines have the capacity to be productive with interchangeable managerial parts. The fundamental premise of this approach is that structured leadership is not needed, just middle management's ability to understand the basic process.

Not surprisingly, however, the search for "leaders" remains an ongoing and somewhat ambiguous process. This search is usually conducted by people who, while they can't tell you exactly what leadership is, "know it when they see it."

In professional football, for example, this search is conducted by those general managers and team owners who believe that there is a single process, scheme, or system that will be successful (i.e., produce the desired number of wins annually), regardless of the coaches or players needed to implement a successful program. Many teams look only to "steal" a coach away from a proven system in the ill-grounded hope that he can bring that system with him and transform a losing organization into a winning one. Unfortunately, many teams look more at a coveted system than they do the individual. Hence, they are doomed to repeat the process through failure after failure.

In reality, no definitive answer exists as to which managerial structure offers an NFL team the best chance of being successful. However, whatever form the paradigm takes, there is one constant that must be in place. At the center of the decision-making process, there must be a primary figure who has extensive knowledge of and expertise in the game. The capabilities of that person will be the measuring stick of the organization. That individual's history of experience, having a basic intellect, and being able to take a proactive, anticipatory approach that enables that person to relate to any point of reference within the organization will be the touchstone for top management and the organization as a whole.

In my opinion, sound leadership is exhibited in three fundamental ways: mentally, emotionally, and physically. It is important to note that each must be adhered to in appropriate measure in order to maintain the overall balance that leadership requires.

First, in order to be a leader you must have a basic knowledge of the environment in which you are expected to lead. In his book, *Why We Win*, Billy Packer presents the results of his interviews with a variety of very successful coaches, and asks them all the same questions. It is fascinating to see the similar mind-set of people with varying backgrounds, ranging from Bob Knight to Joe Gibbs to Tommy Lasorda to Pat Summitt. Each in their own way isolated a fundamental knowledge of their profession as being at the core of their abilities to lead. None, however, intimated that they alone had some intuitive ability or knowledge that separated them from their peers.

Too many individuals mistakenly believe that successful coaches possess fundamental knowledge that provides them with a level of intellectual superiority that affords them the ability to instantly assess a predicament, and out of some sheer burst of individual brilliance formulate the right course of action in every situation. This type of genius may indeed exist, but I have never seen it. What I have witnessed firsthand are individuals like Tom Landry, Bill Walsh, Denny Green, Dan Reeves, and others, who possess a fundamental understanding of their profession after years of study and countless experiences with the painful process of trial and error. Though they may not have individually always had the right answer to every dilemma, they did know how to go about finding the appropriate solution to a particular problem.

Possessing the essential mental attributes for a leadership role may collectively involve something as simple as knowing enough to ask the right questions. As someone once observed, "While you go about learning the tricks of the trade, don't forget to learn the trade." This fundamental knowledge leads to the "synergy" that Winston Churchill spoke of when he observed: "The genius of a great leader consists in the constant harmony of holding a variety of great purposes in mind all at once."

Next, you must have a passion for the work you do. All leaders have passion for their calling in life. There's a story told of Ray Kroc, the founder of McDonald's, who one day was traveling in his car visiting some of his restaurants, one of his common habits. On this occasion, he happened to drive through the parking lot of one specific restaurant. He noticed there were papers strewn and blowing up against the fence that surrounded the restaurant. He called the office to find out who the manager of this particular restaurant was and the telephone number.

Following that, he phoned the restaurant and invited the manager to join him in the parking lot to clean up the papers. What a picture: both the manager of the restaurant and the founder of McDonald's, down on their hands and knees—Ray Kroc in his suit—cleaning up trash. Did this story have impact? You bet it did, because it was retold many times throughout the restaurant industry. Ray Kroc's passion for cleanliness and his passion for providing customers with a clean environment was lived out in this example.

As a leader, your goals and aspirations must be strong enough to sustain you through the toughest of times. And trust me, if your goals are set high enough and your aspirations are worthy enough, there will be tough times. The source of that passion can be as varied as the personalities of the individuals involved. The NFL, for example, has 32 head football coaches, each with a very diverse set of individual attributes and personal characteristics. Yet, to a man, each possesses a tremendous passion for what he does. Whether it's the cool, intellectual demeanor of a Tony Dungy or the squinty-eyed, intense glare of a Jon Gruden, the common denominator is their passion for the game.

"Greed is good," declared the corporate raider Gordon Gekko in the movie *Wall Street*. Greed clarifies, crystallizes, and purifies. Greed heightens the senses and is the most consistent of emotions. For me, greed is a euphemism for passion. There may be a better term for this trait that sounds less self-serving, but I don't know what it would be. It is left to the individual to judge the worthiness or moral justification of the source of that passion. Personally, I trust greed.

When I came to the Baltimore Ravens in 1999, there were two major ingredients missing from the team: passion and accountability. It is the very first thing I addressed as their new head coach. In professional sports, it is very easy to become what I term "pro-ized"—i.e., to not let your emotions show in order to demonstrate that you are always in control and that you are above the emotion of the moment. Certainly, as a coach, I can not let my emotion override my judgment. Accordingly, one of the basic tasks that you, as a leader, have is to develop a balance between the two factors that allow you to execute your responsibilities, all the while maintaining the vital elements of both passion and judgment. However, the day passion leaves the equation in my job is the day I seek other challenges.

The point to keep in mind is that anything worth doing is seldom achieved without passion. As our 26th president, Theodore Roosevelt, once noted: "Far and away, the best prize that life offers is the chance to work hard at work worth doing." Passion is the lubricant of success.

Finally, you must have a level of physical energy that will not only sustain you through your endeavors, but will also set the pace for those around you as well. That energy must above all else be constant. After my first year as a head coach in the NFL, the question I was most frequently asked was, "What was the biggest thing that surprised you about the job that you did not know going in?" The answer, for me, was simple. I had prepared my entire professional life for the rigors of being a head NFL coach. I came into this job understanding and prepared for the long hours, the constant scrutiny, and the never-ending pressures associated with this high-profile position. What I did not expect, however, was how much my emotional and physical energy level would dictate the mood of those around me. This unforeseen circumstance was true not only of the players and coaches, but also of the entire organization, ownership, media, and fans.

Master military strategist Karl Von Clousewitz stated in his book, *On War*, "The personal physical exertion of leaders must not be overlooked. It is as important as any strategy or tactic." If you are not prepared to exhibit a constant level of energy, those around you will respond in kind. Sound leadership cannot be sustained on will alone. Accordingly, everyone in a leadership position should have a consistent conditioning routine to maintain their physical and emotional health. In the Minneapolis Airport there is an advertisement promoting an exercise club that shows an executive going through a workout with a quote, "I don't have the time *not* to work out."

There are countless times when an individual can find a thousand reasons during the course of a day to not take the time to work out. In the short term that may seem to be a reasonable option in your opinion. Ultimately, however, the physical demands imposed by the responsibilities of leadership will take their toll, and your physical and emotional strength may betray you when it counts the most. Winston Churchill had a daily routine of taking a two-hour nap. Many attributed this to age and fatigue. In truth, it was a masterful step that allowed Churchill to keep a consistent schedule of cramming 14 to 16 hours of quality work into a single day. In the process, his support staff used to have to work in shifts to keep up with England's renowned former world leader.

One meaningful benefit of leaders achieving an enhanced level of physical conditioning is that it allows you to better monitor the stamina of your associates. If you are tired or fatigued, there is a reasonable chance that your troops are also. Maybe you both need a break. In years past, the mentality in pro football was that a team will outwork and out-tough its opponents. This concept has proven to be naïve. In the NFL, everyone works hard and is tough. To think otherwise is to set yourself up for defeat. What has evolved in the league is the realization that teams should focus on the concept of working more intelligently in order to get their players to the game healthy and fresh. This process must be monitored and gauged by leadership, which itself must also be healthy and fresh for battle.

One aspect of the position that did not surprise me was the need for achieving and sustaining a high level of performance in my various leadership responsibilities. In that regard, philosophically, I believe that "perfect" can sometimes be the antithesis of "good." As such, the best way to become a skillful leader—whether as a coach, an executive, a politician, or whatever—is not to set out to become "perfect," but rather to aim to be effective *all of the time.*

Perhaps no one better exemplifies this philosophy than John Wooden, the great UCLA basketball coach, who set a standard for success in sports that will never be matched. Wooden's record of winning 10 national championships, (7 consecutively), 88 consecutive victories, and four perfect seasons defines the word "dynasty" that so many people want desperately to apply to teams today. Wooden's career and writings have been a major source of inspiration to me and to so many others. In his masterful tapestry on life and leadership, *Pyramid of Success*, it is interesting to me that the most successful of all coaches did not list "winning," "championships," or "success" at the top of the pyramid. Instead, he used the term "competitive greatness." That term is brilliant in its simplicity, yet limitless in its interpretation. It encompasses all of the elements of winning and success, but transcends those terms in a more personal way that embodies all that we strive to achieve on our way to self-actualization.

Applying the specific concepts of leadership to this theme is the underlying principle of an approach to influencing the behavior and actions of others I have termed "competitive leadership." As such, the primary focus of this book is to present a detailed overview of the traits and qualities I believe are essential to competitive leadership. It is important to note that while skillful leaders tend to possess most (if not all) of these attributes, the absence of merely one of these can compromise a person's efforts to be an effective leader. As a leader, you cannot afford to disregard any of the attributes that constitute the essence of leadership.

chapter 2

BE VALUES-ORIENTED

*"Try not to become a man of success,
but rather to become a man of value."*

—Albert Einstein
Nobel Prize winner in 1922

If you were to read through the *Harvard Business Review* for the past 10 years, you would find dozens of articles extolling the merits of value-driven leadership. One of the major points that is emphasized in these articles is the fact that skillful leadership involves a moral dimension.

This moral dimension is anchored by the presence of certain internalized traits. The Center for Creative Leadership in Greensboro, North Carolina, states that the highest predictor of success in an organization is leadership that functions with integrity and honesty. Three other core traits that are frequently attributed to sound leadership are trustworthiness, loyalty, and pride.

While no two leaders are exactly the same, one similarity that is almost universally found in most leaders is the presence of ethically grounded principles. In other words, a major reason some leaders are more effective than others is because of who they are as people. All other factors being equal, principle-centered leaders are more capable of inspiring confidence and rallying others to achieve a common purpose.

In that regard, how you lead and how effective you will be in the long run in your leadership efforts will ultimately be affected by whether your words and actions reflect a strong, personal commitment to such values as integrity, trustworthiness, honesty, loyalty, and pride. If they do, your efforts will be accorded a sense of legitimacy and moral authority that emanate from your values. These core traits constitute what being professional is all about.

The phrase "I am a professional" is a very popular one in today's society. Whether it refers to an attorney or a hooker, people use it to give legitimacy to their position regardless of the stature they may hold or deserve. It is a way of demanding that they be treated with a level of respect that the previously mentioned core traits signify.

I believe that it's very important for an organization to identify what being a professional is. In my opinion, being a professional involves three main components. First, being a professional means having respect for the full scope of each other's responsibilities. Obviously, it's important for a coach to understand the physical, mental, and emotional stresses and demands that his players face. Likewise, players should be sensitive to the pressures and obligations that a coach works under. They must appreciate the fact that even though a decision might have an adverse effect on them individually, the scope of a head coach's responsibilities dictates that he keeps the greater good of the team as his paramount concern.

A coach should also be aware of the responsibilities and pressures on the media. They have a job to do and face pressures that accompany their job. Likewise, as a coach, you would hope that the press would appreciate that answering their questions may not be your highest priority at a particular moment in time. For example, if a member of the media is digging around trying to find out what free agents the Ravens might be interested in signing, I have to appreciate the fact that they have their own valid reason (e.g., competition with other media sources), even though I might want to keep that a secret for equally valid—yet far different—reasons.

Understanding and appreciating the scope of the responsibilities of others reflects another major component of being a professional: not putting others at risk. If you let your vested self-interest or personal concerns override your obligations to your team or organization, you are putting them, and ultimately yourself, at risk. If I have a player who arbitrarily decides to take a day off because he is tired, not only is he not preparing to the utmost, but he will force someone else to take his reps. Chances are that person is just as tired or fatigued, but is now compelled to extend himself physically beyond the limits of what might otherwise be safe.

Finally, being a professional involves the ability to recognize that team and individual goals must be interactive. In other words, what's good for the individual must also be good for the team by the same token, what's good for the team must also be good for the individual.

It has been said that physical courage is courage in the face of personal danger, while moral courage is courage of responsibility to others or a purpose. In that regard, the attributes of integrity, trustworthiness, honesty, loyalty, and pride are the core ingredients of that moral courage that will define you as a professional.

Some people mistakenly believe that leadership and the power that accompanies an organizational position are synonymous. In fact, an individual can occupy a position of power and not have the respect of those directly affected by that power. Respect is the essential linchpin of authority and leadership that is perceived to be legitimate.

One of my favorite phrases is, "Employees do not want a motto, they want a model." They want an individual whose value-orientation commands a sense of respect and regard. As a leader, you should be that model. An examination of several of the basic core values that most skillful leaders possess can lead to a better understanding of the basis for such respect and can define you as a professional. Hall of Fame coach John Wooden perhaps best articulated the need to have core values when he said, "Be more concerned with your character than your reputation. Your character is what you really are, while your reputation is merely what others think you are."

INTEGRITY

Integrity can be defined as having an unwavering adherence to your moral and ethical principles. You keep your word and your agreements. If you have integrity, you know what you stand for, and you live by the standards you set. You say what needs to be said, not simply what people want to hear. Among the more common synonyms for integrity are virtue, honor, and morality. More simply stated, leaders with integrity are strongly committed to doing what they know is right. Not surprisingly, a leader with integrity is trusted.

A common slang term that is used a great deal by my players is "my bad." It is their quick and direct way of saying, "I am sorry; I made a mistake." On NFL teams that have integrity, players and coaches are compelled to take personal responsibility for a mistake they might have made in order to not let blame fall elsewhere. Such accountability is a sign of respect. It is a reflection of the team's integrity when individuals take responsibility for their actions.

TRUSTWORTHINESS

*"To be trusted is a greater compliment
than to be loved."*

—George MacDonald
Scottish clergyman and poet

Individuals want leaders that they can trust . . . people in whom they can believe. Trust involves affirmative answers to such basic questions as, "Can I count on you?" "Will you keep your commitments?" "Can you hold sensitive information in confidence?" etc. Skillful leaders inspire trust in their followers. They realize that if they don't do what they say they will do, the trust that other people have in them will gradually diminish. Furthermore, once these individuals decide that they can't trust them, they will deal with them as little as possible.

Competent leaders are also aware that trust is a two-way street. Individuals want leaders who trust them. They prefer leaders who will listen to them—to their explanations and to their suggestions. They want leaders who will take them at their word.

Finally, effective leaders spend the necessary time and energy to establish a trusting atmosphere. A number of steps can be undertaken in this regard. For example, individuals should lead by encouragement—not criticism, fear, or blame. Skillful leaders create a relationship characterized by openness with those with whom they interact. Value-oriented leaders tell the truth at all times (i.e., they avoid lying under any circumstances).

Earlier in the book, I discussed my desire to instill a sense of accountability among my players and coaches. Obviously, trust is at the core of that accountability. By doing away with the time-honored "bed check," a traditional practice among most professional-level sports teams, I indicated to my players that I trusted them. I told them that as men, I would trust them to police themselves with regard to the curfews that exist during training camp and the night before games. As long as they acted like men, I would treat them like men. This small act created a very clear line of demarcation that could be used as the litmus test for the trust I wanted to establish between us.

The rationale for building a high-trust environment is both compelling and straightforward. A trusting atmosphere helps make every contact less constrained, less stressful, and more productive. It facilitates a spirit of cooperation. It elevates the basic level of cordiality and satisfaction among all those involved. It inspires people to perform at their maximum level.

HONESTY

"Honesty is the cornerstone of character. The honest man or woman seeks not merely to avoid criminal or illegal acts, but to be scrupulously fair, upright, fearless in both action and expression. Honesty pays dividends both in dollars and in piece of mind."

—B. C. Forbes
founder, *Forbes* Magazine

As a leader, you have a fundamental responsibility to be both truthful and law-abiding. Honesty, however, involves more than adhering to laws and not telling lies. You should avoid intentionally parsing your words and quibbling. Furthermore, not only should you be an individual whose words and behavior are free from deceit, fraud, and dishonesty, you must be intellectually honest. When you evaluate information (i.e., ideas, feedback, etc.), you should keep an open mind and resist compromising your judgment with your own personal biases. Even when you think you are sure that you know the answer, you should thoughtfully consider the input of others.

Similar to trust, honesty should also be a two-way street. Not only should you be honest with other people, you should expect the individuals with whom you interact to be totally honest also. You should neither foster nor condone unethical behavior. Keep in mind that if you fail to respond to or overlook a dishonest act, you are implicitly approving it.

On the other hand, honesty in the workplace can be a very sensitive issue. For example, during the offseason after winning the Super Bowl, we had to make a fundamental decision about the direction we wanted to go with our quarterback position. Trent Dilfer had done a masterful job of playing within himself and the structure of the team that we had created and had played a major role in the Ravens' championship run. Indeed, he helped orchestrate an 11-1 record as our starter.

At face value, it would seem foolish for us to contemplate a change at that position. The old adage of "if it ain't broke, don't fix it" has its merit. However, we made an organizational decision that we needed more dynamic play at the quarterback position and that free agents would be available that would enable us to improve at this critical position. Subsequently, the unexpected availability of Elvis Grbac presented an exciting opportunity to validate that decision, and we were thrilled to be able to acquire his services. That issue aside, dealing with the right way to let Trent go became a major concern for me.

Trent Dilfer deserved to be treated in as direct and honest a way as was possible. He was a valued member of the Ravens during our championship season. Furthermore, he is as quality an individual as I have ever been around. Had we not been able to attract the services of Elvis or Brad Johnson (the former Washington Redskin quarterback), we had every intention of bringing Trent back. Hence, we were dealing with the tenuous balance of wanting to replace someone, yet at the same time leaving the door open for his return.

To have been brutally honest in this situation just for the sake of directness would have been disrespectful to Trent and may have adversely effected the Ravens' chances of getting him to come back. To string Trent and his agent along in negotiations in order to slow-play the possibility that we may have indeed ultimately needed him to come back would have been unethical. No matter how you frame and present bad news, it is sometimes impossible to do it in a way that takes the sting out of the message and that eventually doesn't create ill will. If you tell a close friend his wife is cheating on him, regardless of the truth, he will never forgive you for it. I have never heard anyone say, "Well, they fired me, but they did it really well." Honesty, like beauty, may be in the eye of the beholder.

LOYALTY

*"Loyalty cannot be blueprinted. It cannot be produced
on an assembly line. In fact, it cannot be
manufactured at all, for its origin is the human
heart—the center of self-respect and human dignity. It
is a force which leaps into being only
when conditions are exactly right for it—
and it is a force very sensitive to betrayal."*

—Maurice R. Franks
associate professor, Southern University Law Center

At the center of the foundation of John Wooden's *Pyramid of
Success* is loyalty. Loyalty to yourself, your most firmly ingrained
principles, and your strongest convictions enhances your efforts to reach your true potential. As Brian Biro states in his
book, *Beyond Success*, "Loyalty gives us the inspiration and
passion to reach for the best in us, even during the most difficult of time."

Being loyal involves being a person who refuses to compromise your values for personal advantage. As such, loyalty can
have a very positive impact on your behavior. For example, it
can help you avoid being an individual who procrastinates or
gives in to weakness. In turn, it can help you become a "can-
do" rather than a "make-do" person.

For example, when the Ravens were in the throes of a three-
game losing streak in the middle of the 2000 season that was
accompanied by a scoring drought of no touchdowns over a
five-game span, we were standing at the edge of the abyss and
everyone knew it. It would prove to be the ultimate test of
loyalty to hold off the "negative" forces that might make individuals on this team begin to point a finger at one another.

The first, and strongest, of these "negative" forces involves
vested self-interest. It is one of the most common and often-
repeated scenes in sports: the star athlete who, in the midst of
a critical loss, jumps on the soap box of self-proclaimed accountability and starts to assess blame on his fellow players
and coaches alike. This self-appointed "savior" will tell you he
is simply trying to motivate his team. In fact, all he is doing is

trying to insure that fans and media alike know he is not the one to blame and that he alone will get this thing straightened out. Bill Walsh was an expert at guarding against this type of selfish behavior by continually educating his players against what he called the "your problem, my solution" mentality.

As a coach, you are always looking for opportunities to teach your team certain lessons. Fortunately for us, and unfortunately for others, there were examples of educational opportunities we could draw from on almost a weekly basis. This factor proved to be a catalyst for the Ravens to not become like so many other teams and take the easy way out by giving in to the impulse to momentarily release tension by lashing out at each other. I did not have to "trick" my players with some effort at pseudo-psychology. Simply discussing with them specific examples of how poorly this approach had worked with other teams made it graphically clear it was not the answer to our problems. Loyalty to our structure, our goals, and each other would sustain us through this tough time. Indeed, one prominent national sports columnist told me, "Of all the things your team accomplished this year, not turning on each other during the difficult stretch was the most impressive. Pro teams just don't do that."

As John Wooden surmised in his celebrated *Pyramid of Success*, "I don't see how anyone can truly make the most of his or her abilities without expressing loyalty at all times to the people, institutions, and principles that are important in one's life." Not surprisingly, when the great teams in life are examined— in sports, business, the military, politics, education, etc., it is abundantly clear that loyalty can be an exceptional catalyst for inspired performance.

Skillful leaders not only inspire genuine loyalty toward themselves, but also extend a demonstrable level of loyalty toward those who follow them. The point to keep in mind is that if you want people to be loyal to you, you must be loyal to them, too. Such loyalty will be reflected in your support (or nonsupport) of them.

Within the workplace, loyalty from leadership sends a very positive message to employees. It enhances the employees' feelings of importance. It facilitates the employees' sense of self-worth. In turn, such loyalty tends to stimulate the employees' own feelings of loyalty to leadership and the organization—feelings that can sharply increase employees' desire to perform well and adapt to their individual circumstances.

An excellent example of this situation involved Marvin Lewis, the Ravens' outstanding defensive coordinator. During the 2000 season, Marvin was constantly facing rumors about the likelihood that he would become a head coach at the conclusion of the season. Professional football can be a very exciting yet distracting environment in which to work. The NFL has very strict rules about tampering that prevent teams from contacting prospective coaches while their current teams are still in season. Like most coaches I have known over the years, Marvin would want to be very proactive about his chances to become a head coach. On the other hand, he was very limited with regard to what he could actually do to improve the likelihood of this occurring. I had been through this particular experience just two seasons earlier when I served as the offensive coordinator for the Minnesota Vikings. Like Marvin, because I was in charge of a group of players that would eventually break the NFL's all-time scoring record (in my case, the offensive mark), I garnered a great deal of attention about my suitability for several potential head coaching jobs.

Naturally, I wanted to be as helpful to Marvin as I could. To this end, I had the Ravens' television production crew put a tape together of Marvin that could be sent to any team that was looking for a head coach. This video would feature Marvin's credentials, interviews with Ravens' personnel director Ozzie Newsome and me regarding Marvin's abilities, and most importantly, a chance for ownership to see Marvin first hand. Marvin is a very intelligent and articulate individual who has an impressive presence. The tape achieved two results—one intended, the other by happenstance.

Once the tape was done, I knew Marvin could feel confident that he had been proactive in the process of becoming a head coach. As a result, he could relax and focus on his current duties. This effect was the one I had hoped for when I initiated the process. The outcome that was unexpected was Marvin's appreciation that the organization would show that type of support and loyalty to his efforts to become a head coach. I think his appreciation for the organization's loyalty to him in this situation played a significant role in his decision to pass up a potential head coach job to remain with the Ravens another year.

PRIDE

Pride involves a feeling of gratification that emanates from your association with something or someone that is laudable, meaningful, and inherently good. Pride is often mistakenly confused with negative terms such as conceit, arrogance, and ego. From an ethical standpoint, pride can play a significant role. As a skillful leader, you should be able to take pride in your behavior, your accomplishments, and the actions of those whom you lead. Pride is the result of being and doing your best.

Pride played a very important role in a situation that occurred during the 2000 season when it became apparent that we had a realistic chance of breaking the all-time defensive scoring record near the latter part of the year. A number of individuals became quite critical of our focus on that record. Unfortunately, this type of criticism is not foreign to me. As a former offensive coordinator you recognize that, particularly with offensive records, some people will interpret having those goals as being selfish and self-serving. A few individuals will even intimate that you would risk a loss to achieve some superfluous statistical record. As ill-informed as such a perspective might be, it can in no way be extrapolated to the defensive records we set in 2000. Not letting a team score is at the very heart of any defensive mind set. It is the ultimate in team orientation in that no one person can take credit for its success. Indeed, it takes individual sacrifice by certain defensive players to maintain this team profile. When you ask a defensive end like Micheal McCrary or a rush linebacker like Peter Boulware to maintain their "contain" principles on a mobile quarterback, you do so asking them to forgo certain incentives that they might otherwise earn by making a preset number of sacks and tackles. Our overall success as a team and certainly as a defensive unit emanated from the pride of players like this who placed the team's objectives and goals above their own personal achievements and potential financial rewards.

Pursuing the shutout record and all-time scoring records became a tremendous motivator for this team. The players on the offensive and special teams were equally motivated to be a part of these records. By running the ball effectively and finishing second in the NFL in time of possession, the offense knew that they were helping the defense and our team, even though it limited their opportunities to be viewed as successful. This type of pride and selflessness symbolized the team concept that would carry the Ravens to a world championship.

GOOD ETHICS, GOOD LEADERSHIP

Values provide leaders with a moral compass that is essential if an appropriate vision is to be created and a suitable plan to accomplish that vision is to be implemented. Most importantly, values enable you to know the difference between merely doing your best and doing what is right.

If an organization is to have these qualities, it must begin at the top, both by way of personal character of leadership and the commitment of leadership to demand that same quality of character of everyone in the organization. There is no better example of this than Art and Pat Modell, owners of the Baltimore Ravens. This family has exhibited nothing but class and family values under the most trying of circumstances.

When the Modells were forced out of Cleveland (and I do mean forced), they came under both personal and professional attack. Through it all, they were able to orchestrate an incredible course of events. They left the legacy and history of the Cleveland Browns for the city and fans of Cleveland. This alone was an unprecedented act of generosity and compassion. They brought professional football back to the deserving city of Baltimore. They delivered a world championship. In the process, they developed an organization of professionally competent individuals while demanding that everyone in the organization—from top to bottom—exhibit the highest caliber integrity, honesty, trustworthiness, loyalty, and pride. In short, people you would like and with whom you would enjoy working. This is truly the foundation on which the Baltimore Ravens' success was built.

Leadership Principle #1:

*Values provide the moral authority
for skillful leadership.*

chapter 3

BE
PREPARED

"Failure to prepare is preparing to fail."

—John Wooden
Hall of Fame basketball coach

Skillful leaders are fully aware of the fact that success is not a matter of desire, but rather the by-product of preparation and hard work. In almost every human endeavor, the more you prepare and the greater the effort you expend, the more likely it is that you will be successful.

Preparation obviously plays a meaningful role in athletics. For example, no aspect of the leadership provided by a coach has a bigger or more lasting effect on the players and their performance than the methodology used, in installing and practicing your system. At the absolute core of any type of detailed preparation is the maximizing of meaningful repetitions. In his treatise *On War*, nineteenth-century military strategist Carl von Clausewitz noted, "Habit gives strength to the body in great exertion, to the mind in great danger, and to judgment against first impression." Maintaining a specific routine and level of preparation gives the players a sense of structure and security.

My father was a test pilot in the early years when things were done by the seat of your pants and no computer simulations existed to diminish the risks that a pilot had to face. He frequently spoke of maintaining an established routine to insure that you did not "miss a step" in the heat of the moment. He often told me that living with an established, well–thought-out structure was always your best chance to survive. Denny Green put it another way: "Plan your work, then work your plan." In this instance, the key is having both the right plan and structure and the courage of your convictions to stay with that structure when those around you want to question it.

The impact of preparation on the accomplishments of an organization can be more easily understood when the relative degree of success that NFL teams achieve is examined. In reality, some teams are consistently more successful than others. Given the fact that every team has dedicated coaches, talented players, and operates under the same league-mandated salary cap, the obvious question is why do some teams consistently win more games than others? Good luck? Possibly. Leadership? Definitely. Preparation? Absolutely.

No better evidence of the value of preparation exists than the legacy of Hall of Fame Coach Bill Walsh. His orchestration for preparation is known by the euphemism "West Coast Offense." This is actually a misnomer. Most people think of the "West Coast Offense" only in terms of X's and O's. Even in that context, it is misused. I have long thought that if you had two backs in the backfield, threw a pass of less than five yards, and have visited Disneyland more than once, you could be considered as a "West Coast Offense" guy. Although his creation of a specific style of offensive play is well documented, it is his development of a premium work structure in the NFL that is the most traceable. Entering the new millennium, over one-third of the entire league has a head coach with his roots linked to Bill Walsh. Those 11 coaches represent six total Super Bowls and four of the last five champions.

If you were to analyze the offensive play of teams like Mike Holmgren's Seattle Seahawks, Denny Green's Minnesota Vikings, or George Siefert's Carolina Panthers, you would see a certain level of consistency, but probably no more so than with any other teams in the league. On the other hand, if you had the opportunity to watch a training camp with Tony Dungy's Tampa Bay Bucs, John Gruden's Oakland Raiders, or my Baltimore Ravens, or if you were to examine the week's preparation for a given opponent by Mike Shanahan's Denver Broncos or Steve Mariuci's San Francisco 49ers, you would quickly recognize that we have all been mentored in the same style of preparation. You would discern that our preparation is paralleled in its attention to detail and innovative in the degree to which very specific and focused attention is given to the situational, contingency, and reactive needs of each of our teams by a process that is designed to maintain the learning curve for the players as its primary objective.

In his book *The Road Ahead*, software-industry magnate Bill Gates defines information as "the reduction of uncertainty." This is a simple but eloquent description of the absolute essence of teaching. All coaches should adhere to this precept as the most basic barometer of their teaching progression. While I feel somewhat certain that Mr. Gates has never coached an athletic team, this simple observation isolates the exact purpose of a coach's responsibilities—to put the players in a learning environment that will condition and prepare them for every possible contingency that they might face in a game situation. By taking this approach, coaches can "reduce the level of uncertainty" that players might face and allow them to be aggressive and assertive in carrying out their obligations. Among the key elements of this process are:

- Being sure that the information you provide measurably reduces the uncertainty or hesitation in your players with regard to their basic responsibilities. Otherwise, it is information that is either not needed or has been presented in an ineffective manner.

- Demanding concentration. Be assertive in your insistence that your players focus on the task at hand.

- Being exact, almost to the point of scientific precision.

- Being sensitive to signs of physical fatigue—a situation that can drastically affect the learning curve.

- Keeping meeting times quality-oriented and making an effort to change the learning atmosphere.

- Constantly monitoring the retention levels of the team members.

As was stated in previous chapters, your success as a leader is affected by whether you have a suitable vision and both the resources and the skills to ensure that your vision becomes a reality. In this regard, it is essential that you afford yourself the greatest opportunity to be a successful leader by being prepared to deal with the myriad of details, circumstances, and challenges that you will face over time that might impact on your effectiveness as a leader. Such preparation involves considerable forethought and planning on your part.

Being prepared requires commitment, perspective, and action. Above all, you must have a firm resolve to be prepared and to be willing to expend whatever reasonable effort is necessary in that regard. "Bear" Bryant, the renowned football coach of the Alabama Crimson Tide, once told his players that his attitude had always been that "If it's worth playing, it's worth paying the price." At a minimum, the price of being prepared is work . . . hard work.

"If I do not practice one day, I know it. If I do not practice the next day, the orchestra knows it. If I do not practice the third day, the whole world knows it."

—Ignace Paderewski
Polish pianist

Adequate preparation also requires that you have a clear idea of the goals (short-term and long-range) that you hold for yourself and for the organization. Furthermore, you must have the ability to prioritize the time, energy, and resources that you allocate to a particular goal. In addition, you must have the foresight to realize that unforeseen events will occur that will necessitate that you adapt to the existing circumstances as needed. Finally, you must have a strategic plan for being prepared.

DEVELOPING A PLAN

"Spectacular achievements are always preceded by unspectacular preparation."

—Roger Staubach
Hall of Fame football player

To a point, it can be relatively easy to have a plan. The difficulty lies in the details involved in developing a sound plan. Fortunately, most skillful leaders are at least somewhat detail-oriented. The key is to identify and then address the various steps that need to be undertaken to enhance your level of preparation.

Keep in mind that however well-intended a plan is, it is only a plan unless it leads to action. Planning should be used as a tool that elicits purposeful activity—in this instance, being better prepared—on your part at the present time. Real plans involve strategic decisions that lead to action now. As characterized by renowned management theorist Peter F. Drucker in his book *Management: Tasks, Responsibilities, Practices*, plans that "talk about action tomorrow are dreams, if not pretexts for nonthinking, nonplanning, nondoing."

Accordingly, in order to be better prepared, you should develop an action plan. This strategic plan should identify what aspects or elements of your life (your professional environment) you need to address (in terms of preparation) and how you should approach each component.

For example, prior to training camp, I have the position coaches outline the specific skills that players at their position need to be successful. They are then required to document the practice drills they will use to develop these skills. Once this is done, they must then take the allotted amount of time dedicated to individual drills (usually about three hours worth over a four-week period of practice) and account for every minute of the individual time available and how it will be used. When I first put a coach through this exercise, more often than not the initial response is, "How the heck do I know what my player is going to need to work on a month from now?" My response is simple: "How can you not know?" As teachers, we are no less accountable in pro football than is the elementary, middle, or high school teacher who has to submit a lesson plan for the semester. By putting it in written form, a coach is provided with an opportunity to document the exact process needed to develop a specific skill. Furthermore, the process gives you greater latitude to revise and adapt this plan if for some reason you need to reemphasize a particular fundamental.

Your first step should be to decide what areas of responsibility or concern merit your time and energy. As a rule, while a leader's overall responsibility may be to establish the vision for the organization and to inspire others to perform in such a way to make the vision a reality, leaders also engage in more structured activities that tend to focus on the achievement of specific goals and objectives (e.g., systems management, human relations, quality control, financial management, long-range planning, project management, etc.).

The dilemma that you may have in this regard as a leader revolves around the fact that you often have a multiplicity of position-related goals. In spite of their occasional similarities, your goals are unique. Some involve a different time frame. Some require more resources from you. Some are obviously more important to achieving the vision of the organization. As such, it is your responsibility to prioritize how to best spend your time, energy, and material resources in order to be prepared to perform your duties in a skillful manner.

From a practical standpoint, one of the most useful ways of assigning a priority to your allocation of resources is to develop a written, task-priority checklist. A number of steps can be taken to facilitate your efforts to establish such a checklist, including:

- Listing all aspects in your area of responsibility for which you need or would like to be better prepared.

- Identifying opportunities that you have to be better prepared for each item on your list. Specify what form that improvement might entail.

- Determining the resources that are needed to turn the opportunity into a reality.

- Assessing the feasibility of actually achieving the improvement detailed in the previous step.

- Deciding, relatively speaking, what possibility exists of you wasting your time on a particular area of concern.

- As appropriate, discussing your list with others within or outside the organization (e.g., superiors, followers, externally based experts, etc.).

- Deleting areas of concern from your list that are unfeasible or inappropriate, and prioritizing the rest.

Keep in mind that some areas of concern that you might otherwise address may ultimately be dismissed from whatever to-do list you compile because of low priority or poor timing. Also, don't forget that as you review your list on a periodic basis, your priorities may change.

Deciding what really needs to be done is only the initial step. The next step is to determine how to achieve your goal of being better prepared. Among the actions that you can take in this regard are to give more attention to a particular issue, to become more informed about a specific area of concern, to allot more resources to a given job-related task, to engage in contingency planning, to adopt a policy of willingly adapting to your circumstances, to surround yourself with more skilled followers, etc. Similar to your task-priority checklist, your plan for detailing how to improve your level of preparation should be thoughtful, thorough, realistic, worthwhile, and in writing.

As a rule, most leaders are list makers. Beyond the physical reminder the lists provide, the very act of making a list of priorities can often clarify or define the process you are documenting. Much like writing this book, or making a presentation to a group of professionals, the act of prioritizing may indeed create the teaching sequence you are looking to establish or enhance.

Another essential aspect of the efforts of an organization to prepare should center on the need to adequately address logistics and support. These issues may not be as glamorous and interesting as the more visible strategic or tactical moves you might make as a leader, but they are of equal importance. Any military leader will tell you that if the support apparatus of an army bogs down, it will stop a campaign as quickly as anything the opponent might do. If your army is not properly fed, your machinery properly maintained, and your communications channels kept open, your chances of success are limited. The "devil is in the details," as the saying goes.

When the Ravens were facing an opening 2000 schedule with five of the first seven games on the road, it was vital that we did everything as smoothly as possible as an organization to handle the logistical demands attendant to the situation. It was obvious to me that if we did not support the travel needs of our team (e.g., accommodations, meals, transportation, etc.), the long-term effects could be debilitating. Bob Eller, the Ravens' director of operations, did a masterful job of orchestrating the logistics involved in our early-season schedule. The players were so appreciative of Bob's efforts that they awarded him a game ball after opening 5–2 during this difficult time. That game ball is something I know Bob was very touched by and values a great deal. The point that should be kept in mind in this instance is that while these types of "behind-the-scenes" jobs normally do not get much recognition, they are extremely vital to the success an organization might achieve.

IMPLEMENTING THE PLAN

"One of life's most painful moments comes when we must admit that we didn't do our homework, that we are not prepared."

—Merlin Olsen
Hall of Fame football player

Once you've developed a strategic plan for enhancing your level of preparation and you've subjected your plan to whatever cross-checking and approval criteria you deem appropriate given your situation, you need to put your plan into action. Implementing your plan involves developing and adhering to a detailed schedule for achieving the objectives of your plan. The basic rule of thumb in this regard is to "do it right and do it now." Start executing your plan as soon as the necessary resources (if any) are in place.

Pay attention to the details in your plan. Relatively speaking, there is no such thing as an unimportant detail. While some details may be more important than others, all are important. The reason some leaders are more effective than others is their enhanced ability to focus on essential details.

With regard to implementing your plan, it is also your responsibility to establish an adaptive organizational structure to ensure that your efforts are successful. Creating a productive organization to accomplish a particular task is no easy feat. Politics can get in the way. Disagreements over the allocation of resources can occur. Your followers may have a different perspective than you. The expectations of the organization may change.

If others in the organization are to have a role in your efforts to be prepared, it is your job to select the people you need to help you and to match an individual's skills with a particular assignment. If specific training will contribute to their ability to perform their assignment and is a feasible option, you should arrange for it. Most importantly, you should keep in mind that in this instance, communicating, coordinating, and cooperating will enhance the likelihood of your plan being successfully implemented.

The situation in the NFL is certainly no different. For example, when creating a game plan for an opponent, there are a myriad of details and situations that must be addressed. You must constantly try to utilize and maximize the talents on your team. This includes coaches as well as players. The Ravens' staff is unique in that every coach has previously been a coordinator or play-caller. This level of expertise is very rare in a combined staff, and it would be foolish on my part not to maximize their input. Offensively, as an example, we break the game plan up into various situations in which different coaches will be the "lead coach" in analyzing that set of variables. Although it is the coordinator's responsibility to make the final determination, time does not allow him to properly research each phase of the game with the attention to detail that those decisions would otherwise demand and merit. Given the time and effort he has spent analyzing his "assigned situation," this "lead coach" serves as the primary resource to determine the best course of action for a given set of circumstances because it can be assumed that he has researched the situation with more detail than anyone else has.

CONTINGENCY PLANNING

"The time to repair the roof is when the sun is shining."

—John F. Kennedy
35th president of the United States

It is a fact of life that things don't always go as planned. As the often-quoted adage states, "The only thing certain about certainty is that nothing is certain." Preparation often involves decisions that are based on assumptions that are predicated on the future. In reality, such assumptions may be based on a set of circumstances that may or may not occur as forecast. Because situations change (just as people change), you need a backup plan to address the unexpected. In this regard, among the issues that may require contingency planning are failure, conflict, employee turnover, marginal performance, and internal and external change involving factors such as availability of resources, natural disasters, etc.

In this regard, one of the keys to our success has been the detailed contingency planning on which we base our play calling. Initially, this planning involves a detailed analysis of any tendencies our opponent might possess. This step goes beyond the normal down-and-distance, personnel and formations, run/pass ratio that most NFL teams do. It also includes such specific tendencies as "What does a team do after an explosive run versus what do they do after an explosive pass? What, if any, tendencies exist after loss by a sack versus loss on a run? Do they have a certain profile after a turnover?" These are all circumstances that might not happen, but you need to have a plan of action ready if they do.

One aspect of contingency planning that you should keep in mind is that people and organizations are creatures of habit. Even though they may spend a good deal of effort trying to show you a different profile early in the game, they will usually revert to whatever tendencies they previously had exhibited in times of great stress. I catalog my game plans not by the teams we face, but by the specific coordinator who is calling the game. The transitory nature of coaching dictates that coaches move around a lot. If I have a history against a specific coach, I will rely more on that history rather than on even more current data on the team that might be available.

The need for a leader to consider habits and tendencies applies to organizations as well as individuals. Even though individuals have strong personal tendencies, relatively large organizations and companies have even stronger inclinations. Even when the leadership changes at the top, if the company is large enough, it is difficult to change the personality of a large corporation in a short period of time. Somewhat similar to a large aircraft carrier that takes 15–20 miles to dramatically change its course, a corporation takes time to fully change its operating policies, practices, and procedures.

ADAPTABILITY

As a skillful leader, you must be able to respond to your circumstances as they exist—not as you would like them to be.

To paraphrase a common street saying, "S_ _ _ happens." While life doesn't always give you roses (even if you deserve a bouquet), you still have an obligation to yourself, your followers, and the organization to act in a responsible manner. You must approach each situation with an open mind and a get-it-done attitude. Whatever the circumstances, to the extent feasible, you must be both able and willing to adapt your behavior and your actions in such a way to position yourself to be successful.

To me, one of the most compelling aspects of my job is that it constantly changes. Though the external factors dictating the game and the league are fairly constant, the landscape of personnel throughout the NFL is in constant flux due to the salary cap and free agency. Because of this, the only one true constant in the National Football League is that things change.

The Ravens' world championship after the 2000 season was a case study in the reality of and the ever-evolving nature of change and the need to be flexible with regard to your circumstances. If prior to the season you would have outlined the sequence of events that transpired for the 2000 Baltimore Ravens, and contended that this would be the scenario to achieve a world championship, you would have faced prohibitive odds as to the likelihood of it being successful.

One of the circumstances that the Ravens organization had to deal with involved a change in the fundamental structure of the ownership of the team when Steven Bisciotti purchased 49 percent of the club, with an option to take full control of the club in 2004. Another challenging circumstance occurred during the offseason following the 1999 season when the Ravens' best player, linebacker Ray Lewis, was indicted and tried on murder charges. Although those charges were subsequently dropped, Ray was ultimately fined a record amount by the NFL. During the season, we faced a first-half schedule that included five of our first seven games on the road, something no other team in the NFL was asked to do. We suffered through a three-game losing streak, went five games without scoring a touchdown, and endured a change of starting quarterbacks and a heavy reliance on a 20-year-old rookie running back who had failed to complete an entire, injury-free season in his three-year college career. In the sports arena, these were long odds at their best (or worst, depending on your point of view).

Countering those obstacles was arguably the best defense in the history of the NFL and a team chemistry that was the best I had ever experienced in 22 years in the business. The odds just got better.

The biggest challenge for me in riding roughshod over this set of circumstances was having to adapt my fundamental beliefs concerning what it takes to win a world championship. No championship team since the 1985 Chicago Bears had been so reliant on its defense. Even though offensively we finished the season a respectable 16th in the NFL in total offense, fifth in rushing offense, and second in time of possession, no team since the eighties had won a Super Bowl with an offense ranked that low.

The NFL, by specific design, has evolved over the years into a league dominated by offensive play. Changes in the NFL's rules on holding by offensive lineman, bumping and contact by the defensive secondary, and even the backing up of the kickoff are all examples of the NFL's desire to enhance scoring and offensive productivity. I grew up professionally with these changes. Early in my career, Bill Walsh impressed upon me the need to develop a specialty, something that would distinguish me in the profession. Subsequently, I decided to make offense my specialty—in particular the passing game. My professional pedigree of having graduated and coached at Brigham Young University and having had the opportunity to work at such institutions and for such organizations as San Diego State, Stanford, and the San Francisco 49ers clearly indicated my preference for offensive-minded philosophies.

That philosophy enabled me to help guide the teams I was working with to record-setting offensive numbers at virtually every career stop that I have made. Certainly, it has never been more evident than in 1998, when the Minnesota Vikings, for whom I was the offensive coordinator, had the highest-scoring offense in the history of the National Football League. It was the Vikings' production that season that afforded me the chance to become the head coach of the Baltimore Ravens the following year.

As any corporate, political, or military leader will tell you, it is vital that you have a firm understanding of the business environment you compete in and what it takes to be successful in that environment. The recent histories of the league and the teams that have ascended to the championship have generally been based on offensive production. Prior to our winning the Super Bowl in 2001, the previous winners have had notable offensive assets—for example, the 2000 world champion St. Louis Rams and their aerial circus led by Kurt Warner. The 1998 and 1999 world champion Denver Broncos had future Hall of Famers John Elway, Shannon Sharpe, and MVP running back Terrell Davis. Prior to that, Brett Favre had an MVP season in leading the Green Bay Packers to the championship. The late eighties and nineties saw names like Steve Young, Joe Montana, Jerry Rice, Troy Aikman, Emmit Smith, and Michael Irvin dominate offensive play and help their teams win championships. This philosophical perspective led me to conclude that this type of offensive production was essential to success in the NFL.

Clearly, each of these champions also had solid play by their special teams and on the defensive side of the ball. Indeed, in just about every instance, the ability of each team to adhere to a strategy where everyone made a contribution to the team was a vital, yet underappreciated, aspect of that teams' success.

Those within the industry recognized the need for some semblance of balance between offensive, defensive, and special teams play, even though there is no clear-cut ratio you can identify as to what that balance needs to be. On the other hand, if you decide to build a statistical analysis of what it takes to win a championship over the last few years in the NFL, the case for an explosive, high-efficiency offense is well documented.

It was this conventional, well-documented, thoroughly established, and statistically valid thinking that I had to overcome in assessing and orchestrating the Ravens' championship efforts in 2000. As a rule, conventional thinking is generally much easier to implement, because there is less resistance to it. When, in the early twentieth century, Winston Churchill accurately anticipated the need to convert his Royal Navy from coal-fired to oil-fired ships, he noted, with a nod to Hamlet, it was like "taking arms against a sea of troubles." Oil-fired ships afforded the chance to develop a faster and better-armed arsenal. The problem was that England had coal in abundance, but precious little oil. This step involved a fundamental change in the way England obtained and maintained a constant oil supply from great distances. Churchill realized that a large oil reserve would have to be established. Had Churchill not done this "unconventional" thinking, England would have been ill prepared to face the challenges of World War II.

The business world has countless stories of products and services that were truly different in their nature and hugely successful due to some manager's adroit assessment of the unique opportunities with which they were presented. There are an equal number of case studies of missed opportunities in the same business world when leadership failed to size up the situation and could not adapt their thinking to accommodate the circumstances. "Thinking outside the box" is a popular phrase that sums up this perspective very well.

As the Ravens progressed through the early stages of the 2000 season and a 5-2 start, it was very apparent that defensively, we had something special going. We were in the midst of an eventual 33-game stretch of not allowing a rusher over 100 yards in a game. The next closest team to this was our Super Bowl opponent, the New York Giants, who were at 11. For the season, we registered four shut-outs, one short of the record, and were clearly on pace to set the all-time defensive scoring record of 185 points in a season set by the 1986 Chicago Bears. In short, the NFL had not seen a defensive unit like this in quite some time (if ever).

Even with this defensive dominance, it was hard for me to think the Ravens could win an NFL championship without dynamic play by the offense. Some people misunderstood my steadfast belief in this requirement as an outgrowth of my ego and my feeling that we needed to win with strong offensive play in order to validate my abilities as a coach. These types of observations are not all together groundless. Many times coaches, particularly assistant coaches who are trying to build a name for themselves, will hold to a particular perspective more for the benefit of themselves rather than for the greater good of the team. In reality, this is not a perspective a head coach will have for long, at least not a successful head coach. As a head coach, you are judged in one way and one way only—by the number of *wins*. Although it is understood, and even expected that the people you work with will press a personal agenda, one of the primary responsibilities you have as the leader of the organization is to channel and focus those agendas into a single, focused purpose.

As the season progressed, I was able to make three key assessments that would prove vital to our overall success. First, it became obvious to me that we did indeed have a truly dominant defense that under the right circumstances could effectively shut down any and all opponents we would face. Second, I observed that we had sufficient offensive assets (e.g., outside speed to make just enough big plays), a solid running game, and solid quarterback judgment to minimize turnovers—all of which would augment our defensive profile. Lastly, it was apparent to me that there was not another team in the league that was playing at such a dominant level as to make us abandon our formula for winning. Parity had truly arrived in the NFL, and we had the assets we needed to take advantage of it. Clearly, it was time to "think outside the box."

Collectively, these assessments meant that I had to fundamentally change the way I would orchestrate the game. Ball control, field position, and clock management became my primary focus. During the course of the week when I might catch a game on television, either pro or college, I would normally be drawn to a formation or a sequence of plays a particular team might be using. Now, I found myself watching how other coaches were using their time-outs or when they were electing to punt or go for it on fourth down.

As the media began to pick up on our change in approach, I began to jokingly refer to it as being drawn into the "dark side" of the game. This interchange was done with a bit of sarcasm on my part for those who believed I was more interested in statistics than wins. Some failed to see the humor in it. They were unable to acknowledge that I was willing to adapt. What they failed to recognize was the terms of my contract. I have sizeable incentives built into my contract based solely on wins, making and progressing through the playoffs, and going to and winning the Super Bowl. I don't make a single penny more for leading the league in any statistical category. Like I said earlier, greed is good. Greed clarifies, crystallizes, and purifies. It may have been the "dark side," but it was profitable.

This adaptability was vital to our ability to string together 11 straight wins and become world champions. Whether this formula can continue to be successful for us or anyone else and whether it becomes a trend for the league as a whole remains to be seen. MacArthur's famous statement, "Adapt or die," is very applicable to the NFL. Two-thirds of the league have changed head coaches just in the two years since I was hired. Some have changed twice. In this age of the salary cap, free agency, and the accelerated expectations of both ownership and the fans, you must be flexible enough to adapt to whatever profile your players' assets dictate. While you should have a determined and consistent approach philosophically to the way you plan to operate your team, it had better include a level of anticipatory flexibility that enables you to adapt to your changing circumstances as needed.

Principle #2:

Proper planning is the most effective way for a leader to approach the future.

chapter 4

BE
SELF-
DISCIPLINED

> *"Don't go around saying the world owes you a living. The world owes you nothing. It was here first."*
>
> —Mark Twain
> author and humorist

Your ability to lead effectively is greatly affected by your moral ethic, your work ethic, and your mental ethic. Your moral ethic is a reflection of your values, while your work ethic mirrors your attitude toward doing whatever is necessary to get the job done. Your mental ethic, on the other hand, emanates from your sense of self-discipline. Accordingly, self-discipline is an indispensable asset for individuals who want to be effective leaders. Regardless of whatever skills you possess, you will never be able to reach your potential as a leader without this essential attribute.

The single most important component of self-confidence is self-control. Simply stated, self-control is your ability to exercise restraint over your impulses, emotions, and desires. Within a leadership setting, self-control can influence a number of other behaviors, such as your capability to control your behavior regardless of the circumstances, your skill at managing your time wisely, your willingness to accept responsibility for your actions (or lack thereof), and your ability to maintain an appropriate level of focus at all times.

Throughout this book, I have talked about the passion that is required to achieve your objectives and the fact that you should not compromise your ability to exercise sound judgment. This cuts to the very heart of being self-disciplined. By setting specific standards of conduct and being able to monitor and regulate those standards, you allow yourself to let your passion and emotions show without compromising your responsibilities.

One of the most amazing examples of this sense of self-control was exhibited in Super Bowl XVI when the San Francisco 49ers, coached by Bill Walsh, faced Bill's protégé and friend Sam Wyche who coached the Cincinnati Bengalxs. As Bill orchestrated a 92-yard drive at the end of the game, he did so knowing this would be his last game as the head coach of the 49ers. Bill had decided that after 10 years and what would soon be three Super Bowl championships, it was time to move on to other challenges. When Joe Montana hit John Taylor in the back of the end zone to take the lead, the predictable euphoria of winning the Super Bowl had everyone on the San Francisco sideline exploding with emotion—everyone, that is, except Bill. He knew that Sam Wyche and the Bengals had a potentially explosive offense that could turn around and execute the same type of drive that the 49ers had just completed successfully. He also knew they had a kickoff and some defensive decisions to make before the game was truly won.

In my efforts to prepare for my part in writing the book *Finding the Winning Edge*, which Bill and I coauthored, I got a television copy of this championship game. Given the sequence of events that would take place and the fact that Bill was doing everything he needed to do while knowing this would be his legacy game, his last game as head coach of the 49ers, I was absolutely amazed at his self-control and demeanor. Looking at the tape and watching him work the sideline with little hint of emotion or adulation will be something I will remember for quite some time.

Bill's actions are a reflection of the fact that your level of self-control is your unspoken voice of conscience that directs you to do the right thing and make the right choices regarding developing and adhering to your priorities, regardless of the circumstances. If your behavior is not guided by your priorities (i.e., if you lack self-discipline), you'll never be able to inspire confidence in your leadership abilities either in yourself or your followers. If you are not a disciplined person, you won't be able to lead by example. As John Maxwell cogently points out in his book *The 21 Indispensable Qualities of Leadership*, you should always keep in mind that "the first person you lead is you."

In that regard, you can get a general idea of how well you're leading yourself by whether your behavior is marked by certain patterns. For example, your ability to exert self-control over your actions is undoubtedly insufficient if you're the type of person who frequently makes excuses for your own behavior, puts doing things that should be done today off until tomorrow, frequently loses your temper, doesn't make the best use of your time, etc.

Being in self-control, on the other hand, involves at least three factors. First, you have standards (i.e., you know what you want to do or should do). Second, you are aware if your behavior does not meet your standards. Third, you are able to correct your substandard behavior whenever necessary (a capacity that is commonly referred to as your "willpower"). You must have command of all three factors in order to be in control of yourself.

At the heart of this process is the accountability, or lack thereof, that I felt was missing from the Ravens when I took over. Regardless of the structure I established for our players, if they did not develop a pattern of self-discipline, both on and off the field, we had little chance of winning. You do not foster this pattern of self-discipline simply by preaching about it. Like all constructive habits in your life, you must establish a behavioral pattern that enables the players to maintain their sense of self-discipline. In other words, self-discipline often depends on setting a routine.

In the previous chapter on preparation, a great deal of discussion was given to the need for attention to detail and providing a learning environment. To a large degree, such a learning environment must ultimately be geared toward your follower's ability to maintain a high level of self-discipline with regard to your efforts to prepare them. For example, when players are required to adhere to a routine, it becomes a covert act to violate the routine, rather than their being able to just dismiss it as an oversight.

Keep in mind that you lose self-control when you take a counterproductive approach to the steps attendant to being self-disciplined. For example, you either fail to set or set impossible goals for yourself. On the other hand, although you might set goals, you don't pay attention to them. You stop working toward achieving your goals because you're tired, stressed, or bored. You focus on your immediate situation, rather than considering your more long-range goals. You misjudge your priorities. You become obsessed with shielding your ego—to the exclusion of fulfilling your responsibilities. You vent your feelings, rather than trying to address the cause of your emotions. You tend to adopt an attitude of not wanting to know the truth about yourself (i.e., your strengths and weaknesses as a leader), and even when you do, you fail to take action to remedy any bad habits or behavioral characteristics you might have. With regard to self-discipline, one of the most unwarranted habits you could have is procrastination.

PROCRASTINATION

"Procrastination is the fear of success. Because
success is heavy, it carries a responsibility with it.
It is much easier to procrastinate and live on the
"someday-I'll" philosophy."

—Denis Waitley
productivity consultant, author, and lecturer

Procrastination can take many forms. As a rule, it generally involves putting off doing something important. It can also manifest itself in a number of other ways, including being reluctant to take risks; getting ill when confronted by the need to perform a task you deem unpleasant; blaming others for your difficulties; avoiding making hard decisions or getting involved in confrontations; and making big plans that never get done. Collectively, such behavior makes it very difficult, if not impossible, for you to fulfill your responsibilities as a leader.

In reality, almost everyone procrastinates to some extent. In varying degrees, everyone is afraid of facing reality—confronting the hard work and uncertainty involved in confronting life's challenges. Procrastination is a way to escape those fears. The key is to find a more appropriate way to deal with your anxieties and defense mechanisms.

Similar to all human beings, I have had to overcome a tendency (or two) to procrastinate at certain times in my life. This past season, for example, I had developed a bad habit of putting off my film study of the upcoming opponent. On Mondays after a game, our normal routine is to come in a little later so coaches can spend a morning with their families since they will not see them again until Friday. They are usually gone in the morning by the time their kids get up and typically get home after they have already gone to bed.

When the coaches get in to the office, they first individually, then collectively, analyze and grade the film from the previous game. I often have several media obligations that I have to address in the afternoon. What I subsequently discovered was that I was finding things to do to put off looking at the first bit of tape on our next opponent. On my part, my behavior was somewhat odd since the chess-match nature of the game planning for an opponent is one of the main reasons I am in this profession and what I enjoy doing the most. What I came to realize was that once I started the process of game planning, the preparation for the coming week is absolutely incessant. The time, focus, and energy it takes to prepare a game plan, once started, is not completed until the gun sounds at the end of the game. Knowing that this process starts with the first flip of the tape machine, I held off initiating this catalyst until the last minute. My dilemma was easily remedied by setting a specific time on Monday afternoon (4:00 P.M.) when all other duties come to an end and by not allowing that self-imposed deadline to pass.

My dilemma that involved procrastinating and my ultimate solution to my problem is consistent with the observations of industrial psychologist Clayton Tucker-Ladd, who astutely points out that the first step in being able to stop procrastinating is to begin with the notion that your procrastination is not the basic "problem," but rather an attempted "cure" for your fears, self-doubts, and aversion to a particular task or work-related goal. In order to overcome your procrastinating behavior, you have to focus on the real factors—your underlying fears, attitudes, and irrational thoughts—that are causing you to act in a certain way. In this regard, no single step or procedure will serve as a cure for procrastination for everyone. However, you can take specific actions that might help solve your "problem," including the following:

- Develop a daily work-to-be-done schedule. Keep records of your adherence to the schedule. Use rewards or punishments (penalties) to reinforce your ability or need to adhere to your schedule.

- Break down the "big" jobs you find daunting into more manageable tasks. Work on getting started. Make getting started early a habit.

- Keep a journal in which you record in detail your feelings and thoughts associated with your fears about performing a particular task. Identify how your fears, excuses, and habits block your ability to conduct yourself in an appropriate manner. Use these insights to deal with these blocks.

- Change the way you think about work (i.e., reduce your dread of work). Have alternate ways of completing a task in case your first option proves unfeasible. Replace pessimism with optimism.

- Take responsibility for directing your life. Take pride in knowing that you did your best.

PERSEVERANCE

"In the realm of ideas, everything depends on enthusiasm; in the real world, all rests on perseverance."

—Johann Wolfgang von Goethe
German author and theorist

Just as procrastination has an extremely counterproductive impact on your level of self-discipline, perseverance is one of the most positive habits you can have if you want to exhibit self-control as a leader. Perseverance involves a demonstrable work ethic characterized by a high level of industriousness and a desire to see the job through to its completion.

Skillful leaders are driven to complete what they have begun. Whatever the circumstances (e.g., imposing challenges, insurmountable obstacles, etc.), they "stay the course." They are able to combine their moral ethic (refer to Chapter 2) with their work ethic (refer to Chapter 3) to fulfill their work-related responsibilities and to set an example for others in the organization.

Not only do effective leaders get their work done, they focus on expending whatever effort is necessary to achieve a given goal in the right way. They demonstrate a consistently high level of persistence and commitment when facing every challenge—however hard the situation may be. They tend to avoid the "law of least effort"—an approach articulated by organizational psychologist Robert Eisenberger, as trying to get things (a payoff) the easiest way we can. Leaders whose behavior is characterized by perseverance fully realize that as a rule, "there is no free lunch" with regard to getting things done.

The energy level that was discussed in Chapter 2 as one of the three primary ways that leadership is exhibited is in tangible evidence in this instance. The long hours coaches tend to keep is legendary. Determined coaches pick through the video and printout sheets looking for any additional bit of information that might enable them to make a better coaching decision or provide their players with any insight or advice that might somehow assist them in their efforts to prepare or execute the game plan. Like many things in life, this commitment to do "whatever is necessary" can also be taken to excess.

In reality, many coaches burn the midnight oil with the mistaken idea that long hours somehow are a proper reflection of their level of determination and perseverance. They fall into the trap of thinking they are going to outwork their opponent by staying and working later. In most cases, what really happens is coaches tend to wear themselves out with the all-night game planning. Subsequently, when they are with their players, when they need to be at their most animated and vibrant, they have to drag themselves into meetings and onto the practice field because of fatigue. To quote the great John Wooden again, "Don't mistake activity for production." Proper use of your time has to always remain in balance with perseverance.

TIME WISDOM

Relative to self-discipline, another skill that every successful leader has is the ability to use time in a meaningful manner. While everyone would like to spend their time wisely, some individuals are much more successful in this regard than others. Regrettably, a leader's poor use of time can have numerous adverse effects on an organization—affecting not only the people involved but also the ability of the organization to accomplish its goals. Accordingly, if you want to be an effective leader, you have to become "time-wise." Becoming time-wise involves not only adopting specific steps and techniques to ensure that you use your time wisely, but also being aware of the barriers that you might face that could otherwise hinder your efforts to manage your time effectively.

If you show me a coach who stays up past midnight every week preparing his game plan, I will give you a coach that doesn't plan his time very efficiently. When I was with the Dallas Cowboys in the late seventies, it was at a time when several coaches were known for their late hours, even to the point of sleeping in the office during the week. Head Coach Tom Landry, who was as meticulous and hard working as any coach in the NFL, was asked if he slept at the office any during the week. Sensing that the reporter was trying to make the inference that Coach Landry didn't put in as many hours as some others, he responded, "Young man, if it took me that long to put a game plan together, I surely wouldn't admit to it. It just doesn't take that long."

My wife has an observation every time we have a Thursday game, when our preparation time is obviously dramatically less than during a normal week. She questions that if we can put a game plan together in time to play a Thursday game following a normal Sunday contest, why can't we do that on a normal week and then rest on the two extra days we have in a normal week? I hate to admit it, but she has a point. Human nature will dictate that if you have three days to do a job you will do it in three days. If the same job is required, but you have a week to do it, you will take the entire week. Of all the things I criticize and analyze during the offseason, how we utilize our time and how we can increase our efficiency with that time heads the list.

In reality, most people who make poor use of their time generally don't understand how important time really is and how relatively easy it can be effectively managed and used. Such individuals tend to be characterized by a lack of planning and self-organization. Whatever attempts they make to manage their time in some sort of logical approach are often limited by one or more of the following confining factors:

- *They rely on mythical time.* They put off important tasks on the incorrect assumption that they will later have a sufficiently large block of uninterrupted time in which to complete their obligations. By relying on nonexistent time, they become lulled into believing that they have plenty of time. When reality rears its head, they quickly discover that they misused their real time.

- *They underestimate the demands on their time.* They take on more than they can realistically expect to do in the time available. In this instance, such a dilemma can result from a number of shortcomings. A major cause is that they overestimate how much time is actually available. Another key contributing factor is that they have an unrealistic perception of their own capability to complete a specific task in a given amount of time.

- *They fail to complete immediate tasks before agreeing to do more.* Often referred to as "task creep," this particular confine arises from an individual's inability to say "no" to others.

- *They go from task to task before actually completing any.* Too many tasks; too little sense of priority.

- *They ignore reality.* They fail to examine themselves critically and objectively. They undermine their chances for success by failing to recognize what could and should be done by them within the time available.

Fortunately, several possible steps exist that can enable you to become more time-wise. Regardless of which approach to becoming time-wise you ultimately adopt, one of your first steps must be to accept the fact that as a rule, time-related problems are *not* beyond your control. Among the techniques that you can pursue to enable you to use your time more effectively are the following:

- *Analyze your use of time.* Collect detailed data on how you spend your time each day. You have to first know how you spend your time before you can decide how to use it more effectively. When data replaces conjecture, you have a much more realistic assessment of your situation.

- *Establish direction in your use of time.* As a leader you need to be aware of what goals and objectives your organization is attempting to achieve. Clearly-defined goals, priorities, and limits can provide you with a well-conceived sense of direction that will increase you chances of using your time in the most efficient and effective manner possible.

- *Maintain control over your work environment.* Take whatever steps are necessary to build and sustain a healthy work environment. Establish an environment where you can concentrate so that you can use "real" (as opposed to "mythical") time to complete tasks before their deadlines. Develop a detailed plan for handling particularly stressful circumstances.

- *Adopt a time-wise approach to performing your leadership responsibilities that works for you.* Everyone has a personal style of leadership. If you truly want to become time-wise, you must use time leadership techniques that fit your personality. Whatever techniques you adopt, keep in mind that becoming time-wise is an ongoing process that requires that you to periodically review what steps you are following and determine what really works for you.

FOCUS

Skillful leaders have the ability to focus on the important factors in their life—both professionally and personally. Not only do they know what's important and what they want, they also have an aptitude for "keeping their eye on the prize." As such, they do not allow themselves to be distracted or dissuaded from their proper role within the organization. In that regard, they are able to systematically expend their time and energy in a targeted manner. As a consequence, they are able to make the maximum use of their strengths while minimizing any weaknesses they might have.

Of all the attributes of the many great coaches I have been fortunate enough to work with, one of the distinguishing characteristics that singled them out from others was their ability to focus. There is no better example in my field than film study (or I should say video or even digital study). It takes a great deal of experience and focus to effectively look at the extensive amount of video that coaches use to prepare for an opponent and not just end up watching endless hours of tape. A trained eye knows what to specifically look for and what to keep your focus on, rather than be distracted by the many other components of a game that might otherwise grab your attention.

The need to be able to maintain your focus is equally important during the game itself. Later in the book, I've outlined several of the specific duties each coach is responsible for with regard to watching a game while it is being played. When a specific piece of information is needed, particularly from one of the coaches observing the game upstairs in the booth, it is very frustrating when that coach does not have the information I need because he somehow became distracted by the game itself, rather than keeping his attention on the specific aspect of the game he was supposed to be watching. All factors considered, I consider myself a pretty easy guy to work for. On the other hand, just ask any of my coaches what will set me off, and they will tell you it is when I find one of them has not kept his focus during a game and, as a result, is unable to provide the information we need from him.

Likewise, the players know the surest way to get me to pull a "blue-veiner" (i.e., the veins in your neck bulge because you are mad) is for them to lose their focus during practice. Somewhat like applying a 2 x 4 to the head of a mule, you occasionally need to metaphorically "slap" their attention back into focus. There are enough things about this game that I have no control over, but maintaining focus is not one of them. Of all the factors that you, as a leader, have to be demanding about, being focused should always remain at the top of the list.

CONQUER THYSELF

It can be argued that within the environs of leadership, a lack of will power has caused more failure than a shortage of ability or intelligence. You should not expect others to be inspired to act as you desire them to if you are not sufficiently disciplined to control your own behavior. In other words, you cannot expect discipline from others if you cannot impose discipline on yourself. This concept is perhaps best expressed in the words of the philosopher Plato, who wrote, "The first and best victory is to conquer self."

As a leader, you must recognize your limitations and either establish a plan for change or surround yourself with people who balance whatever deficiencies you have. I once worked for a head coach who had a tough time during practice keeping track of when one period needed to end and the next should begin. He would become so absorbed teaching during a specific period that he would just keep extending the period until he was done with whatever he felt he needed to do. He tried just having the manager blow the horn when the schedule called for a period to finish, but became frustrated when he was not able to finish his training sequence. He compromised by having me monitor the period, and when I said it was time to move on, he did so without question. What impressed me was that the head coach removed his ego from the situation and created a format that accounted for his inability to handle a situation. He did not care how it looked; he simply wanted to create a structure that got done what was needed to be done.

Principle #3:

Self-discipline is the bedrock foundation on which successful leadership is built.

chapter 5

BE
KNOWLEDGEABLE

"Real intelligence is a creative use of knowledge, not merely an accumulation of facts. The slow thinker who can finally come up with an idea of his own is more important to the world than a walking encyclopedia who hasn't learned how to use this information productively."
—D. Kenneth Winebrenner

There is a traditional and often-quoted adage that claims that "knowledge is power." To the contrary, the more appropriate way of stating that point would be "knowledge properly used can be power."

For a skillful leader, the source of that power is the competence and credibility that comes with the impact that knowledge can have on your ability to handle the diverse demands of leadership and to motivate others to follow your call for action. All other factors being equal, the more knowledgeable you are, the better able you will be to engage in rational decision making and problem solving and conduct yourself in a suitable, principled way. In turn, people will gain an enhanced level of respect for your leadership ability. As your credibility as a leader rises, your followers will be more likely to respond in a positive manner to your actions as a leader.

Understanding the relationship between knowledge and leadership involves several factors, including knowing the various components that constitute "knowledge" and being aware of how a leader acquires knowledge. Collectively, your knowledge is the sum total of all the information, facts, ideas, and insights you have acquired over the course of your lifetime. You obtain knowledge in two primary ways—education and experience.

When you discuss education, you normally are referring to the knowledge and learning ability that you acquire during formal schooling. In reality, however, formal education all too frequently is characterized by a process that essentially is designed to reward those individuals who are able to regurgitate information gained by rote memorization. This situation is where the concepts of "quantitative managerialism" are fostered. On the other hand, this type of knowledge is typically of little use in those situations that require imagination and judgment (two of the most critical cognitive components of overall intelligence). The point is even more dramatized in the words of industrialist and inventor Charles F. Kettering, who once observed: "The difference between intelligence and education is this: intelligence will make you a good living."

While pursuing my degree in communication at Brigham Young University, I had the good fortune of having a number of very competent professors. One specifically stands out in my mind because of his incredible capacity to recall various pieces of information and their sources. On more than one occasion, I would be discussing a concept or idea with this mentor when he would suggest a book or article on the subject. In some instances, he could recite a specific page number or chapter that was relevant to our conversation. Whenever I looked into one of his recommended sources, it was uncanny how his reference would strike at the absolute heart of the issue I was exploring.

After graduating from BYU and experiencing life in a non-academic setting, I questioned whether the admired professor could actually survive in a non-educational environment. He had several degrees, but had never worked outside academia. As I recalled, I never read any original material by him. This recollection is not meant to either criticize or diminish his skills or value as an educator. I truly appreciated his guidance and think of him as a valued mentor. I offer this comment simply as an observation questioning whether his lack of "real-world" experience would limit his ability to discern the practical application of what was a considerable reservoir of theoretical knowledge.

In this regard, the point to keep in mind is that your collective experiences generally have a more meaningful effect on your level of knowledge than education. Your "experience" can be defined as what you learn collectively—intellectually and emotionally—from the information- gathering opportunities to which you are exposed. As such, your experiences contribute to your knowledge and heighten your ability to process information. As John Wareham points out in his book *The Anatomy of a Great Executive*, your experiences enhance your reserve of *tacit knowledge*—the sum of "inside" practical information that you have absorbed during your lifetime. To a degree, your experiences can foster emotional growth and improve your capability of reacting positively and quickly in changing (and sometimes more demanding) circumstances.

How you react to changing circumstances is, to some degree, a reflection of the extent of your experiences and how much confidence you have in your gut feelings. The idea of taking a chance based on gut feelings and educated guess-work begins to seem less and less credible in this age of instant and total information access. Admittedly, gut feelings can be overrated, but so can substituting the endless analysis of data for the instinct born of experience. There are any numbers of examples of decisions I have made over the years that, at the time, I might have dismissed as being based on my gut feelings, but upon reflection can identify a specific previous experience that impacted a particular decision.

In the 2000 AFC Championship game versus the Oakland Raiders, for example, we had moved into potential field-goal range with the score at 10–0. A field goal would have made it a two-touchdown game early on and could have potentially devastated the Raiders. Our kicker, Matt Stover, had earned a Pro Bowl spot with his outstanding performance during the 2000 season. Although we were approaching his range, I decided to punt instead. Kyle Richardson, our punter, had led the league in punts inside the 20-yard line. Kyle's demonstrable skills, coupled with our record-setting defense, led me to opt to attempt to pin the Raiders down deep in their own territory. At the time, it just seemed like a "gut feeling." In fact, in my normal routine of reviewing my decisions the day after any contest, I was reminded of an instance in our second regular-season game against the Pittsburgh Steelers. Late in that game, trailing by three points, I decided to punt in hopes of backing the Steelers up and kicking out of their end zone. Unexpectedly, because of the way our defense normally played, they were able to work the ball down the field and punted from the 50-yard line, thus putting us 90 yards from the winning score. Even though we lost the game (a painful third loss in a row), I determined that it was still the right decision given the circumstance. In retrospect, I believe that I drew on the analysis that I made after the Steelers' game to make a similar decision in the playoff game against Oakland. Subsequently, we pinned the Raiders deep and got the ball back in a much safer field position to kick the field goal and take a 13–0 lead on the way to a 16–3 victory.

MORE THAN EDUCATION

"What is all our knowledge worth? We do not even know what the weather will be tomorrow."

—Berthold Auerback
German author

While "book smarts" can certainly play a role in your efforts as a leader, the business world is full of examples of accomplished businessmen who were somewhat "short" in formal education, but "long" on success. In this regard, two exceptional examples are Ray Kroc and Walt Disney, the founders of McDonald's and the Disney Corporation, respectively. Although neither had formal business training, both were strong leaders who initiated and led their organizations through periods of incredible growth and development. Their success occurred because they understood their businesses and they understood people.

Knowledgeable leaders do not have to have a comprehensive understanding of all aspects of their organizations (businesses). It is beneficial, however, for them to have a broad, working knowledge of the basic activities of the organization, as well as the ability to apply that knowledge as appropriate.

This factor is why job rotation is a relatively common practice in large corporations for those individuals who have been identified as potential leaders (i.e., those who will possibly be accorded executive-level positions). The primary objective of job rotation is to move people from activity to activity, from area to area, throughout the organization to give them a general understanding of the basic activities of the organization. The process is designed to provide individuals with a broad awareness of the nature of the organization's functions.

On a personal basis, I have a somewhat more varied set of experiences in the NFL than the average NFL coach. As was mentioned in the Preface, my first job in the NFL was not in coaching but in administration. At the time, I was working on my masters at BYU and serving as a graduate assistant on the Cougars' coaching staff. Like most GA's, I was looking to hook on with a program in a full-time coaching capacity when I became aware of the fact that George Heddleston had recently been hired as the director of public relations for the San Francisco 49ers under new head coach and general manager Bill Walsh. I met George when I was playing in Dallas and he was the assistant public relations director for the Dallas Cowboys.

At the time, I had a friend that was also working on his masters in communication and was looking to get on with the NFL in an administrative capacity. The 49ers had advertised an opening in their public relations department, so I called George on my friend's behalf. He indicated that he wasn't interested in talking with my friend, but asked if I would be interested in the job. Up to that point in my life, I had not considered doing anything but coaching. After flying out to San Francisco to meet with him and Coach Walsh, however, it seemed like a unique opportunity.

In those early years with the 49ers, we were very small organizationally. In fact, I was the only assistant administrator in the building. Hence, I became everyone's assistant. To be truthful, the word "assistant" may not be the right job description. An assistant infers some level of authority. I was, in fact, little more than a gofer for most of the organization.

That having been said, I can honestly tell you that those two years of being exposed to every aspect of the organization, from public relations to marketing, finance, personnel, travel—and yes, even coaching, were two of the most informative, tangibly useful years of my life. I look back at the time as though I were on sabbatical from coaching. I am especially grateful to Coach Walsh for allowing me to keep my fingers in coaching by letting me sit outside his player meetings and listen to him install what would become a world championship prototype system.

LIFELONG LEARNING

"I don't think much of a man who is not wiser today than he was yesterday."

—Abraham Lincoln
16th president of the United States

Effective leadership also involves an awareness of the need for lifelong learning, a commitment to establishing an organization with a suitable environment for group learning, an acceptance of the value of critical thinking, and an understanding that learning is reciprocal. Skillful leaders tend to share a number of characteristics, including a thirst for relevant knowledge concerning their organization, a desire to learn, and a willingness to be teachable. Effective leaders are committed to continual learning and self-improvement. To a point, being a leader involves recognizing the importance of maintaining a competitive edge with regard to knowledge. In other words, leaders are never content about how much they have learned. They understand that they don't know everything and that the ever-evolving body of knowledge is an invaluable asset that should be inculcated, processed, and utilized. As such, skillful leaders are fully aware of and accept the fact that learning is an ongoing process. Keep in mind that as John Wooden once noted, "It's what you learn after you know it all that counts."

As part of my own personal commitment to lifelong learning, I try to do as many coaching clinics and seminars in the offseason as my schedule permits. This goal was made easier after winning a Super Bowl, based on the number of people that seem to be willing to pay you unbelievable amounts of money to come lecture. I feel a little guilty taking their money (but only a little) because I have never been to a clinic or seminar, whether I was the main speaker or not, that I did not learn at least one new thing that could help me better myself. A few years ago I was asked to be a presenter at the American Football Quarterly Clinic in Fortworth, Texas. While there, I heard a coach just casually mention performing a drill at "coaching speed." In fact, a number of times exist during the course of a practice when you want to repeat a play, but you want to slow it down to less than full speed for teaching purposes. On one hand, you don't want your players to walk through the play, but on the other hand, you don't want the play to be performed too fast either. The term "coaching speed" is one my players now know. As a result, they can immediately give me exactly the tempo for which I am looking. Somewhat ironically, I learned this term from a high school coach whom I was supposed to be teaching.

To some people, however, learning is not always so easy. As Lin Bothwell surmises in his book *The Art of Leadership*, learning can be a difficult, sometimes painful, process. Learning involves at least two steps that many people find distasteful—thinking and changing.

Learning requires thinking—an activity that educational psychologists suggest most individuals devote very little of their time to on a daily basis (less than 40 minutes daily for the average person and probably much less). As opposed to processing information (where your mind is engaged in a series of actions, such as retrieving, sorting, labeling and storing information), thinking involves more complex undertakings, such as solving a complicated problem, making a difficult decision, struggling with an idea, etc.

Learning also involves changing. To learn, to develop, to grow, you must change. To a degree, change involves an element of risk. Although skillful leaders tend to be risk takers, most individuals are relatively uncomfortable dealing with situations that may involve an abandonment of their normal way of doing and thinking about things.

Skillful leaders, however, embrace change as a growth opportunity—not as a challenge to their level of authority or personal comfort zone. Keep in mind that the next time you run into someone you haven't seen for a long time and that person says, "You haven't changed a bit," you are *not* on the receiving end of a compliment. The only time you ever grow in life is when you change. As a leader, you must be a positive agent for change in your organization.

GROUP LEARNING

Effective leaders also appreciate the need for creating an environment where their followers have the opportunity to learn not only from their leadership, but also from the group as a whole. In such an environment, learning is a mutual process in which leaders and followers "learn" from their interaction with each other. Leaders not only serve as teachers of the group, they also learn from the members of the group. The point to keep in mind is that everyone a leader meets should be viewed as a potential source of valuable information.

As such, leaders should foster learning and the exchange of knowledge. They should create an environment where learning has perceived (as well as actual) value. They should act as a conduit for information so that everyone in the organization addresses a problem from the same general perspective.

One example of the need for everyone to be on the same page concerning information and perspective involves the leader's vision for the organization. In that regard, one of the most meaningful steps that a leader can take to ensure that a particular objective is accomplished over the long term is to promote and facilitate group learning. When group learning is effective, problem solving is improved. Communication efforts are enhanced. The followers' acceptance of the organization's goals is heightened. In the process, the leader gains, the followers benefit, and the entire group performs better.

This premise is best evidenced by the laying out of the weekly game plan for a given opponent. If the formulating and calling of the game is mainly performed by one individual, that person will inevitably make the costly mistake of not having all the information needed to make a calculated decision even though that information might be readily available. An often-repeated scene throughout the NFL takes place the day after any contest, when the coaching staff is reviewing the game film. On a particular play, say a draw, the offensive line coach may make the observation, "I knew the draw was not going to work here because they had not been rushing up the field aggressively." At this point, the offensive coordinator often goes ballistic, taking the comments as a criticism, and lashes back, "Great, that does me a lot of good now, a day later. Where was that brilliant observation yesterday?" In fact, it may indeed not be the fault of the offensive line coach if the offensive coordinator has not been as inclusive as he should have been in his game planning and play-calling intentions. In other words, group learning should play a role in all organizations—including sports.

In order for group learning to be effective, however, leaders must understand that learning involves both a leadership decision and a way of leading. If you take a "controlling" approach to leadership (characterized by an authoritarian, dictatorial view of imposing decisions) rather than a "guiding" approach (a style of reaching a decision that features encouraging and considering input from your followers), then you severely limit any learning that might occur.

The point to remember is that you, as a leader, need to develop and implement a plan for group learning that makes learning a strategic choice for your organization. As a rule, individuals are learning new things all the time. You can tap into the process, however, by undertaking specific steps to maximize the opportunity for learning, the desire for learning, and the channels for learning within your organization.

CRITICAL THINKING

"If everyone is thinking alike,
then somebody isn't thinking."

—George S. Patton, Jr.
general, U.S. Army

One of the most valuable traits that a leader can possess is the ability to be an independent thinker. Independent thinking involves reaching decisions and making objective judgments based on your own experiences and observations, rather than simply relying on the statements or opinions of others. It involves being a nonconformist to the extent that you have faith in your own ability to make judgements even if your decisions contradict what others believe.

Once this factor is achieved, it is important to take the next step and think three-dimensionally rather than two-dimensionally with regard to your interaction with your subordinates. In my opinion, most people react in a two-dimensional way with regard to their dealings with other people in an organization. Initially, most people in an organization are in a dependent mind frame. In other words, any action they take is generally dependent upon the directions of those above them. The longer people are in an organization and their responsibilities grow, the more likely they will evolve into an independent mode, where they are able and willing to initiate action for those underneath them independently without directions from some controlling authority above them given the expanded scope of their responsibilities.

Too often, when individuals reach this position, they think that they have attained the highest level of interaction in the organization. In fact, there is a third level: interdependent interaction with those around you. This level involves having such confidence in your own abilities that you're not afraid to initiate interaction with those around you. You are willing to consider their initiatives and perspectives, fully aware that they may offer the best way to proceed. Subsequently, you incorporate their input into the directives that you set forth.

Too many times, I've seen situations where a coach will hesitate to initiate directives because it wasn't their idea, fearful of the concept that others, in seeing it wasn't his idea, may question his abilities. This quality is most apparent to me in game planning for a given opponent. I've always believed in the philosophy that whether it's as a head coach or as an offensive coordinator, on game day anybody could call the game. As you prepare for an opponent during the course of the week, if you're doing your job appropriately, you're interacting with the other coaches—each of whom will have a designated aspect of the game plan in which they are expected to be the expert.

Putting out the game plan in an efficient manner—not only during the week to the players but on game day—enables everyone to have a better understanding of the full dynamic of the plan. As a result, everyone can be more anticipatory as to what might need to be adjusted during the course of a game because they know what the overall game plan is.

When people feel like their ideas are being acted upon and can be implemented into the game plan, it heightens both their learning curve and their level of productivity. If a coach or player is led to believe that his input isn't sought and that he's simply a device used to orchestrate the game plan without making any contributions, he generally won't execute it at the level he would if he felt like he played an interactive role in it. When submitting an idea for consideration, a head coach, a coordinator, or a position coach (who's hoping to interact with the game plan) must not let their position or ideas be so closely aligned to their ego that if an idea is shot down or not accepted, their feelings are hurt. If your employees or coaches are made to feel the lesser for coming up with an idea that's not accepted (for whatever reason) then you will slowly and steadily inhibit them from wanting to bring forth any new ideas. Likewise, it's incumbent upon the leader to make everyone appreciate the fact that while a person's ideas may be sound, it is impossible (if not impractical) to implement everyone's ideas into a single game plan. It's the specific job of either the coordinator or the head coach to make sure that the game plan is constructed in a synergistic fashion that enables it to be consistent with a specific set of philosophies.

I've always had an appreciation for those coaches that could come up with idea after idea, and even though they may not have been accepted, were not hesitant to come back in subsequent weeks with more ideas, knowing at some point their input will be of value. As a leader, you should shy away from those people who when they bring forth an idea that is not accepted, simply sulk and pout and then discontinue to bring up ideas, given their feelings that since their ideas aren't going to be accepted anyway, why should they bother. Jerry Rhome, a longtime NFL coach who was my receivers coach for a year in Minnesota, was the best I have ever been around in this regard.

I was a young first-time coordinator, and Jerry had already served many years as a successful coordinator in his own right. Naturally, Jerry had a lot of ideas, many of which we incorporated into our scheme. I can honestly say I learned as much football from Jerry as from any coach I have ever been around. Yet, as a new coordinator, I was trying to put my stamp on the offense. There were any number of ideas that Jerry would have that I did not employ for one reason or another. These rejections never deterred Jerry from suggesting something else. Many times, he would come into my office and suggest something. I would reject it and before he could get back to his office, he would turn around and come back and suggest something else. At times, it was tiring keeping up with Jerry, but I truly appreciated his enthusiasm. Jerry applied one of General Colin

Powell's basic 13 rules of leadership: "Never let your position be so closely tied to your ego that when your position is defeated, so is your ego."

In other words, you should apply critical thinking as a reasonable means to help you solve problems, consider new information, or process new ideas. You are introspective of what you see and are told. You question your assumptions and values. You stand up for your beliefs, while being tolerant toward those who hold divergent viewpoints. You take a rational, analytical approach to assessing the accuracy of the information you must process. With regard to your ability to challenge your thought processes, you exhibit a willingness to think "outside the box." You are constantly looking for a better way. You don't do something in a particular way just because that's the way you've always done it or the way everybody else does it.

LEARNING IS RECIPROCAL

A reciprocal relationship must exist between you as a leader and those whom you lead if learning is to be maximized within your organization. The essence of this relationship is that both parties must take responsibility for the success of each other. The relationship is characterized by open lines of communication and mutual involvement in the planning and decision-making processes. It is a process that depends on developing a relationship that is based on trust and respect.

For example, a major reason for the success we have had with the Ravens is the relationship between Ozzie Newsome and myself. Newsome, the Hall of Fame tight end for the Cleveland Browns, has become one of the top personnel men in the NFL. Ozzie and I balance each other very well on both a personal and professional level. Ozzie is one of the most "egoless" men I have ever met, preferring to stay out of the limelight as much as possible. His lack of ego is a perfect balance for my over-exaggerated ego. On a professional level, Ozzie has spent a few years in coaching, much as I have spent a few years on the administrative side of an NFL organization. I believe that our broadened perspectives enable us to better appreciate the demands and pressures we both face individually, as well as collectively, in our respective positions.

Because of the way that Ozzie and I trust and respect each other, we communicate more readily—a factor that makes the decision-making process in the Ravens' organization much more effective, particularly in pressure situations. For example, in our first draft together, the clock had started on our second-round pick. This meant that we had 10 minutes to make our selection before it passed to the next team. We were in the process of finalizing our pick when the Atlanta Falcons called with an offer to trade their next year's first-round pick (2000) for our current second-round pick (42nd) in 1999. Atlanta had been in that year's Super Bowl and was picking 30th. It was reasonable to assume that the Falcons would be close to that level the next year. My concern was we might be giving up a needed body now for virtually the same pick the next year. I did not want to make the trade.

We did not have enough time to discuss it. Ozzie immediately sized up the board in the way only a top director of personnel can. We had wanted to take either Edward Mulatolo, an offensive lineman from Arizona, or Brandon Stokley, a wide receiver from Southwest Louisiana. Ozzie said we could still get both in later rounds. I disagreed and could have forced the issue. Even though we had not worked together very long, I knew Ozzie had conviction about his opinions and had the expertise to evaluate the draft board in much more detail than I could. We made the trade, and it turned into a brilliant move. Because Atlanta suffered a number of injuries the next year, the trade yielded us the fifth pick of the 2000 draft—a pick that turned out to be Jamal Lewis who, as a rookie, became a major part of our Super Bowl season. Just to add emphasis to the point I'm trying to make about the value of reciprocal learning, we also ended up getting both Mulatalo and Stokely in later rounds. Both have become starters and are excellent young players. If Ozzie and I had not based our relationship on trust, open communication, and a deep respect for each other's abilities, we would not have handled that situation as effectively as we did.

When I interviewed for the job, I told Ozzie that I would not compromise. Initially, I think my comments caused Ozzie to feel that I was saying that it would be "my way or no way." In fact, I subsequently explained to Ozzie that it was our obligation to develop a relationship whereby either he would convince me of his point of view or I would convince him of mine. When you compromise on major decisions, there is no accountability. As a result, no one is happy with the decision. This was the first situation that put that theory and relationship to the test and was a major stepping stone toward building a championship team.

Principle #4:

*Knowledge is a potent source of
competence and credibility for a leader.*

chapter 6

BE PERFORMANCE-ORIENTED

> *"If a man has done his best, what else is there?"*
>
> —George S. Patton, Jr.
> general, U.S. Army

A distinguishing characteristic of skillful leaders is that they are able to create a vision, to identify steps for achieving that vision, and then to assess the progress of the organization in accomplishing that vision. Vision is what defines the future of an organization and enables groups to pursue continued growth and to willingly confront challenges.

In other words, effective leaders plan for an organization's future by establishing a vision. They then use that vision as a standard of excellence by which the efforts of everyone within an organization can be judged. The vision is the benchmark that keeps everyone on track. It is the touchstone that helps guide the behavior of the leader.

Having a sense of vision is the essence of leadership. It's what distinguishes a leader from a manager. Managers ask, "How?" and "When?" while leaders inquire, "What?" and "Why? What are we doing and why are we doing it?" Competent leaders also want to know "how well are we doing it?" Because of their responsibility for establishing the guiding force that pulls the organization forward, leaders—by nature—are results-oriented. As such, skillful leaders are not only passionate about the dream (i.e., the vision) they've created for the organization, but also dedicated to ensuring that their grand plan is successful.

In our book *Finding the Winning Edge*, Bill Walsh and I listed the establishment of the "primary directive" of the organization as one of the most fundamental decisions an organization can make. It is vital that at least at the top level of management, a "prime directive" is established. Without it, it is impossible for subordinates to prioritize their obligations and decision-making processes.

An excellent example of this prioritization was noted recently by the president of a well-known major airline. Although the airline industry has multiple goals and priorities—such as providing timely service, adequate meals, comfortable surroundings, profitable routes, and obviously a profitable bottom line—each has to take a secondary position to what must be the "prime directive" of every company in the airline industry: getting people from point A to point B *safely*. Being aware of this enables people within an airline company to align their behavior and actions to always position the prime directive above any other obligation that may otherwise come into conflict with it.

In the NFL, there are a number of organizations whose prime directive is winning. Others place a higher value on remaining profitable. At face value, these directives may seem wholly compatible. However, at some point in the process, these two priorities will come into direct conflict with each other. Notable examples of this dilemma have arisen in recent years due to factors associated with the NFL's free-agency process. It is not too difficult to identify the organizations that constantly let their developed talent get away, not because they don't recognize their skill level, but because they won't or can't commit to the financial structure it would take to keep these athletes in their organization. In reality, it is cheaper to let your developed talent get away and then simply fire the coach and his staff for not winning enough games. A team can often replace an entire coaching staff for the cost of keeping one key player. Somewhat inexplicably, teams that continually adhere to this particular prime directive have a hard time recognizing why they are continually at the bottom of the NFL success curve.

As such, leadership must clearly define the parameters regarding what their prime directive is so that the principle individuals involved in guiding the organization can make their decisions accordingly. For example, if the head coach fools himself into thinking that the prime directive of his organization is winning, when in fact the ownership is more concerned with its financial spreadsheet, he is not going to be able to adequately anticipate the needs of the organization and make decisions that are consistent with those needs. In this instance, my observations are not meant to be offered in a judgmental way. I realize that some clubs exist in an economic climate that makes it very difficult for them to have winning as their prime directive. The changing nature of the salary cap in the NFL is forcing some teams to reevaluate their ability to sustain an acceptable level of productivity. In this regard, they are having to reexamine their short-term versus their long-term commitment to their prime directive.

For good or bad, right or wrong, leaders must accurately identify and assess the prime directive of their organization if they are going to make the right decisions within the framework in which they have to function. Frankly, the only thing worse than being in an organization that *will not* or *cannot* compete financially is not being able to recognize that fact.

CREATING A VISION

"Always bear in mind that your own resolution to succeed is more important than any other thing."

—Abraham Lincoln
16th president of the United States

The relationship between leadership and an organization's vision can be illustrated by making an analogy where leadership is an arrow and the vision is the target you're trying to hit with the arrow. As a leader, you have the responsibility of identifying and articulating the target toward which the organization should direct its resources and energies. Your vision is a by-product of both your knowledge (experience and formal education) and your creative imagination. Your imagination enables you to conceptualize the possibilities that await an organization at the end of a particular destination.

Your imagination is the creative ability of your mind that enables you to combine the existing facts available to you with your mental ability to perceive a variety of possibilities in a way that enables you to envision different circumstances. Imagination works in its most practical form if it's maintained within a unity of purpose. Otherwise, your imagination can become defused and unfocused.

In order to be viable, the vision you establish must meet several criteria. First and foremost, it must be achievable. Within the context of your skills as a leader, the capabilities and enthusiasm of the group you are leading, and the resources of the organization, the dream that you've visualized must be "do-able."

Your vision for the organization must also be tangible. It must have a perceived reality that emanates from an intelligible mission statement—a statement that summarizes goals that, when accomplished, fulfill the vision of the organization.

Another feature that your vision for the organization must satisfy is that it must meet the expectations of your followers, your superiors, and yourself. With regard to having trust in you and the vision that you establish, your followers have a right to expect certain things from you. They have the right, for example, to expect that their leader has chosen an appropriate goal for them and the organization. Furthermore, they also have the right to expect to be kept informed about what behavior and actions are required of them and why. In addition, they have a reasonable expectation that their leader will have at least a comparable sense of urgency as they do concerning the mission of the organization. Followers also have a right to expect that their leaders are intellectually honest, dependable, values-oriented, and have the ability to exercise good judgment.

As a coach in the NFL, I have had the opportunity to gain a degree of insight into the expectations of followers. For example, dealing in free agency over the last eight years has taught me at least two things. First and foremost, free agency is always about the money. No matter what a player says about liking the city, the team, or its coaches, a free agent will almost always go with the top bid. Having said that, the second factor I have learned about free agency is that a small minority of experienced players exist who have the money, the records, the Pro Bowl appearances, but lack one thing—a championship ring. For this select group of athletes, the team's ability to convey its commitment to winning a championship can make a major difference. Since our victory in the Super Bowl, the response we get from players and agents has been tangibly different now that we have earned a world championship, and they can readily discern our firm commitment to achieving another one.

Your superiors will also typically have certain expectations of you relative to your role in establishing and implementing a vision for the organization. They expect you to fulfill that role in an expeditious manner. They expect the organization to achieve demonstrable, continuous improvement—relatively quickly. They also expect you to marshal the resources of the organization in a way that maximizes their use. Finally, they expect you to keep them informed about what's going on. They don't want to be blindsided by unforeseen problems.

You also have your own expectations concerning the vision you have created. You expect your followers to perform certain actions or behave in a particular way in order to accomplish the mission. You have a right to expect your followers and your superiors to believe in and accept your vision if you have taken the appropriate steps to establish and implement the vision. In that regard, it is reasonable for you to expect that your superiors will provide you with the resources and support essential to accomplishing the vision you have developed for the organization.

As a leader, one of your primary responsibilities is to keep everyone focused on ensuring that the organization's vision becomes a reality. In that regard, you should try to get everyone's expectations on the same page. The more these expectations are in accord, the more likely you will be able to establish a level of trust between all parties that will minimize any conflict and misunderstandings.

For example, the day after we concluded our 8–8 season in 1999, I stated in my year-end press conference that our goal was to make the playoffs in 2000 and that anything else would have to be considered a failed season. This record and the accompanying goal might have seemed to be a modest proclamation to some, but you should remember that the 8–8 record represented the first time in the history of the Ravens' organization that they had not had a losing season. In my opinion, it was a carpe diem moment; we had to seize the day.

I also attempted to put the value of our record in the previous season in proper perspective by stating that our initial 8–8 season could be considered successful only if it led to a playoff berth in 2000. Otherwise, it was just another mediocre season. My actions were vital for the organization because we needed to recognize that even though an 8–8 season was a good start, relatively speaking, it was only an initial step in the ultimate direction we wanted to go. Our overall vision had to be maintained, rather than to be defused by a momentary accomplishment.

The media appeared to love this declaration because it gave them just the angle they needed to criticize me regardless of how the season might go. If we did not accomplish our goal of reaching the playoffs, the media could attack their perceptions of my "failures" as a coach for not only this season but for the previous one as well. If we were successful, they could criticize me for not setting our goals high enough by limiting it to just making the playoffs.

Frankly, some of my coaching brethren questioned the logic of me putting this kind of pressure on myself, particularly since I was only in the second year of a six-year contract. Usually, those types of declarations are saved for someone who is at the end of a contract and expects to get fired if he doesn't reach the playoffs anyway. As a rule, it is good to have a plan for success based on the length of your contract. For example, if you have a three-year contract, you had better have a three-year plan. In fact, success had better start rearing its head in two years or you may be in trouble.

The difference for me was that I didn't believe that this organization, these players, this city, and these fans could have gone into the season with less than defined and lofty goals. The fans in Baltimore had supported losing Ravens' teams with four years of continual sellouts. They had paid the PSL's, bought the tickets, donned the colors, and been supportive throughout four frustrating seasons. In my opinion, it was time to provide a winner, and they needed to know what the standard of expectations and success were going to be.

One of the many things I learned from Denny Green is that if you're not willing to talk about the success you expect to achieve, it is unlikely you are going to be able to accomplish it. Corporate America has a number of skillful leaders who understand the necessity of being resoundingly committed to success. For example, Andy Grove, the successful CEO of Intel, once made the observation that, "Most companies don't die because they are wrong; most die because they don't commit themselves . . . You have to have a strong leader setting a direction. And it doesn't even have to be the best direction—just a strong, clear one." GE's dynamic leader Jack Welch called this factor "edge." "A leader has to have edge. Without it, nothing else matters. That is what separates, for me, whether or not someone can lead."

I wanted to communicate to the Ravens organization that regardless of the individual success in each department, everyone was being put on notice about our expectations and would be judged accordingly. It didn't matter if you were in the ticket office and we had sellouts, or if the publications were the best in the league, or if the suites were sold out. If this team did not succeed on the field, then neither did you. There would be one barometer for success—winning. I am sure some individuals in the organization tired of my typical greeting to them: "What have you done to get us into the playoffs today?"

A fourth factor that should influence your efforts to establish a vision for the organization is the fact that the vision should consider the "big picture." For example, a properly conceived vision is based on strategic thinking and planning. Strategic leadership involves the ability to think conceptually, interpret a multiplicity of ideas, insights, and information, and reach a reasoned, straightforward plan of action.

The ability to effectively manipulate the salary cap is an excellent example of the need to deal with an often contradictory set of priorities that involve both short- and long-term objectives. In fact, no set formula exists for handling the cap successfully. The strategies and tactics for dealing with it are as fluid and changing as anything that happens on the field of play.

You should keep in mind that even if the vision you created satisfies the aforementioned four criteria, it can still fail for any number of reasons. For example, your vision may be superceded by a better vision by another organization. Your vision may have been too grand, thereby rendering it unachievable. In such an instance, if your vision is perceived to be too grandiose, your followers may become discouraged and decide that "buying-in" to your vision would be a waste of their time. On the other hand, your vision may have been too limited. As a result, it may have been insufficient to adequately inspire your followers to perform as you intended.

SETTING GOALS AND OBJECTIVES

"Goal setting is the strongest force for human
motivation. Set a goal and make it come true."

—Dan Clark
in *Chicken Soup for the Soul*
by Jack Canfield and Mark Victor Hansen

Once the vision for an organization has been developed and articulated (via a mission statement), the next step is to decide how that vision will be realized. The most effective way to reach that decision is to establish specific guideposts by which particular courses of action can be advanced and the results of those actions gauged. The two most commonly employed guideposts in this regard are organizational goals and objectives.

As a rule, goals are positive statements that articulate what needs to be accomplished over the long run to achieve the vision of the organization, while objectives are clear, relatively specific statements, the completion of which will lead to the achievements of the organization's goals. Unlike objectives, goals are purposely stated in generalities. Objectives, on the other hand, are short-range, challenging (but realistic) statements that focus on immediate accomplishments.

The difference between a goal and an objective can be more readily seen by examining the following statements concerning the on-the-field performance of the Baltimore Ravens. A desirable goal might be "to continue to play at a highly competitive level for the foreseeable future." A measurable objective, on the other hand, that addresses the same fundamental issue might be stated as "to win at least 12 (75 percent) of our games next season." When considering any differences between goals and objectives, the key point to remember is that both are integral aspects of strategic planning.

As a leader, you play a critical role in setting the direction your organization will take. By extension, one particular point is obvious. If you're going to provide skillful leadership, you must know which way you are going and which path you want the organization to follow. Goals and objectives are the tools that enable you to define the parameters of that path.

Setting goals (and objectives) is neither a particularly complex nor a time-consuming process. In fact, setting goals is a relatively straightforward endeavor that can be done in a minimal amount of time if done thoughtfully.

Similar to establishing a vision for an organization, the task can involve several factors and considerations. For example, goals should be reasonable. Idealistic goals that can't be attained can be counterproductive and demoralizing. They should be compatible with the abilities of your followers and the resources of the organization.

Goals should also be manageable. If they're too large, they should be broken down into several smaller goals that can be more easily handled (each of which should contribute and lead to achieving the next larger goal). In addition, goals should motivate and challenge individuals to do their best. Goals that are too easily attained are often either temporal or perceived as meaningless (i.e., not worth the time or effort involved).

Setting goals effectively involves more than simply ensuring that the goals you set are consistent with a particular set of attributes or features. Your goal-setting efforts should also adhere to a number of broad guidelines for establishing goals. In that regard, one of the best overviews of the factors that should be considered when setting goals is provided by Gary Blair in his book *The Ten Commandments of Goal Setting*. Among the guidelines for goal setting that Blair recommends are the following:

1. *Thou Shalt Be Decisive*
   Success is a choice. You must decide what you want, why you want it, and how you plan to achieve it. No one else can, will, or should do that for you.

2. *Thou Shalt Stay Focused*
   A close relative to being decisive. Your ability to sustain your focus from beginning to end determines the timing and condition of your outcomes.

3. *Thou Shalt Welcome Failure*
   The fundamental question is not whether you should accept failure. You have no choice but to expect it as a temporary condition on the pathway of progress. Rather,

the question is how to anticipate failure and redirect re-sources to grow from the experience.

4. *Thou Shalt Write Down Thy Goals*
   Your mind, while blessed with permanent memory, is cursed with lousy recall. People forget things. Avoid the temptation of being cute; write down your goals.

5. *Thou Shalt Plan Thoroughly*
   Planning saves 10-to-1 in execution. Proper planning pre-vents poor performance.

6. *Thou Shalt Involve Others*
   Nobody goes through life alone. Establish your own "Per-sonal Board of Directors," people whose wisdom, knowledge, and character you respect to help you achieve your goals.

7. *Thou Shalt Take Purposeful Action*
   Success is not a spectator sport—achievement demands action. You cannot expect to arrive at success without having made the trip.

8. *Thou Shalt Reward Thyself*
   Rewards work. Think of what you will give yourself as a result of your hard work, focus, and persistence—you deserve it.

9. *Thou Shalt Inspect What Thy Expect*
   The shelf life of all plans is limited. No plan holds up against opposition. Everything changes. Therefore inspect fre-quently and closely; it's an insurance policy on your success. You must keep shaping, molding, and adapting your goals as appropriate to the ever-changing times.

10. *Thou Shalt Maintain Personal Integrity*
    Maintain your commitment to your commitment. Set your goals; promise yourself that you will achieve them. Elimi-nate wiggle room and excuses. That's a step that reflects well on your personal integrity.

As Blair's points suggest, goal setting is an important pro-cess that involves planning, preparation, and passion. Anything less may compromise the vision that you have created for the organization.

With the Ravens, I use a very specific approach to decide what goals are set for this organization, both individually and collectively, by making sure that these goals are S.M.A.R.T. This acronym outlines the need for goals that are specific, measurable, attainable, realistic, and timely. Every goal that I set for this team must fit those criteria. To a large degree the people in your organization will measure your competency based, at least to some substantial degree, on the goals you set. With the Ravens, I certainly believe that my players judge me in that way.

Understanding and applying the S.M.A.R.T. criteria will enable you to establish more meaningful goals. For example, a goal must be specific so that the players know exactly what is being put before them and what they are being asked to do. You can't be vague about the goals that you set. Your goals must also be measurable. There must be a way the player can look at and tangibly recognize whether he's achieving or not achieving a specific goal that has been established. Next, a goal must be attainable. The players must have a realistic expectation that a particular goal can be achieved and that they have the capabilities to do whatever is necessary to accomplish that goal.

A perfect example of the application of this factor occurred in the 1999 season, when we gave up 56 sacks. That was clearly an area that needed to improve in order for us to be successful in the 2000 season. On the other hand, to simply go out in front of my team and do my best Knute Rockne imitation by stating, "We're going to go out there and not give up a single sack," would have been ill-advised and a waste of everyone's time. By setting such an unrealistic goal and sharing it with them, my players would have immediately questioned my abilities to lead. In the first place, it would be totally unrealistic to think that a team could go through an entire season without a sack. While the goal might have been specific and measurable, it certainly was not attainable or realistic.

With regard to setting a team goal for how many sacks we would allow in 2000, what we did do was identify a level of sacks that we felt was realistic—two a game—that put us in the mid-30 range for the season. Although we would like to allow even fewer than two sacks per game, I believed that at that level we had a chance to be successful in every game. The goal we set gave them a very specific and measurable task to accomplish, one that was both attainable and realistic based on what the rest of the league was doing and what we thought our capabilities were. Although we did not meet our goal in 2000 when we gave up 43 sacks, the focus on this particular goal was clearly important and helped reduce the number of sacks we allowed from the previous season.

As a leader, you should consider a number of factors when setting goals for the organization. For example, when establishing goals and monitoring their progress, you must be careful not to give in to excessive perfectionism. As coaches, we too often employ an unattainable level of perfection to gauge the success of our teams, or worse yet, set such large and sweeping goals that we create an environment that is too big for those within the organization to effectively comprehend. The need to keep your goal-setting efforts in proper perspective is reflected in the words of Winston Churchill, who cautioned that the phrase "nothing avails but perfection" is nothing more than a euphemism for "paralysis." There are times when satisfying minor goals can lead to a more desirable end than a more grand and sweeping initiative.

When setting S.M.A.R.T. goals, you should recognize that in many instances a particular goal can be met, but you could still lose. For example, consider our sack goal in 2000. Although we did not achieve our goal, we still won the Super Bowl. Keep in mind that if you set too many secondary goals for your players or organization, it can become confusing as to what their real priorities should be. Eventually, they will either dismiss or slight your regard for those goals. Players call this "coach speak"—that useless chatter that players have to endure from coaches who are not prepared and simply talk off the top of their head.

Several of the coaches I have worked with over the years employ different grading systems for monitoring the performance level of their players. I have always attempted to discourage them from sharing those evaluations with their players. A serious problem can occur when you have a player of limited ability who is doing the best he can struggle to grade out well because of his lack of ability. Sharing the results of player evaluations with a particular individual can be an acceptable practice if you have someone to replace that player. If not, however, all you are doing by letting him know how well he graded out is to cut his confidence to the bone when he has to sit in meetings and hear how bad he is compared to his teammates. He can't help but begin to feel like any and all losses are at least partially his fault.

In my initial season with the Ravens, I had such a player. He was a great young man who gave the team everything that he had, but he had extremely limited abilities. The problem was that he was the best available player for the job. During one particularly tense time in the early part of the season, my frustration boiled over and I yelled into the head set for his position coach to get him out of the game. His coach answered back, "Fine, and just whom do you propose that I put in?" He was right. I had demanded that a coach make a change based on some arbitrary observation that I had made when in fact, he had no other personnel options available. At that point, that coach had to wonder about my ability to size up our talent base and whether I really understood the situation that he was facing.

The "T" in the S.M.A.R.T. acronym refers to the fact that any goals you set must be timely. A truck driver will tell you that he doesn't drive directly from Los Angeles to New York because that seems to be too big a task for him to undertake. Accordingly, common sense would dictate that no reasonable person would attempt such a huge task. What he does is drive from L.A. to Salt Lake, Salt Lake to Denver, Denver to Chicago, Chicago to Philly, and finally Philly to New York. The truck driver's point can be applied to those leaders who want to achieve relatively large goals. By breaking a large goal up into increments, that particular goal becomes more attainable and more realistic.

As the head coach of the Ravens, I take an incremental approach to our 16-game season. It's a long season, so it's difficult to think only in terms of it as being a single entity of 16 games. Like many coaches, I break the season up into phases or quarters and attack it two, three, or four games at a time. I have measurable and specific ideas about what I think we need to do to ultimately be successful over a 16-game time frame.

Our schedule in the 2000 season was like no other in the league. We were asked to open with five of our first seven games on the road. Because our last two preseason games were also on the road, the cumulative effect was seven games on the road in a nine-game stretch. At the tail end of this difficult stretch loomed a three-game road stand that included two contests against the Washington Redskins and the Tennessee Titans—the two teams that were favorites to be in the Super Bowl.

We broke our season into several mini-seasons beginning with the first five games, when we had an even balance between road and home games. We then focused on the three-game road stretch. The third phase of our season involved the eight games in the last half of our schedule. During training camp, we discussed the ways we would have to adapt our schedule to account for the varied circumstances, depending on which mini-season we were in (such as shorter practices, more rest at home, and increased study time to balance the lack of practice time).

With that many road games so early, we also recognized that we would have a good string of home games in the key months of November and December that could ultimately prove to be a huge advantage for us. The key was to get through the first half of the season in good shape and to then take advantage of the second half of the season.

In the first mini-season, we opened with a 4–1 run. We did not fare as well in the next mini-season, with three road games, going 1–2 with two 7-point losses. To some, a 5–3 record may not have seemed like a major accomplishment, but we had left ourselves in a position to take advantage of the remaining part of our schedule by not having worn ourselves out with the first half of the season or panicking about our early-season record. By cutting up the season and getting our players to understand that there was a plan in place to account for the tough part of our schedule, they gained confidence in their abilities to handle the challenges that they would face. This step proved successful and helped us go not only on a 7–1 run the rest of the regular season, but also an eventual 11–1 stretch that enabled us to go to and win the Super Bowl.

Another key to sound leadership is to find the right balance between short- and long-term goals. Some teams sacrifice their positive, short-term goals for ambiguous long-term objectives that never happen. Other teams allow the all-important prime directive of the organization to be eaten up in a never-ending series of short-term projects that lack the essential synergy with regard to achieving an overall objective.

A perfect example of this factor involves what approach a team takes to deal with the salary cap that exists in the NFL. The cap must be constantly monitored and dealt with using a level of evenhandedness that achieves a balance between addressing the short-term personnel problems a team might face and understanding the collective impact that a lack of attention to the long-term effects of any given signing might have on the future ability of the team to stay competitive. The two individuals in charge of monitoring the salary cap for the Ravens, Ozzie Newsome and Pat Moriarty, do an outstanding job of projecting the cap on a 3–4 year basis for any given signing. While we many extend ourselves cap-wise on a specific occasion, we never sign anyone with a blind eye to the future concerning the effects of such signings.

ENHANCE YOUR OPPORTUNITIES FOR SUCCESS

Your ability to be a performance-oriented leader can be enhanced if you understand and apply Pareto's Principle to your life. Also known as the 80-20 rule, Pareto's Principle is based on Italian economist Vilfredo Pareto's observation that in almost any set of human activities, 20 percent of the activities to be undertaken account for approximately 80 percent of the results. In turn, the remaining 80 percent of the tasks will produce only 20 percent of the results.

As such, skillful leaders identify those activities that will yield the greatest payoff (relative to expended effort) and devote their time, energy, and resources to those tasks. In reality, too many people spend too much time with the inefficient end of the 80-20 continuum, with too little to show for it. Effective leaders, on the other hand, are able to achieve more because they maximize their use of time, thereby elevating the likelihood of them being successful.

At the heart of your efforts to be successful is the ability to surround yourself with competent people. The faith you have in the capabilities of your staff will allow you to focus on the initiatives with which only top leadership can deal. It is one thing to be aware of all aspects of your organization and how they affect the performance of your team. It is something all together different when you have a compulsive need to orchestrate each and every action taken by a member of your team under the misconception that only you can do things right. I recently read about one coach who was so obsessive with his attention to detail that he even handpicked the type of soap that was used in the showers. It will be a shame if this detail-oriented and hard-working coach fails because key decisions affecting his organization (e.g., involving personnel, strategies, and tactics) go unmade while he is needlessly obsessed with what soap his players use.

My philosophy concerning the need to hire good people and to allow them to do their jobs led to my decision to allow Matt Cavanaugh to call the offensive plays for the Ravens. Matt is an outstanding coach with 14 years of experience in playing quarterback in the NFL. Even though my background and primary interest lie on the offensive side of the ball, I found that I was letting too many important decisions be affected by my limited perspective. I realized that I had to find a formula that would enable me to have the input I thought was needed based on my successes and experiences, but, at the same time, allow Matt to deal with the never-ending attention to detail that calling a game requires. Part of this equation is for me to accept the fact that for better or worse, Matt will not call the game the exact same way I would. I can help analyze and suggest things at key times, but I must not constantly second-guess his actions with the perfect 20/20 vision of hindsight. That type of skill is best left to the media.

Subsequently, during the middle of our championship season we experienced a five-game scoring drought, when we failed to score a single offensive touchdown. What is even more amazing is that we still won two of those games. During the week leading up to a crucial game at Cincinnati, Matt designed a play on third down that utilized our young wide receiver Brandon Stokley's quickness. I did not particularly care for the route because I didn't think he could get the depth needed to get the first down. Matt, on the other hand, had a lot of faith in the route. By the end of the week, I joked with Brandon that it would probably be the play that broke our scoring drought, even though I still did not like it. As it turned out, I was at least right about one thing: it did prove to be the play that broke our drought. On the play, Brandon scored our first touchdown in five weeks from 26 yards out—a touchdown that started us on the 11-game winning streak that led us to the Super Bowl.

The importance of this point goes beyond any discussion of the concepts and relative merits of micro vs. macro leadership. It is vital that you let your people make their own calls and "pick their own soap." If you can't adhere to this precept, you are probably surrounded by the wrong people—a factor that will get you beat long before any strategy or tactic will.

Principle # 5:

Vision defines the future of an organization and serves as the standard of excellence by which everyone in an organization can be judged—leaders and their followers alike.

chapter 7

BE A
COMMMUNICATOR

*"The greatest problem in communication is
the illusion that it has been accomplished."*

—George Bernard Shaw
British author and socialist

The ability to communicate effectively is an indispensable requirement for sound leadership. As a point of fact, it could be reasonably argued that many of the world's most talented and ambitious people fail to achieve their potential simply because they don't master the art and practice of skillful communication. In other words, you cannot prevail—much less excel—as a leader without superior communication skills.

For example, from a technical standpoint, you may be the best coach in the industry, but if you cannot effectively communicate with your players, coaches, and management, your understanding of the game is of little use. It is important to keep in mind that your ability to communicate effectively involves more than just your verbal skills. There are any number of coaches who are outstanding clinicians who are able to lecture effectively about a given topic. The point where they fail to take the next step is to utilize their entire array of communication skills on different levels to reinforce their message, thereby increasing the effectiveness of their efforts to communicate.

As a head coach in the National Football League, the form, intent, and recipients of my communication efforts are wide and varied. For example, the tone and tempo of my communication with Shannon Sharpe, our future Hall of Fame tight end, may vary greatly from that which I have with Jamal Lewis, our star rookie running back. By the same token, the direct and aggressive tone I take with one of my assistant coaches might crush the spirit of my secretary if I exhibited the same temperament with her. On the other hand, the detail and specificity that might be appropriate for my efforts to communicate with the Modell's, the owners of the Ravens, would be counterproductive or useless if I employed a similar approach with the *Baltimore Sun*, the local newspaper.

As a leader, the point you have to be aware of is the fact that effective communication, similar to competitive leadership, is an amalgam of several essential attributes—each of which can have a varying degree of impact on the demonstrable level of leadership involved, depending on the situation. A list of the more consequential elements of skillful communication includes the following aspects: verbal communication (face-to-face, telephonic, and presentation), listening, writing, feedback, memory, electronic messaging, and nonverbal communication. Most people who are placed in a leadership role typically have the ability to employ at least some of these skills at an acceptable level, while those individuals who are consistently able to demonstrate effective leadership tend to have mastered most, if not all, of them.

VERBAL COMMUNICATION SKILLS

Most verbal communication involves an interchange between one individual and either another person or a small group of two or three people. On occasion, such communication may entail addressing a relatively large group presentation-style. For example, my job requires that I communicate with a single player, an entire team, a whole city, or even millions of fans via television or radio. In any setting, the key is to identify what constitutes effective verbal communication and to determine what steps you have to undertake to ensure that your message is both conveyed properly and received and understood as you intended.

Obviously, not all successful leaders communicate in exactly the same manner. Important similarities exist, however, in the way these individuals communicate that can serve as invaluable guidelines for anyone who aspires to be a skillful leader regardless of whether the communication involves face-to-face contact or a telephonic exchange. Among the suggestions that can enhance your ability to communicate verbally are the following:

- *Keep in mind that effective verbal communication runs in both directions.* If you talk at someone, that is a monologue—not communication. Avoid coming across as a one-directional communicator.

- *Keep your communication simple.* Don't confound the main point of your message with a maze of meandering or complicated words.

- *Avoid a patronizing tone.* People tend to resent (and tune out) an individual who exhibits a superior, haughty manner. Know the difference between showing deference and being patronizing.

- *Match your tone to your intentions.* Employ a tone (e.g., straightforward, analytic, effusive, dogmatic, impersonal, accusatory, placating, etc.) that is consistent with the way you intend to come across.

- *Hear silence as it is intended.* As a response, silence can leave several meanings. Try to decipher what the other person's silence means.

- *Recognize the difference between defending ideas and being defensive.* Defending ideas reflects resolve and analytical forethought on your part. Being defensive puts you in a negative light.

- *Make the words you use an asset—not an impediment.* For example, avoid words that suggest lazy thinking, such as et cetera. Don't employ empty words (e.g., sort of, more or less, you know what I mean, etc.). Reduce your use of an excessive number of adjectives and adverbs. Employ powerful verbs (e.g., use "will" instead of "should," "I doubt" instead of "I don't know if," etc.).

- *Be specific.* Because people are not mind readers, don't mask your message in abstractions. Concrete words should always be used instead of abstract, muddled ones. Employ precise words. Don't buy into the premise that "just any word will do." It won't.

- *Get to the point.* Be concise. Don't beat around the bush. Don't waste words. Speak plainly. Confusion often increases in direct proportion to the number of words you use.

- *Get your thinking straight.* Muddled thinking can obscure your message. Organize your thoughts. Think before you speak.

- *Say what you mean and mean what you say.* Establish a track record for truthfulness. Don't exaggerate. Don't parse your words. Don't quibble. Be yourself.

- *Employ proper grammar.* Poor grammar can diminish your ability to get your message across clearly and effectively. As such, avoid using double negatives, adverbs without "-ly," unnecessary prepositions on the end of sentences, improper pronouns, and improper verbs.

- *Choose your words carefully.* Use positive action words to shape a positive image of yourself.

- *Us an appropriate tone of voice.* Tone is collectively the by-product of speaking rate, volume, inflection, choice of words, and body posture.

- *Enunciate.* Avoid sloppy diction. Proper diction involves both your choice of words and your manner of speaking (i.e., enunciation). Using imprecise or inappropriate words, mispronouncing words, or sloppily uttering your message will create a negative impression of you. Substitute different words for those you have difficulty pronouncing.

- *Speak with an appropriate level of formality or informality.*

- *Project success.* You don't just sound like you feel, you also think the way you sound. Speak with the expectation of success.

Within the confines of my responsibilities as a head coach, I have a number of opportunities to exercise my verbal communication skills. One such example involves the message I personally deliver to my team on Wednesday mornings. The main theme of my message is whatever focal point I decide to make throughout the week and then reemphasize on Saturday night in our last team meeting. These messages will vary from week to week. One week we may be facing a particularly hostile crowd. Another week, we may be up against a team who is a prohibitive favorite or underdog. Yet another game may involve a particularly physical style of play, while another may require an unduly aggressive or conservative game plan.

My Wednesday morning message is the best tool I have for providing a focal point, which may be crucial to our chances of winning. If the point I want to make is of particular importance, my message must be very well thought-out and presented. If I don't present it in a capable manner, the players will know that I didn't prepare well and thus will likely ignore my message. One way that I know I have gotten my point across is when I see the theme I emphasized being repeated by the players in the media (newspapers, radio, and television) interviews they give during the course of the week.

It is also important to keep in mind that your communication efforts must sometimes touch those with whom you are attempting to communicate emotionally as well as physically. It is not enough to just communicate a certain concept. Your message must also be internalized and remembered. During the course of a season, for example, I sometimes use a movie clip from a popular film to emphasize a particular point. If you can employ such a device or practice to elicit a specific emotion or a reaction in those with whom you are communicating, it can help reinforce an emotion or response that will be much deeper than even the most eloquent of speakers could evoke.

One of the film clips I used in my first year with the Ravens was a scene from *The Fugitive* with Harrison Ford and Tommy Lee Jones. Early in the movie, Ford's character (the fugitive) was holding a gun on Jones, who played a U.S. marshal who was pursuing Ford. A very tense moment occurred in the film when Ford, in an impassioned voice said, "I didn't kill my wife." Jones, looking down the barrel of the gun, looked up without flinching and responded, "I don't care!" The message I was trying to convey in showing that clip to my players was that Jones' singular purpose was to hunt down and capture Ford. The fact that Ford was innocent was of no interest to Jones. He was going to do his job regardless of the facts.

Like Jones' character, our fundamental purpose is to do our job—win games. It simply doesn't matter if you're tired, we are on the road, our flight is late, your bed is too short, you didn't like the pregame meal, your wife is mad at you, you're playing opposite an opponent who's better than you, or any other number of possible factors that you can conjure up as an excuse to not perform. From that point on, whenever I invoked the "fugitive rule," they knew that regardless of the reason they might want to advance for not finishing the job, I didn't care. They should quit feeling sorry for themselves and just "finish the damn job."

The night before Super Bowl XXXV, I showed the players a short video produced by CBS for the next day's telecast. It chronicled the history of the Super Bowl, featuring memorable moments in Super Bowl history. I knew that some of those moments would be ones that carried a strong emotional tie to any player who grew up dreaming of playing in this game and who had probably seen every Super Bowl ever played. This short clip connected my players to their soon-to-be legacy in a way no speaker could, no matter how gifted.

TELEPHONE SKILLS

Without question, the telephone is potentially one of the most effective communication tools that a person can employ. Properly used, a telephone can help you link up and transfer information, ideas, concepts, or feelings with anyone you deem appropriate. Improperly used, miscommunication, wasted time, emotional stress, and poor manners (possibly contributing to a negative impression of the offending individual) can result.

Personally, I have had several profound professional moments that involved using a telephone. One such moment occurred during my first interview with the Ravens. Like most coaches, I spent a considerable amount of time over the years preparing and daydreaming about the way I would present myself to an owner, general manager, or athletic director when given the chance to interview for a head coaching position. I would practice my mannerisms and gestures and the way I would communicate verbally and nonverbally. It never occurred to me that I would actually be doing this via the telephone. As fate would have it, that is exactly what happened.

After unexpectedly losing the NFC Championship game against the Atlanta Falcons in 1999, the opportunity to interview for a head coaching position came much more quickly than anyone had anticipated. There were several bidders for my services, and time was of the essence. After the game, I sat in a hotel room and interviewed for four hours over the phone with the Baltimore Ravens. Owners Art and David Modell, Director of Personnel Ozzie Newsome, and Director of Public Relations Kevin Byrne tag teamed me with questions into the wee hours of the morning. I had visions of them pounding away at me and when one tired he would turn it over to another, then go out and get a rubdown, a quick shower, a bite to eat, and then come back into the room and take over for someone else.

In all my efforts to prepare for an interview for a head coaching position in the NFL, it never occurred to me that this might take place over the phone. This situation required a tremendous amount of focus on my part to be able to effectively verbalize my abilities without the aid of my physical presence.

My interview with the Ravens was clear evidence to me that using the telephone (either a conventional phone or a cell phone) involves more than dialing the correct number. In fact, if you want to be able to get the most out of your use of this powerful communications tool, you need to adopt certain techniques and strategies for perfecting your telephone skills. The majority of individuals in a leadership role spend a great deal of time on the phone—and very little time improving their telephone skills.

Fortunately, the telephone does not have to be such a counterproductive instrument. Turning this piece of equipment into one of your most effective communication tools can simply be a matter of training and technique. As an NFL coach, I spend a lot of time on the telephone. For example, for every interview I do face-to-face with the media, I do three or four over the phone. In reality, the telephone is one of the main conduits I have with our fans. Unfortunately, it is also one of the biggest intrusions on my day. The number of people who want to "just touch base with you," "talk briefly," etc. can be overwhelming at times—particularly after you win a Super Bowl.

For most people (me included), one aspect of using the telephone effectively that is an almost universal problem is how to use the phone in a time-efficient manner. In reality, time is an extraordinarily valuable resource for most individuals. Accordingly, time waste is a major issue for many individuals. Inefficiently using someone's time on the telephone is not only inconsiderate to the person you're talking to, it can also be very counterproductive to you and your possible relationship with that individual.

The most straightforward method you can adopt to avoid wasting time on the telephone is to approach every nonsocial call with a four-step action plan: (1) get to the point; (2) clearly state your problem and your needs; (3) identify yourself and your organization; and (4) get on with it. The following strategies/techniques can also help you make the best use of your phone time:

- *Develop a "telephone time team."* If you have an administrative assistant or a secretary, possibly your best opportunity to save time on the phone will involve working together with that individual. Identify and review the exact procedures you want your assistant to follow in handling your calls. Develop an effective call-management system. Have your assistant screen your calls. Make sure your assistant is aware of which calls (if any) you wish to receive. Organize a callback system to eliminate the time-wasteful nightmare of phone tag. Custom design a telephone message form that will best meet your unique needs. Develop a method for prioritizing callbacks. Develop an office checklist for efficiently handling phone calls.

- *Manage your inbound calls.* Whenever possible, limit the number of inbound calls that you take. Not only are inbound calls somewhat disruptive, they put you in a "reactive" mode, where you may not be as prepared as you would be if you were the caller. Accordingly, whenever possible, make a callback. If you receive a call, make sure that you and your caller outline the major subjects you want to cover in the call. In other words, as soon as you can, impose some semblance of structure on the call. If appropriate, set limits on how much time you will actually be willing to spend on a particular call.

- *Organize your outbound calls.* Get the maximum results from every minute you spend on the phone. Be prepared to take notes and listen. Design and use a form that allows you to plan and organize your objectives for a given call. Write down your primary and secondary objectives for each call. Use this form for taking notes. Keep your focus on the objectives. Save the small talk until last—accomplish your objectives and then get into the informal exchanges.

- *Develop an appropriately organized workstation.* The physical layout of your workstation—including where your conventional telephone is situated—can have a substantial effect on what you're able to accomplish on the phone. Your phone should be located to the side of your desk—away from the possible distractions that are stacked on your desk. Place your phone so that you cannot see others in the office. Make yourself appear inaccessible or uninviting to others in your office when you're on the phone. Keep a notepad and a favored writing tool in a handy place adjacent to the phone. Keep a rapid-access file of relevant information on people who are likely to call you next to your workstation. Keep a clock in plain view. If possible, place a small mirror next to your phone. Considerable evidence exists that indicates that the shape of your mouth influences how you sound. If you're smiling, you'll sound friendly. Keep in mind at all times that your phone station is your sanctuary. Keep it neat and organized—ready for concentrated action.

- *Develop and use effective listening skills.* A majority of the time actually wasted during a phone call emanates from poor listening skills. Essentially, communication involves one or more of four skills: writing, reading, speaking, and listening. Of the four, most people do more listening than anything else. Unfortunately, for most people listening is also the least developed skill. Effectively listening will enhance the likelihood of accurately hearing what is being said and what is not being said—all the while keeping yourself and the caller organized.

Listening, however, involves more than simply shutting up and letting the information flow in. At the minimum, you need to do the following: prepare to listen; focus on the call (turn away from other distractions); consciously keep an open mind; let the other person speak without interruption; provide feedback (i.e., low level auditory messages/sounds that let the speaker know that you are intently focused on the message); take notes during every call; and repeat and verify all facts.

- *Close the conversation.* If you receive a call, quickly determine through questioning the purpose of the call and what the caller expects from you. When your conversation has accomplished its objective, bring the call to a quick and courteous close. Summarize what's been discussed. Review any relevant points. End with a cordial comment. Let the caller hang up first. Be sure you've actually hung up the phone once your call has ended.

- *Making the telephone work for you.* Using a phone effectively is generally a process that can be achieved through creative thought and determined organizational efforts. By simply taking charge of the situation, you can make either a conventional phone or a cell phone one of your best—if not *the* best—communication allies. Accordingly, it is critical that you give the right impression when using a phone. In addition to several of the points listed in the previous section, there are at least six steps you can take to make a better impression on the telephone:

  - *Remember that "how" you say something can be more important than "what" you say.* The same words can convey a totally different message depending on your tone, volume, and inflection.

  - *Take control of your voice variables.* Your voice has a profound effect on how well your message is heard. You are not stuck with the way you currently sound. Your voice is a matter of choice. Your voice volume, choice of words, rate of speech, enunciation, and voice tone can be changed through instruction and practice.

- *Develop rapport with the person with whom you're speaking on the phone.* Use explicit techniques to open the channels of communication.

- *Speak at an appropriate rate for the situation.* Speak too slowly and you may lose the other party's attention. Speak too fast and you may lose rapport with the other party. As a general rule of thumb, adjust your speaking rate to the other person.

- *Use an appropriate level of volume when speaking.* Your volume level when speaking can enhance or destroy rapport. Speak too loudly and you may be perceived as overbearing. Speaking too softly may give the impression of indecisiveness. As a general rule of thumb, adjust your volume to the other person's volume. If you speak just slightly louder, you will tend to project confidence.

- *Remember that you talk with your body.* Your voice is like a window that enables the other party to see you as you are. Your posture is projected through your voice.

PRESENTATION SKILLS

"It takes three weeks to prepare a good ad-lib speech."

—Mark Twain
American writer

What is a presentation? In its simplest form, a presentation is an opportunity to sell yourself and your ideas to others—usually a group. As someone in a leadership role, your skill at selling yourself and your ideas will greatly affect how successful you and your organization are. Fortunately, you'll only need two tools to make a presentation—a mind and a voice. How well you use these tools will determine your effectiveness.

When I address my team, I am constantly reminded that I am standing in front of 53 athletically gifted millionaires to whom I am selling my program at every meeting. During each meeting, almost every player looks at you with a piercing set of eyes that says, "Why should I be sitting here listening to you?" When I was growing up, if a coach said "Jump," the classic answer was "How high?" In today's athletic climate, if you say "Jump," athletes are just as apt to ask "Why?" or "What's in it for me?" Frankly, those are legitimate questions, and if you expect to survive in today's competitive and intense professional sports environment, you had better have the right answers.

In reality, you are required to prove yourself with each and every encounter you have with a player. Your competency and the competency of your program are not enough. If you and your program are not presented effectively, neither will have much of a chance of succeeding. I am constantly prodding my coaches to spend as much time finding the most effective *way* to teach as they do in determining *what* to teach.

In my opinion, current advances in technology provide one of the best means for improving our ability to teach. For example, one of the most effective tools I have come across for presenting our game plans is PowerPoint software installed on a laptop, in slide-presentation format. Those of us in the coaching community often lag quite a bit behind corporate America. This particular presentation format has been in use by many businesses for quite a while. The PowerPoint presentation software is an invaluable tool for coaches as well because it allows you to heighten the learning curve of your players. Anytime you can insert color and movement to animate your subject matter, it can increase your players' ability to comprehend and retain the game plan almost tenfold.

By using the most advanced tools and technology to help me communicate with my players, I have been given the nickname of "Compu-Coach" by the media. The fact of the matter is that with each ensuing year, more and more of our players are coming to us computer savvy. Indeed, many of our players almost demand that we use the latest technology to teach. This format is the one with which they are most comfortable. This factor can be seen by simply walking down the aisle of any team charters during our road trips. Given their financial means and personal disposition, you will see every electronic device known to man being used by our players—from laptops to palm pilots.

Technology or no technology, however, no magic formula or potion exists for making a good presentation. Speaking before a group is a learned skill—one that sometimes takes years of training. The fundamental premise of making an effective presentation involves at least three factors: know your subject, set and meet high standards for you talk, and work hard to prepare your talk. The key is preparation.

Planning an effective presentation can be an involved process. Taking sufficient time to fully consider and answer the six basic questions (who, what, where, when, why, and how) in a detailed manner will help ensure that your planning efforts are successful. Essentially, the answers to these six questions serve as the guide posts to the eight-step process for preparing an effective presentation.

Step #1. The first step is to identify the objectives of your presentation. Before you can develop a good presentation, you must know why you are making it. Some of the common objectives of giving a talk are:

- to inform or instruct
- to sell or persuade
- to arouse interest
- to make recommendations
- to initiate action
- to set the stage for further action
- to interpret or clarify
- to gather ideas
- to explore ideas
- to entertain

Most presentations are a combination of objectives. For example, to a point, you may attempt to entertain your audience while simultaneously focusing on one or more additional goals. Your objectives should be realistic, attainable, measurable, and hopefully in writing. Whatever your objective, keep in mind that a presentation is *not* a lecture. Rather, it is an exercise in interaction with you attempting to present your ideas in an interesting, positive way.

Step #2. Your next step is to know your audience. Regardless of the number of people in your audience (large or small), it is virtually impossible for you to know too much about your audience. Adequate information on the backgrounds, interests, and needs of the members of your audience will enable you to be better able to examine your presentation from *their* viewpoint. In turn, you will be better able to meet their needs and your objectives.

Step #3. Next, you need to define (in general terms) what you're going to say. Basically, this involves answering the five "what's:" what does your audience need to know; what do they already know; what do they want to know; what do they not need to know; and what should you not talk about? Keep in mind that too much detail can easily (and completely) stifle the interest and attention level of your audience.

Step #4. Your fourth step is to gather information on your subject. In this regard, the key is legwork. Using the Internet to surf the web, personal observations, interviews, and questionnaires are the typical means for obtaining information. A simple rule of thumb is that you should collect more material than you will ever need and then be selective to identify exactly what it is you need to use. Keep in mind as you gather your data that you need to evaluate it by asking yourself how accurate, objective, authoritative, and current it is.

Step #5. Once you have gathered the information for your presentation, you need to organize your material. Generally, individuals take two approaches in organizing their materials. They either organize to suit the material and its subsequent treatment or organize to suit the audience. In most instances, a combination of the two approaches is recommended. Whatever method you adopt, many experts suggest organizing your material by beginning at the ending and working backwards to the start. This sequence is designed to enable you to keep your focus on your primary objectives and to minimize any sidetracking en route.

Step #6. Your next step is to develop your presentation. You need to decide how you're going to shape all of your ideas together into a continuous flowing script—not unlike sewing together a patchwork quilt. Your presentation should be developed in such a way as to make your audience listen, understand, and be influenced. Eventually, you need to develop an outline of the step-by-step sequence in which your ideas (and the subject matter) should be presented. Once you have completed your outline, you should show it to several colleagues for their review, comments, etc.

Step #7. When you reach a point where you have basically defined the points you are going to make in your presentation and the order in which you plan to make them, you need to decide what kind of visuals you will use to enhance your talk. Keep in mind that individuals learn through their senses, using each one to a varying degree. Taste and touch account for only 1 and $1\frac{1}{2}$ percent, respectively. Smell and hearing involve an additional $3\frac{1}{2}$ and 11 percent respectively. The remaining 83 percent of the information that the average individual inculcates is from sight —lending credence to the fact that learning is largely a visual phenomenon. The literature suggests that visual aids (e.g., PowerPoint slides) can communicate ideas faster, more effectively, and more memorably.

Step #8. Your final step is to rehearse your presentation. At first, practice going over your talk alone. You may choose to video or audio tape your presentation at this point. During this stage, as you're practicing on your own, you'll often find little things that will make your presentation clearer, sharper, and more focused. Next, you should give your talk to others (associates, friends, etc.) and ask for critical comments. Finally, you should go through a final run-through in which your rehearsal presentation is simulated as closely as possible to the actual presentation you want and plan to give.

Presentation guidelines for selling yourself and your ideas. Audiences tend to form an immediate, general impression of your leadership skills by how well you present yourself during your presentations. To that extent, your presentations are a reflection of your ability to influence the behavior and actions of others. Accordingly, you need to ensure that your presentations are an accurate reflection of the image you wish to project. The following basic guidelines for selling yourself and your ideas to your audience are recommended:

- *Be positive—sell weddings, not funerals.* Transfer your own positive outlook to the members of the audience and entice them into giving you a positive reaction. Think in terms of cans . . . "I can," "You can," "We can." Avoid hedging. Don't appear to be either wishy-washy or uncommitted.

- *Understand and implement the process of persuasion.* Use the force of other individuals' opinions and prejudices to make your points and to win your argument.

- *Assess and focus on the needs of your audience.* Basic marketing theory consists of identifying the needs of those people you are attempting to influence and then influencing those individuals to work with you to satisfy those needs.

- *Acknowledge the importance of your audience.* Treat them with respect. Be prepared. Don't waste the time of those in your audience.

- *Capture the interest of your audience.* Ideas are like eggs—they can be served in several ways. Make positive points as early as possible in your presentation in order to effectively let the members of your audience know why they should listen to you.

- *Read your audience.* Don't overwhelm them with too much information or rhetoric. Know when enough is enough.

- *Allow your audience (if appropriate) to reach their own solution to a problem or point you want to make.* Instead of forcing an answer on them, provide your audience with information that will enable them to select your approved solution on their own as their own.

- *Be flexible; give your audience an opportunity to speak.* Don't neglect the importance of listening before, during, and after your presentation. Spend a moment or two reflecting on why God gave everyone two ears and only one mouth.

- *Sell by semantics.* Using the wrong words in a presentation can severely hinder (or totally block) the points you are trying to make. Select your words carefully and wisely.
- *Be honest.* To paraphrase Mark Twain, you have a lot less to remember when you tell the truth. Honesty, truth, and sincerity go a long way in presenting you and your ideas in a positive light.

LISTENING SKILLS

"Conversation in the United States is a competitive exercise in which the first person to draw a breath is declared the listener."

—Nathan Miller

No matter what your situation, no matter what the objectives of your organization, every working day is a constant, ongoing flow of information. As a leader, the better able you are to enhance the dissemination of information from both the sender and the receiver, the more likely it is that your organization will be a success. Many individuals tend to focus on the "communications exchange" as essentially a by-product of a person's ability to speak or write. In the process, they ignore what many communication consultants refer to as the single greatest attribute of an effective leader: the ability to *listen.*

You should keep in mind that it is impossible to gauge someone's comprehension of the information and concepts you are presenting to him if you don't listen to his reactions. When a player who has made a mistake comes off the field, it is of little value to him (or anyone else for that matter) for you to simply jump on him and outline what he should have done. You should first listen to his perspective to determine what both his temperament and his mindset are. We see this situation all the time in our games. An offensive lineman will come off the field after making a mistake—say blocking the wrong man. He will swear on a stack of Bibles that a defender was in a certain alignment, and that he's sure that that's the way it was. You then look at the Polaroids that we make of every play and determine that what he claims he saw truly didn't exist. It never ceases to amaze me that in some situations, an offensive lineman is unable to discern that a man is lined up over him when that player is probably 6'5" and 300 pounds. If you truly listen to someone, you can ascertain whether he is simply mistaken or if he is panicked and confused. There is a major difference between the two.

In reality, listening is both an art and a skill. Listening is the art of obtaining meaning from a situation in which the spoken work conveys meaning. It involves the skill of being able to separate fact from statement, innuendo, and accusation. It also involves the skill of creating an environment for the two-way exchange of information in which both parties involved are continually receptive to the thoughts, ideas, and emotions of the other. To be an effective listener, you not only must open the lines of communication, you must compel others to do likewise. Unfortunately, as communications experts point out, listening is a natural process that tends to go against human nature. But it is also a vital component of effective communication.

Listening is important for countless reasons. Contrary to the old saying "What you don't know can't hurt you," what you don't know *can* hurt you. Creativity is stifled. Individuals are talking when they should be tuning in. The communications process is disrupted. Time is wasted. The potentially endless supply of ideas, suggestions, and solutions is at least partially untapped. Your ability to communicate effectively is compromised.

A more pragmatic way of looking at the value of listening would be to hypothesize the net effect on your organization if each of your employees prevented just one $10 mistake a week by better listening. A $10 mistake can be as simple as a few minutes oversight in the time of a critical meeting, placing an item of stock in the wrong place, having to retype a letter, or misdirecting an important sales contact. If you had just 20 employees, the cumulative negative drain on your organization's bottom line would exceed $10,000 annually.

Effective listening, however, affects more than the financial resources of an organization. Properly utilized listening skills can have an impact on other factors within an organization as well. It can improve productivity, boost morale, enhance co-operation, teach, and inform—all essential goals at one time or another for most leaders.

Since the ability to listen effectively is so important, the question arises concerning what factors keep you from listening. On the surface, the process seems simple enough—people talk, and you hear what they say. Listening involves more than hearing, however. Hearing is passive; listening is continuously active. Listening is what you do with what you hear. As such, a number of factors can keep you from listening—some external, others internal.

External obstacles to listening involve disruptive distractions in your immediate environment; for example, noise in the office, telephone calls, a loud meeting, etc. The effective listener plans for listening. Effective listeners, whenever possible, select an environment that minimizes external distractions. They find a place where every individual involved in the exchange of information can listen without distractions.

Internal distractions involve matters like preoccupation, pressure, and priority. Although not as easily managed as external distractions, they can be controlled to a certain extent. The easiest way is to schedule your listening in concert with your other commitments. If you have something of a higher priority, do it first—listen later. If you have specific times of the day that tend to be more pressure-packed, schedule those communication situations where listening would be particularly critical to avoid those times.

With regard to listening, one of the most critical components of game management is the filtering of information from your assistant coaches. When processing information, it's almost as important to disregard the useless input as it is to discern the useful information. During a game, there is a lot of information to sort through. If you can quickly disregard those things that aren't important to your decision, you will be better able to focus on the data that is important to the outcome of your decision. As a part of your desire to glean what you need from what you hear, you should never underestimate the filtering effect of fear or anxiety. This factor can best be dealt with by developing your listening skills.

Once you accept the premise that listening is an invaluable skill that can make the difference between being a mediocre leader or an effective leader, you should make listening-skill improvement one of your primary personal and professional goals. Conscious, deliberate application of relevant suggestions and techniques for effective listening is the key to better listening.

Most people are simply poor listeners. Identifying good listening habits and incorporating those habits into your daily lifestyle is critical if you are to improve your ability to listen. Keep in mind that for most people, listening is about the hardest work they'll ever do.

The ability to listen is an asset I look for in my assistant coaches. If an assistant coach has a pattern of simply formulating a response to prove his point while another is outlining his position, he will miss any valued insight into the possible solving of the problem. Far too many valuable observations are lost because those in a position to act on them are not listening. This is too heavy a price to pay.

> *"When you're talking, you ain't listening."*
> — A sign on the wall of Lyndon Johnson's office

Improving your listening skills. The ability to listen is a learned skill that requires considerable personal commitment to develop. The strength of that commitment for most active, effective listeners tends to be based on answers to several fundamental questions, including "What's in it for me?"; "What can I learn?"; and "Will it be helpful?" Positive responses to questions such as these will enable you to keep your mind focused on the matter at hand. Knowing that the effort to listen is worthwhile makes the practice of the techniques for effective listening a more meaningful, realistic process.

A wide variety of techniques exist for developing listening skills, including the following:

- *Listen for what you'll get from the speaker.* Don't just listen to be polite.

- *Listen critically to an effective delivery.* Don't permit the type of delivery (eloquent words, training aids, etc.) to override your ability to decipher the message. Some people say nothing but with a style that obfuscates the true content. Others say a lot, but have a difficult time saying it. Know the difference.

- *Listen skillfully to a poor delivery.* Listen for ideas and information, not for entertainment.

- *When others speak, listen.* Don't compromise your listening time by thinking about what you're going to say next.

- *Focus your attention on the ideas being presented by the speaker.* Don't just sit back and be a passive observer.

- *Work at listening.* Listening is hard work. Effective listening requires that you apply yourself.

- *Schedule your listening (when possible) during your best times for listening—around competing priorities, pressures, and preoccupations.*

- *Minimize the number of external distractions that interfere with your listening.* When possible, find a good place for listening.

- *Listen for meaning—the whole meaning.* There is a substantial difference between the two phrases "I heard what you said," and "I see what you mean."

- *Ask questions to clarify meaning.* Listeners can (and often should) speak as well—but without commenting evaluatively on the speaker's ideas. Appropriate questions help the speaker get meaning across.

- *Be patient.* Everybody can't talk at the same time. Some must withhold their comments. Even though you may have something you want to express, sometimes you must be the listener.

- *Paraphrase.* If you can give the speaker back the meaning he or she intended to convey in your own words (not the speaker's), then both the speaker and you are more assured that you listened for the actual meaning. Paraphrasing allows you to check the accuracy of your listening.

- *Remember that the feelings, attitudes, and emotions of the speaker are part of the message.* Emotions and feelings are part of communication. They're normal parts of human living and as such are often reflected in messages.

- *Remember that the gestures and mannerisms of the listener are part of the communications process.* Lean forward rather than back. Nod occasionally to indicate comprehension. Smile. Look directly at the speaker.

- *Never end a conversation without being sure of what was said and why.* Don't pretend to understand when you don't.

WRITING SKILLS

"You don't write because you want to say something; you write because you have something to say."

— F. Scott Fitzgerald
American writer

Good written communication doesn't come easy for most individuals. And the ability to write is frequently identified in nationwide surveys as one of the single most neglected communication skills in leadership settings. Yet the ability to write effectively is one of the most valuable skills a leader can possess.

The importance of the written word is reflected in an observation of Winston Churchill, who once declared, "Nothing of any consequence was done by me by word of mouth." Futhermore, in his renowned book *The Second World War*, Churchill proclaimed, "I am a strong believer in transacting official business by the written word." Like Churchill, I am a very strong believer in documentation. I know my coaches often get frustrated with what might appear to them to be a "paper chase." However, it is my experience that when you take the time to document what you are doing, you bring clarity and definition to the situation in a way that verbalizing alone cannot accomplish. It is rare when I sit down to document a plan of action or process that I don't find additional observations about that process that I would not have otherwise considered. It also provides a degree of accountability that helps to remove any sense of ambiguity as to the scope and purpose of any given action.

Within the workplace setting, the question arises concerning why writing well is important? At the very least, poorly written correspondence is counterproductive to sound leadership practices. It can waste time and money. It lowers the efficiency of your organization both through misunderstandings and any resultant unnecessary follow-up efforts (e.g., telephone calls and letters) to correct those misunderstandings. Poor written communication can also impede relationships with both those with whom you work and everyone else with whom you interact because any resultant misunderstandings can lead to unwarranted (and unwanted) confrontations and mistakes.

In contrast, because good business writing is clear, concise and accurate, it tends to be both efficient and cost effective. When individuals with whom you are attempting to communicate know exactly what you mean to say, you foster goodwill, promote better relations, and elicit improved efficiency. In other words, the ability to effectively communicate in writing is not simply a nice-to-have luxury for those individuals who wish to influence the behavior and actions of others, but an essential prerequisite for anyone who truly wants to be successful in a leadership role.

If you're among the majority of individuals, whose writing skills are somewhat less than you want them to be, the obvious question is what—if anything—can you do to improve your ability to communicate in writing? An acceptable approach to your dilemma would be to learn as much as you can about effective writing principles and then resolve to apply those principles to your writing efforts.

In general, effective writing should encompass three basic steps: plan it, write it, and refine it. Each step, in turn, involves general adherence to certain rules, techniques, and principles, which, if successfully applied, will lead to effective writing.

The first step is to *plan* your written communication. As simple as it may seem, effective writing involves considerable initial thinking. The basis of clear writing is clear thinking. Before you begin to write a business letter (or any other form of written communication), you need to ask yourself three fundamental questions: what is the purpose of your letter, who is your intended audience, and what result do you want the letter to achieve?

You need to know why you are writing a particular letter before you begin to write. Is your letter intended to inform, inquire, direct, or persuade? Once you have a clear purpose in mind, it will be easier for you to organize your letter around a specific focus (as opposed to rambling around a topic so that the intended objective of your letter is missed).

You also need to spend a few moments considering who your intended audience is. When you identify your audience, you will be able to tailor your communication to your intended recipient. The basic rule of thumb is to write for your reader rather than for yourself. Generally, this involves considering what your readers already know about the topic, what they need to know to satisfy your intended purpose, and what the likely response of the readers will be toward the subject of your letter. Your answer to this final question will influence how persuasive you will need to be in making your point(s).

You should also think about and identify what action(s), if any, you want the reader to take as a result of reading your letter. Similar to knowing why you are writing a letter and to whom, knowing what you want your letter to achieve will enable you to more effectively organize and focus your writing. If, for example, you want a specific response, your letter should lead up to and reinforce the action you want the reader to take.

Once you've addressed the fundamental issues of "why," "who," and "what," you need to do some further groundwork to write effectively. Ideally, this endeavor will involve a certain degree of creative ideation (e.g., brainstorming, mind mapping, free writing, etc.), an effort to evaluate your ideas to determine which are appropriate for your letter and which aren't, and an undertaking to organize your material (via an outline). Keep in mind that all good writing typically has an outline at its core.

After you've decided on the content of your letter, the next step in effective writing involves actually *writing* your letter. Although countless textbooks have been written on the subject of "how to write," there are a few basic (and relatively painless) rules of writing that you should consider. First, "write the way you speak." The flow of ideas and your choice of words to express those ideas should reflect the natural communication pattern of the writer—in this case, you. In essence, your letter involves you having a brief (written) conversation with someone. To a point, it can be validly argued that the best letters tend to write themselves.

Another good rule of effective writing is to "get to the point." Start your letter as close to your intended point as possible, and also state your point as soon as possible. As a result, your letter will be less cluttered with unimportant information. In the process, you increase the chances that your point will be made. In addition, all factors considered, you'll appear to be more decisive. You'll also show more respect for your readers by not wasting their time and yours.

Effective writing also requires that your letters should be "clear and concise." Letters that are full of redundancies, tangential information, etc. frequently cloud what it is you are attempting to say. Don't overwrite. Excessive writing can weaken your message.

Finally, good business writing should be "positive." Positive writing involves using a generally upbeat style and tone. To a point, your letters reflect a specific attitude on your part. With no exception, this attitude should be both courteous and professional. Even bad or negative information should be communicated in as positive a manner as possible. Keep in mind that every communication effort has at least some public relations aspect to it.

The third and final stage of effective writing involves *refining* your letter. Refining includes three basic elements: editing, creating a specific "visual" look, and proofreading. Refining can enable you to turn an ordinary letter into an outstanding one.

Editing is the antithesis of the credo "More is better." Editing is designed to achieve several objectives, including eliminating unnecessary words; making your text more natural (and less pretentious) by decreasing the use of stuffy, complex words; and ensuring that your sentences do not exceed a maximum length (e.g., 20 words).

Creating a specific "visual" look involves formatting your letter so that it has an appropriate amount of white space. White space enables your readers to rest their eyes, as well as providing them with some visual variety. A one-page, solid block of type may obscure the message you're trying to convey. Effective writers increase the amount of white space in their letters through a number of fairly simple techniques, including breaking up a paragraph into several smaller paragraphs, using lists, etc.

The last step after you've finished writing, is to proofread your letter at least once. Use the spell check feature on your word processor to help ensure that the words in your letter are spelled correctly. Finally, take a few last minutes to make a final inspection of your efforts. Make sure that you adhered to the objectives you originally established when you started to write and to the rules and guidelines for effective writing.

Guidelines for Better Writing. Effective writing is the end-product of the careful choice and use of the basic building blocks of written communication: words, phrases, sentences and paragraphs. Among the guidelines you can employ to write more effectively are the following:

- *Choose your words carefully.* The foundation of all good writing is effective word selection. Clear, simple words will make your writing easier to read and comprehend.

- *Use short, conversational words.* All factors considered, everyday words enhance your communication efforts. Never use technical terms unless you are certain that your reader will understand them and that they are appropriate for a particular piece of writing.

- *Select the word that best fits what you mean.* Focus on using simple and specific words to clearly communicate your thoughts. Don't force your language. Don't worry about impressing your reader with "academic-sounding" words.

- *Avoid using words that are either overused or may be misunderstood.* Overused words often lose their meaning and effectiveness. For example, the excessive use of certain modifying adjectives when describing a new product or service (e.g., super, new and improved) has diminished their impact. The use of words that are misunderstood is both incorrect and sloppy and may ultimately lead to confusion.

- *Use simple active verbs.* Writing that uses clear, simple, active verbs tends to be perceived as energetic and powerful. As the central word in a sentence, a properly chosen verb can enhance a sentence tremendously.

- *Write actively.* Using active verbs and an active voice constitutes what is referred to as active writing. Active writing provides energy, clarity, and directness to your message—all desirable traits in good business writing.

- *Use clear, natural phrases.* Phrases—similar to words—should come naturally from the way you speak. The best phrases tend to be simple, direct, and easy to visualize.

- *Write clear, complete sentences.* Sentences are most clear when they communicate a single idea in a simple, direct way. If your writing is difficult to understand, you can usually clarify your message by simplifying what you are saying and the order in which you are saying it. When in doubt, shorter sentences are preferred over larger ones.

- *Write good paragraphs.* Each paragraph should center around its own theme—usually stated in the first sentence of the paragraph. Your paragraph structure should reflect an organized flow of thoughts. Get your reader's attention with a direct and interesting opening paragraph and then retain it with subsequent appropriate paragraph structure. As a rule, shorter paragraphs are used for emphasis or ease in reading; longer paragraphs are used to explain more complex topics.

- *Use transitions to connect your thoughts.* Transitional words, clear topic sentences, and effective paragraph openings enable your writing to flow from paragraph to paragraph. Your use of specific transitional techniques should help your reader to move easily from one idea to the next.

FEEDBACK SKILLS

Communication is often defined as a two-way transfer of information, ideas, concepts, or feelings. In other words, communication is an interactive process with information both being sent and returned. One of the best ways to determine whether your communication efforts are achieving their intended results is to obtain feedback. Not only can feedback enable you to know whether those with whom you are communicating heard and understood what you said, it also can tell you whether the recipients of your message responded the way you wanted them to respond.

I was quickly exposed to the potential impact of feedback when I became a head coach. One of the first things I had to adjust to was that if I observed that a certain thing needed to be done, even if it was just a casual observation, someone took it as a directive and went about doing it. At times, this reaction set in motion a series of expended efforts that would have been better spent on other projects. I then developed and implemented a directive that all initiatives I gave were to be taken to "their *logical* conclusions." By that, I meant my associates should, if need be, simply question my orders with regard to their intent, if for no other reason than for me to reconsider the value of my initiatives and possibly vacate them.

As a leader, it is vital that you don't let the authority of your position prevent effective feedback. For example, as an offensive coordinator, I fostered an atmosphere that required me to challenge, and if need be argue, with any given idea. Mike Tice, the outstanding offensive line coach for the Minnesota Vikings, played for me and got his first coaching job with me. Mike is from New York and played in the NFL for 14 years—a fact that he will remind you of on a continual basis.

Mike and I would routinely argue about various aspects of a game plan. We had a basic rule. If we did not "dog-cuss" each other at least twice a day, we were not working hard. It is my style to challenge an associate's point of view, even if I strongly believe in it. This approach is designed to find out how strongly he or she believes in their opinions. In other words, I want to test the courage of their convictions. Because of the friendship and respect Mike and I have for each other, we could continually challenge each other, and yet, at the end of the day, always come to a consensus and not take our interchanges personally. This type of interaction was vital to our orchestrating the most productive offense in the history of the NFL in the Viking's 1998 season.

When I became a head coach, it was hard to foster the same degree of feedback because my staff was more hesitant to challenge a head coach than they would a coordinator. Because such a lack of feedback was obviously counterproductive, I worked hard to establish a comfort zone for my assistants, one that enabled them to feel comfortable giving me feedback, even if it were critical of something I was advocating.

To a degree, feedback should be viewed as an insurance policy to ensure that your communication efforts are working. In effect, feedback is the mechanism employed to determine the answers to four questions posed to the person with whom you are communicating: "Did you hear what I said?"; "Did you understand what I meant to say?"; "Do you concur with my message?"; and "What is your response?"

The communication feedback cycle must be a continuous process. Not only do you need to receive feedback, you also need to give it as well. Communicating clearly and effectively entails real effort and requires a basic understanding of the fundamental elements involved in getting and receiving feedback.

For example, to be of benefit to the individual receiving it, feedback should be hearable, testable, and usable. *Hearable* means that the recipient is able to overcome any internal (e.g., the individual's own defensiveness) or external (e.g., noise) interference that might otherwise compromise the recipient from "hearing" the feedback. *Testable* refers to the fact that feedback is most valuable when it can be evaluated, verified, and corroborated (or refuted) by someone else. Finally, to be of most value, feedback should be *usable* by its recipient.

A number of effective strategies and techniques exist for facilitating your efforts to give and receive feedback. Among the factors that you should consider in this regard are the following:

- *Be as specific as possible.* As a rule, the more specific you can make the feedback you give, the more effective it will be.

- *Don't be overly judgmental (good or bad) of the other person's behavior or feelings.* Focus on the specific point you want to make, not on your subjective evaluation or judgment.

- *Don't guess at the other person's thoughts or motives.* To the extent possible, use directly observable data to bolster any inference you might make.

- *Be sensitive to whether the feedback is actually wanted.* The more a specific incidence of feedback is asked for and wanted, the greater its benefit.

- *Share negative feedback as soon as possible after the relevant incident.* While such feedback does not have to be provided immediately, it should not be saved for possible use as a counterargument or counterattack.

- *Be able to recognize when the recipient gives the response you desire.* Give the necessary forethought to identifying both the response you want and then the feedback that will tell you whether you've received that response.

- *Look for valid feedback.* Don't look for feedback that reinforces your biases, strokes your ego, or provides misleading favorable information. If the feedback is unfavorable, don't dismiss it as unduly unfair or inaccurate. If feedback is going to be helpful, it has to be viewed through an unvarnished perspective.

- *Ask for feedback in an appropriate manner.* The key is to employ words and phrases that call for a response in the listener's own words (or language).

- *Know your audience.* Focus your communication efforts to appeal to your audience. If the feedback you receive suggests that your message didn't get through, determine why and identify ways to improve your "connection" in the future. Keep in mind that if your message isn't getting through, it's seldom the audience's fault.

- *Ask for feedback that enables you to assess recipient's understanding of what you said, not how you said it.* Try to obtain usable information.

- *Keep in mind that feedback is relatively useless unless it is used.* Gathering feedback for feedback's sake is a hollow exercise. Feedback should enhance your efforts to achieve your specific goals.

- *Utilize negative feedback to turn the situation around.* Analyze what went wrong. Identify how to prevent the problem from occurring again. Build on future successes.

- *Stifle the urge to give premature feedback.* Listen to all the information before you offer your feedback. Don't jump to a conclusion until you've received the available information.

- *Don't give mixed signals about whether you want feedback.* If you don't want feedback, say so firmly but in an appropriate manner.

- *Ask for the specific kind of feedback you want.* In order to save time and avoid hurting someone's feelings (including your own), be specific concerning the type of feedback you need.

- *Thank people for their solicited feedback.* Express your appreciation to the specific individuals who provide you with feedback. Keep in mind that individualized expressions of thanks sound much more sincere than global praise.

- *Keep in mind that feedback can be either verbal or nonverbal.* Examples of nonverbal feedback include a nod, a smile, a look of dismay, etc.

MEMORY SKILLS

"Somewhere along the way to bigness,
information overload sets in. Short term
memory can't process it all, or even a small
fraction of it and things get very complicated."

— Tom Peters,
from his book *In Search of Excellence*

As a leader, if your memory is poor or inadequate, you are at a distinct disadvantage when communicating—either as a sender or a receiver. In order to be an effective communicator, your mind must serve as a vast storehouse for the knowledge and information you have accumulated in your lifetime (both in the short term and in the long term). That storehouse is commonly referred to as your memory.

A good memory can be an exceptional leadership tool. At a minimum, it can help you navigate the daily deluge of information, enhance your ability to learn, make the most of your efforts to influence the actions and behavior of others, and help make the best use of your time.

Similar to other elements of skillful communication, your memory can be improved by adhering to selected techniques and guidelines. Among the steps you can undertake to improve your memory are the following:

- *Repetition.* Rote learning (i.e., repetition) is a key to remembering. Repeat what you want to remember. Then, repeat it again. For example, if you want to enhance your ability to remember a name, say it immediately. Then, say it again and use it immediately when speaking to someone else.

- *Visualization.* This technique involves developing a mental picture of something you want to remember. Make strong and very specific images. Whenever possible, personalize the images.

- *Association.* This procedure involves associating new information with something you already know and mentally linking the two.

- *Exaggeration.* An extension of the association technique, exaggeration entails assigning an even more embellished (in some instances comical) image to a piece of information you want to remember. To a point, the more exaggerated the image, the easier it is to recall.

- *Linking.* This technique involves picturing information (items/ideas) and linking it with something you already know. Keep in mind that the linking association doesn't have to be logical to be an effective memory enhancer.

- *Acronyms.* This method involves spelling out a memorable word or phrase by using the first letters of the topics/items you want to remember. Initially, you begin by writing down the ideas/items you want to remember and isolating a key word or phrase in each idea/item. Next, you take the first letter of each of the key words and create a recognizable word (to the extent possible).

- *Rhyming.* A form of linking, this practice involves associating something you want to remember with a number (or some other item). The number and the key element you want to remember should rhyme (e.g., seven and heaven, nine and wine, etc.). This technique can be particularly useful when you want to remember something in a specific order.

- *Key words.* Your ability to recall details that you want to remember can be enhanced through the use of key words. For example, you can associate a particular detail with a key word (e.g., create a connection between an activity that is familiar to you and a specific piece of information you want to remember).

NONVERBAL COMMUNICATION

"When the eyes say one thing, and the tongue another, a practical man relies on the language of the first."

— Ralph Waldo Emerson
American poet, philosopher, essayist

Much of the communicating you do is wordless. In fact, over 90 percent of your communication is nonverbal. While verbal communication enables other people to learn about your thoughts and ideas, nonverbal communication helps to paint an image of who you are and your feelings. As such, nonverbal communication is an essential component of skillful communication. Nonverbal communication involves four broad elements: voice qualities, body language, facial expressions, and clothing and grooming.

How you say something sometimes conveys more meaning than what you actually say. For example, individuals who speak with a low-pitched, well-modulated voice are perceived to exemplify calmness, strength, and confidence. On the other hand, a voice that rises to a high pitch is thought to reflect an elevated level of excitement, a sense of panic, and a lack of control.

In other words, certain voice qualities tend to convey particular feelings, moods, and attitudes. A list of those qualities includes the volume and pace of your voice, intonation (voice pitch), stress (points of emphasis), juncture (the way vowels and consonants are joined in the stream of speech), and throat noises (e.g., sighing, laughing, yawning, etc.). Collectively, these qualities can have a powerful impact on your attempt to communicate effectively.

While your voice is conveying a verbal message, your body is talking too. Your body language has a critical impact on your efforts to communicate. How close you stand to someone with whom you are speaking, your posture (i.e., an alert, upright posture signifies interest and involvement, while a slouching posture reflects a lack of interest), voiceless signals (e.g., diverting your eyes, rising from your seat, etc.), and gestures (e.g., fidgeting, talking with your hands, etc.) are examples of body language–related factors that can influence your ability to get your message across effectively.

Another form of nonverbal communication involves facial expressions. Some estimates suggest that the average human being is capable of more than 20,000 different facial expressions. As such, the face and eyes can be powerful conveyers of intended messages. For example, a smile can be construed as a powerful expression of pleasantness. A steady gaze is often seen as a sign of sincerity, while darting eyes are often perceived as a reflection of untrustworthiness. Steady eye contact can be viewed as a manifestation of your level of interest or assertiveness. Looking at the floor while you're speaking is typically viewed as a trait of someone who has an inadequate level of self-esteem. A glaring expression, on the other hand, is generally seen for what it is—an expression of extreme dissatisfaction.

The final major category of nonverbal communication involves the way you dress and how you groom yourself. One of the first things that people tend to notice about you is your clothing and grooming. What you wear and how you wear it says a lot about you and how you feel about yourself and your relationship with others. By the same token, your personal grooming habits and personal hygiene also play an important role in the visual impact that you have on others (and by extension, your ability to be a skillful communicator).

One of the ultimate examples of nonverbal communication in my life occurred during the 13th week of the 2000 regular season in a game against the Cleveland Browns. Up to that point in the season, we had achieved four shutouts and had a chance to tie the all-time record of five shutouts set by the Pittsburgh Steelers in 1976—a team many experts consider to have had the best defense of all time. We were also on the way to breaking the all-time defensive scoring record of 186 points set by the 1986 Chicago Bears. Eventually, we shattered the record for the lowest points allowed by yielding only 165 points. If we had either tied or broken the shutout record, coupled with the record for fewest points allowed over the course of a season and our subsequent victory in the Super Bowl, this defensive group could truly be considered the best defensive squad of all time, with little or no argument. Needless to say, getting a shutout was important to this team.

In the game, the Browns orchestrated a masterful, four-play, 86-yard scoring drive in the first 1:42 minutes of the game. As I worked my way down the sideline to chastise our record-setting defense for allowing the score, the nonverbal communication from my team encompassed every aspect of listening and feedback. The look in their eyes and the way they carried themselves screamed, "Don't screw with us." They were very angry. Their message came through to me loud and clear, and they responded with the most dominant defensive effort I have ever been a part of. The Browns were only able to muster a meager 12 yards of total offense in the remaining 58 minutes and 18 seconds, while we were on our way to a convincing 44–7 victory.

EFFECTIVE COMMUNICATION

Skillful communication involves many dimensions. The more you can master each of these dimensions, the greater your advantage as a leader. I had a professor in college who observed that if you got your message across and it solicited the response you wanted, it was effective communication. For me, my efforts at communicating sometimes involve the use of "blue" language. Frankly, it is not something I am proud of, and it causes me to constantly work at improving the language I use on the field. Yet, sometimes, "locker room language" seems to be the only verbiage that fits the situation. I would love to have the time and demeanor to approach a player and coolly and calmly comment: "Gee, because you are playing in a manner that would indicate that you are not fully focused on the task at hand, I would like for you to endeavor to regain some semblance of focus on your duties." All factors considered, it is just more telling (and expedient) to say, "Hey, get your g_ _ d_ _ _ head out of you're a_ _." The former may be civilized, but the latter seems to be a lot more to the point and more effective. Besides, I know I feel a whole lot better about it. As George F. Patton once said, "Give it to them loud and dirty, that way they will remember it."

Obviously, I am taking a somewhat lighthearted approach to a discussion of the subject because I am embarrassed occasionally by my language. I find it interesting, however, that the television people will almost always hone in on a coach at just those moments when they are sure of showing him making some unguarded, emotional outburst that will typically be laced with profanity. To that end, I have pledged $100 to the United Way charities every time I am caught on camera using foul language. My daughters are the ones who keep the tally, and believe me, they miss nothing.

In any instance, the way I communicate is at the absolute core of my abilities to lead a team. In whatever form you choose to communicate, you must be trained and nurtured to be instinctive. These terms may seem contradictory to one another; but like an athlete who must be trained to be instinctive on the field, you too must train yourself to communicate your message in an instinctive way. If a player's reaction to any situation is always measured and calculated, he will never be able to adapt to his situation quickly enough to be an effective player. If the only way you can communicate with your team or organization is in a purely structured or academic setting, you will not be able to adapt to the many situations your organization may face in a way that gives them the immediate direction they need.

One of the most intense and hectic environments a team will face during the course of a game involves the two-minute drive at the end of a half or game. Of all the possible contingencies you face during a game, the two-minute drill has the largest number of scenarios. You could be ahead or behind by a limitless number of combinations, on one of literally a hundred places on the field and in a multiple of down-and-distance situations. The communication involved in this situation is very hectic, almost panicked. If your players have not been schooled in the likelihood of a change in your demeanor or tone in such situations, they may very well perceive your actions as panic— a reaction that could heighten their sense of anxiety. Though hurried and frenetic, your communication efforts must still be concise and precise, even to a greater degree than they would be in calmer times.

University of Michigan Business School Professor Noel Tichy characterized this type of communication best when he referred to it as having a "teachable point of view." He observed that, "Having a teachable point of view is both a sign that a person has clear ideas and values and a tool that enables him or her to communicate those ideas and values to others. It is not enough to have just knowledge or experience: leaders must draw appropriate lessons from their experiences, and then take their tacit knowledge and make it explicit to others."

Related to having a "teachable point of view" is the concept of a "teaching moment." A teaching moment is an isolated moment or opportunity to stress an idea or a value that is enhanced by a particular moment in time. Such a teaching moment availed itself at the halftime of our first game against the Jacksonville Jaguars in the 2000 season. Our organization had never beaten Jacksonville either since it relocated to Baltimore or before, when it was still in Cleveland. I had made the statement prior to the season that we could not think of ourselves as a playoff-caliber team until we beat the Jaguars. Regardless of how our season might turn out, our road to the Super Bowl was, to some degree, always going to go through Jacksonville.

We came into our first game with them, at PSINet Stadium in Baltimore, with great hope and anticipation, only to have the first half go as it had during all of our other games against Jacksonville. Mark Brunell and company torched us for 421 yards on the Jaquars' way to a 23–7 halftime lead. As we made our adjustments in the locker room during halftime, I gathered the players around me before we went back on the field. I told them that regardless of how the game ended, how we conducted ourselves in the second half of this game would determine the character and the ultimate success of this team in the rest of the 2000 season.

The Ravens then came out and played a masterful second half that culminated with a 75-yard drive in the last minute and 30 seconds of the game that enabled us to achieve our first win against a first-class organization like Jacksonville. The sequence and timing of events provided an invaluable learning opportunity that could never have been manufactured artificially.

The point to keep in mind is that a "teachable point of view," when combined with the proper "teaching moment," makes for an optimum learning environment that can have a positive impact on the organization if you communicate quickly and effectively at an instinctive level.

Principle #6:

Effective communication is the cornerstone of leadership.

chapter 8

BE
A MOTIVATOR

"Knowledge alone is not enough to get desired results. You must have the more elusive ability to teach and to motivate. This defines a leader; if you can't teach and you can't motivate, you can't lead."

—John Wooden
Hall of Fame basketball coach

An organization, no matter how well structured, will ultimately be only as good as the people who work for it. In turn, the employees of an organization will perform well only to the degree that they believe the organization is meeting their personal needs and to the extent that they "buy into" the vision established for the organization. By definition, a leader is integrally involved in both factors.

Without question, the two most fundamental responsibilities of a leader are to create the vision for the organization and to inspire the individuals within the organization to act in a way that enables the vision to be achieved. Skillful leaders are able to perform both duties very effectively. Not only do they have the insight and ability to set the vision and identify challenging, but achievable, goals for the organization, they also have the faculty for influencing the behavior of others.

Accordingly, one of the most essential duties of a skillful leader is to be a motivator. As a leader, you must be able to motivate individuals to do things in the interest of the organization. Your ability to address this objective in a straightforward, meaningful manner can be affected by a number of issues. For example, how well you understand and can respond to the various factors that impact the motivational level of those individuals within the workplace is particularly important.

MANAGING MOTIVATION

"A leader has two important characteristics;
first, he is going somewhere; second, he is able to
persuade other people to go with him."

—Maximilien François Robespierre
principal figure in the French Revolution

If leaders want to improve work performance and attitudes, they should take an active role in managing whatever steps and processes may exist for enhancing motivation in the work place. Efforts to manage motivation should involve reasoned, planned action on behalf of a leader. Such action is not something that just happens. Leaders should be aware of and accept their responsibility for giving direction to an organization's motivational efforts.

The single most consequential way that you as a leader can affect the motivational level of an organization depends on the theory of human nature in which you believe. Do you ascribe to the authoritarian, traditionalist viewpoint that employees respond best to a carrot-and-stick approach—in other words, are your employees motivated by either fear (stick) or rewards (carrot)?

A more commonly accepted theory concerning human nature is based on the premise that human behavior is governed by needs. The central idea behind need theory is that unsatisfied needs motivate people until their needs are met. As such, your key is to get to know your followers well and to try to couple the circumstances for achieving their wants and needs with the vision and goals of the organization.

In the late fifties, Abraham Maslow identified five major areas of needs that all human beings have. According to how important or more basic they are, these needs are arranged in a five-tiered hierarchy. The base of the triangle that Maslow designed to illustrate the ordered ranking of these needs consists of the physiological needs of the body (e.g., food, water, air, rest, etc.)—all of which must be satisfied before an individual becomes concerned with the needs at the next level of the hierarchy. No matter how ambitious a person you may be, no matter what goals you've set for yourself, those goals will become secondary if your physiological needs are not met.

Once your physiological needs are met, you then advance to the next category of needs in Maslow's hierarchy—a "sense of security." This category includes such needs as shelter, safety, stability, and predictability. The third level in Maslow's pyramid of human needs addresses social needs such as loving, being loved, belonging, and inclusion. When you're dealing with needs at this tier, you tend to be asking yourself questions such as, "Where do I belong in the group that I'm dealing with?" and "What is my role?"

Maslow identified ego needs (e.g., self-esteem, power, recognition, prestige) as the core of the fourth tier of his hierarchy. At this level, you are concerned with issues such as "Am I good at this role?" and "Am I successful in what I'm doing?" Finally, at the apex of Maslow's hierarchy are those needs he categorizes as "self actualization." Encompassing our developmental and creative needs, self-actualization factors motivate us to strive for the dreams and ambitions that we all have.

Our players are confronted with the same pyramid of needs. For an athlete, the physiological level is clear-cut. Can he survive in the world of the NFL? Does he have the physical, emotional, and mental tools to endure in a highly competitive, and in many instances, violent environment? We spend a great deal of time conditioning our athletes so that they can survive at this level of needs.

The next need level for our players is security. On one hand, you can talk all you want about team goals and winning a Super Bowl. On the other hand, if a player isn't sure that he's going to be a part of your team (i.e., he is worried that his financial welfare may be in jeopardy because he may be cut), his primary concern is going to be security—no matter how much he may appear to be interested in discussing team goals.

Once a player feels secure and knows he's a part of your team, he will then devote his attention to his need to define his role on the team and to be socialized into the team. As a point of fact, every successful team must have role players. Those role players need to understand that, while they are not called upon to be starters, it's both acceptable and reasonable for them to strive to do so. On the other hand, they need to understand that if their primary role is to be a special team's player or a backup third-down receiver, they must fill that role in order to maintain their value to the organization. Not only must they accept their role, they must want to excel in it and recognize that performing well in their designated role is their entrée to reach the next level of self-esteem.

Only after a player has satisfied his needs on these four levels can he begin to focus on his need for self-actualization (e.g., being a Super Bowl champion, being recognized/ honored for his performance, etc.). In this regard, I still prefer to use John Wooden's term for the top of his pyramid of success—competitive greatness. As a coach, what you need to recognize is that on a team of 53 players, you're going to have players who are at varying levels of needs compared to the next. Someone like Rod Woodson, who's a future Hall of Famer, who's been named to the NFL's All 75-Year Team, and whose sole motivation for playing is to achieve a Super Bowl, is obviously at a different level in his hierarchy of needs than is a rookie who's just satisfied to be playing on the team. In between these two extremes on the need hierarchy are those individuals that know they are secure on the team but want a larger role in order to garner the financial rewards that come from being a starter, a pro bowler, or a superstar. It's vital that a coach be able to recognize where each of his players is in this pyramid of needs.

SELF-MANAGEMENT

"If you wish to succeed in managing and controlling others—learn to manage and control yourself."

—William H. Boetcker
lecturer and industrial psychologist

Any efforts by leaders to improve the motivational levels of their followers should be preceded by self-examination by the leaders themselves. For example, they should be aware of their own strengths and weaknesses as motivators. The issue that must be considered in this instance is to what degree would these strengths and weaknesses limit or enhance a leader's attempts to affect motivational levels. In reality, different types of personalities, different skill sets, and different styles of leadership may call for different approaches to the same problem—depending on the circumstances.

Leaders should also attempt to develop a clear understanding of their own role within the organization before they try to deal with the motivational levels of others. What are their own wants, needs, and expectations? Are their own perceptions of themselves consistent with the perceptions that others have of them? Recognizing and dealing with these aspects of reality will enable leaders to be more effective motivators.

The needs and motivations I experienced as a first-time head coach in the NFL and those that I currently hold as a Super Bowl–winning coach are dramatically different. As a result, the financial considerations, my perceived position of acceptance and recognition among my peers and within the pecking order of the league as a whole, and the more national presence I now have in the media all dictate that I constantly monitor the effect of such factors on my personal level of focus and self-motivation.

Any fears that I might have previously held, such as losing my job and dealing with the financial burdens that being without a job might place on my family, are far different for me now that I have certain contractual guarantees and options for my future that did not exist prior to becoming a head coach in the NFL or winning a Super Bowl. For most people, fear is a tremendous motivator. Accordingly, if fear was indeed an integral factor in my motivation to succeed, I now would have to find a different catalyst to replace that factor in order to avoid becoming complacent. Complacency is something that I am constantly on the lookout for in an individual who has struggled through his career to become a top player in the league, only to have his level of motivation change when he finally reaches a point where he garners "big" money and feels more secure about his future.

RECOGNIZING DIFFERENCES

With regard to motivation, it is important that leaders recognize that differences exist between individuals. Leaders should be sensitive to the divergence of needs, interests, and skills among their followers. As such, leaders have a responsibility to get to know each of their subordinates and to treat them as individuals. Leaders should be aware of the fact that the most effective, productive way to deal with a human being is to treat that person as a unique resource.

In order to maximize the impact of a particular resource (person) on the vision and goals of the organization you, as a leader, should identify the strengths and weaknesses of your followers and take advantage of your assessments. Furthermore, you should create a system of motivation that is designed specifically to address each follower's unique characteristics and potential contributions to the organization. Such a system must be based on an awareness of the fact that in order to be effective, motivation has to focus on people's own needs and goals—and people's needs and goals differ. In that regard, a major part of a coach's responsibility to manage his team effectively involves his ability to recognize at what point each player is in his level of individual and professional development.

REWARDING PERFORMANCE

Nearly everyone wants something from work in addition to their paycheck. What they want can span a wide range of feelings and expectations. To the extent that individuals see a clear connection between successful performance on their part and their ability to satisfy their wants, they will be more motivated to perform as expected.

Accordingly, leaders should be sensitive to the various ways their followers' wants can be met. In general, the factors that help satisfy a person's needs can be grouped into two broad categories—intrinsic motivators and extrinsic rewards. Intrinsic motivators come from the job itself and include an individual's internal motivations, such as interests, values, and drives (e.g., feelings of accomplishment, opportunities to employ essential skills, desire for security, etc.).

Extrinsic rewards, on the other hand, are tangible incentives that are not inherent in the nature (structure) of the job. Examples of such external rewards include salary, bonuses, recognition, gifts, compensatory time off, etc. In some instances, such rewards do not have to be costly to have value as a motivating factor. For example, when I was with the Minnesota Vikings, I worked with special team's coach Gary Zauner. Gary was a longtime college coach and brought a certain collegial enthusiasm to his job that some thought might not be as effective with professional players. One of Gary's motivational tools was to provide specially designed

T-shirts to reward certain outstanding play on special teams the day after a game. These T-shirts had dynamic graphics that highlighted big hits, special plays, or overall effort. At first glance, most people might think that a big-time, million-dollar athlete would not be motivated by such "college" tactics. In fact, it was amazing to watch the way these players coveted the T-shirts as a sign of accomplishment that was acknowledged just among their peers. The use of T-shirts proved to be a tremendous motivator in a group that you might not otherwise think would be motivated by such an inexpensive gimmick.

While the use of extrinsic rewards is certainly an invaluable tool for motivating people within the organization, overreliance on such a practice can have a negative effect on the motivational level of those individuals working for an organization. External rewards, for example, can cause people to focus too narrowly on the task that is connected to a reward. People may be inclined to perform the task as quickly as possible and to minimize taking any risks. As a result, their willingness to be creative may be stifled. As a general rule, the greater the emphasis placed on the reward, the more likely a person will do the minimum work necessary to obtain the reward.

Another potential problem with the use of external rewards as a motivating agent involves the fact that extrinsic rewards can diminish an individual's intrinsic interest in work. Research suggests that people who view themselves as working primarily for money tend to perceive their tasks as less pleasurable and, as a result, they do not perform them as well. In other words, depending upon the circumstances, money can actually be a demotivating factor to a degree.

A third reason why the use of external rewards can have a negative effect on a person's motivational level arises from a situation where the rewards are perceived as an intrusion on the feeling of freedom held by an individual. If people come to view themselves as being controlled by a reward, they feel less autonomous. Such a feeling may interfere with their work performance. To some extent, the more freedom individuals have in the workplace, the happier and more productive they are.

STRUCTURING THE JOB

"Unless the job means more than they pay,
it will never pay more."

—H. Bertram Lewis

One of the most effective steps leaders can undertake to have a positive impact on motivational levels is to consider the tasks that they ask their followers to perform. As a leader, if you want subordinates who are motivated and enthusiastic about their work, who are focused on doing the job properly, who look forward to confronting the challenges and opportunities inherent in the tasks that they are asked to do, then you must find ways to incorporate those factors into the work. To the extent feasible, you should provide your followers with jobs that have been structured to afford them personal need satisfaction.

Furthermore, you should ensure that everyone in the organization understands exactly what is expected of them. Generally speaking, increasing role clarity on a job has been shown to have a positive effect on task performance. For example, in the NFL, not having a precise and explicit chain of command that is accompanied by a detailed outline of responsibilities is a surefire way to lose. This factor not only applies to your basic organizational structure but to game-day orchestration as well.

Typically, the head coach will have the offensive coordinator/quarterback coach and either the running back coach or the tight end coach in the booth. The offensive coordinator/quarterback coach is responsible for charting coverages and identifying match-ups in the defensive secondary. The tight end or the running back coach will switch between talking with the play caller and the offensive line coach (both of whom are on the field). While the coaches who are on the field also talk frequently to each other on the phone, the offensive line coach is not directly on the phone with the play caller due to the amount of conversation that exists between the play caller and the coach in the booth who is responsible for identifying and charting the overall front.

The offensive line coach is responsible for the point of attack. A remaining coach will be responsible for watching the drop and exchange between the quarterback and the running backs. It is vital that each coach does not get caught up in watching the game like a spectator and stays focused on his particular task. Accordingly, the head coach can quickly obtain an answer about what is happening in regard to any single aspect of the play (e.g., front, coverage, point of attack, and backfield action).

ENHANCING WORK ENVIRONMENT

"Find something you love to do and you'll never have to work a day in your life."

—Harvey MacKay
author and entrepreneur

Another way that leaders can enhance motivational levels in the organization is to cultivate an environment of motivation within the workplace. In other words, the climate within the workplace should be such that it facilitates job performance. Furthermore, any barriers to that objective should be remedied if possible. For example, if the existing group dynamics in the workplace are having a negative effect on task performance, steps should be undertaken to change the dynamics of the situation.

Among the practices and policies that you as a leader can adopt to improve the workplace environment for motivation are the following:

• Have an open-door policy. Make sure that everyone in the organization actually believes in your open-door policy (even if your open door is only an e-mail address).

• Never make promises that you know you can't keep.

• Establish an atmosphere of mutual respect between you and your followers.

- Adopt a positive attitude toward the organization's vision and goals and the ability of people to perform in a way that enables the vision and goals to be achieved.
- Lead by example. Work hard. Be punctual. Be a can-do (rather than a make-do) person. Get things done.
- Give people the attention they require.
- Challenge people—but not to the point of exhaustion.
- Keep the channels of communication open at all times. As appropriate, emphasize two-way communication.
- Have an open mind. Don't let your biases, prejudices, or opinions cloud your judgment.

MONITORING JOB ATTITUDES

"One of the illusions of life is that the present hour is not the critical, decisive hour. Write on your heart that every day is the best day of the year."

—Ralph Waldo Emerson
American poet, philosopher, essayist

Skillful leadership needs a feedback mechanism (system) that enables leaders to act from an enhanced position of knowledge and understanding. With regard to motivational levels within the workplace, the information gained by assessing individual attitudes toward their jobs can be used by leaders as a motivational barometer to identify potential problematic areas and issues. As such, leaders should take advantage of the various sources of information that are available in an organization relating to job attitudes.

A checklist of places a leader could look for feedback concerning work attitudes might include written behavioral opinion surveys; objective performance indices (e.g., performance history, performance against goals, etc.); face-to-face meetings with individuals or small groups; direct observations made in the workplace of worker behavior and actions; absenteeism levels; worker complaint levels; employee turnover rates;

etc. The key for a leader is to use this feedback in a timely, strategic fashion to shift job attitudes as needed.

A common mistake made by many leaders is to fail to follow up an organizational directive with personal interaction with key members of the staff whose job it is to carry out those initiatives. Typically, such initiatives may expose a staff member to an additional amount of stress or may be contrary to that staff person's personal opinions or recommendations. In either case, the leader needs to interact with the staff members involved with the initiative to ensure that they are adequately motivated to carry out their duties.

This problem exhibits itself around draft time for most NFL teams. A great many scouts and coaches spend a good deal of time and energy evaluating the college talent. As you might imagine, each coach and scout develops a certain affinity for players they have seen, a bond that lends itself to some degree of disappointment if and when you ultimately decide to draft other players. It is important to allow these scouts and coaches the opportunity to express their opinions and enable them to be a part of the overall decision-making process concerning which players should be drafted.

Phil Savage, our director of college scouting, is one of the best in the business. It is Phil's job to oversee the scouting of all college players and to help us maintain our perspective throughout the draft. Like most teams, we are also forced to augment our talent pool by either signing free agents or, whenever necessary on occasion, trading draft choices for players we want. Part of our checks-and-balances system is for Phil to argue his position of not giving up draft choices and the future assets they represent. Phil does this passionately. If Ozzie Newsome and I ever create an atmosphere whereby Phil feels compelled to keep his mouth shut because he doesn't want to rock the boat, then both Ozzie and I have done a great disservice to the organization. It is also incumbent on Phil to recognize that once the decision is made to either trade or keep a draft choice, he must move on to the next issue.

ELICITING COOPERATION

"Coming together is a beginning; keeping together is progress; working together is success."

—Henry Ford
American industrialist

Perhaps the single most important action a leader can take to motivate individuals in the organization is to involve them more fully in the steps that are undertaken to establish individual (or group) goals and responsibilities. In all likelihood, an enhanced level of employee cooperation and support will result from such involvement. Furthermore, the cooperative process should reinforce the attitude of the individuals involved in the process that they have a real stake in what happens to the organization. Skillful leaders are aware of the fact that eliciting cooperation from others is a process of offering "something for something."

Sometimes, eliciting cooperation involves dealing with spatial considerations. For example, we have a unique physical setup with the Baltimore Ravens in that most of our business offices (ticket office, sales and marketing, stadium operations, etc.) are located in our downtown offices. On the other hand, our training camp, where the players, coaches, personnel department, public relations, and football operations are all located, is about 20 miles outside the city of Baltimore in the suburban community of Owings Mills, Maryland. This has created a dynamic whereby we must consciously work at being inclusive of the downtown personnel in order to ensure that they feel that they are a part of the more well-known and visible environment at our training camp. David Modell, president of the Baltimore Ravens, has done an excellent job of merging these two groups and referring to everyone in the organization as "associates." This designation gives those in a less-visible position a way of feeling more connected to the pride and recognition of being a Baltimore Raven.

THE ABILITY TO MOTIVATE

To be a skillful leader, you must be able to inspire others to accomplish meaningful goals. In this regard, you must understand people and human behavior. Such an understanding is the foundation of knowing what energizes individuals to perform in a certain way, what factors shape such behavior, and how this behavior can be maintained. Effective leaders can have no more valuable tool in their arsenal of essential skills than this ofttimes elusive insight.

My ability to motivate emanates from three key factors attendant to leadership. First, my fundamental knowledge of this industry allows me to set goals and establish directives that give my players the confidence that they have a structure that will allow them to be successful. Finally, the passion and energy I attempt to display on a daily basis contributes to a positive atmosphere that heightens the learning curve.

Principle # 7:

*The essence of successful motivation
is understanding human behavior.*

chapter 9

BE A
PROBLEM
SOLVER

"The measure of success is not whether you have a tough problem to deal with, but whether it is the same problem you had last year."

— John Foster Dulles
former secretary of state

A large measure of the duties and responsibilities of a leader is devoted—by necessity—to dealing with and solving problems. In the ofttimes complex and diverse world of a leader, problems are inevitable, if for no other reason than the fact that no one can possibly control all of the situations that they face.

Accordingly, it is absolutely essential that a leader is able to solve problems in a timely, competent manner. What does this skill involve? John Maxwell, author of *The 21 Indispensable Qualities of a Leader*, suggests that leaders with problem-solving abilities tend to exhibit certain specific qualities.

First, good leaders anticipate problems. They acknowledge the reality of the existence of problems and try to make things better. They don't get so bogged down in the details attendant to a particular situation that they lose sight of what's important. They tackle problems in a systematic fashion, making sure that they resolve the issue they're working on before moving on to the next one. Finally, they don't make important decisions when they're unduly emotional. Such a set of circumstances may impair their ability to clearly focus on the relevant issues and to exercise sound judgment.

The aforementioned qualities are essential if leaders are to have the capability of addressing the three basic levels of problem solving: recognizing a problem, solving the problem, and foreseeing and preventing problems before they occur. Each level involves a certain degree of skill and systematic thinking.

RECOGNIZING THE PROBLEM

The initial skill required in the problem-solving process is the ability to recognize a problem when it exists. This also encompasses the capability to determine to what degree the problem is worthy of examination. Relatively speaking, a problem may be seen as somewhat inconsequential, not meriting much attention. On the other hand, it may be deemed serious enough to warrant a definitive problem-solving effort. As such, a leader must have the insight and the perspective to know when such an effort should be undertaken. In reality, some problems require more immediate attention than others.

For me, part of the problem-solving process during the season is what I call "ghost busting." One of the most difficult aspects of preparing a team for an opponent is deciding what you should focus on among the many potential problems your team may face. Because teams in the National Football League over the years have advanced both offensively and defensively, they will show many different looks in a game—looks that will evolve and change over the course of the season.

The need to be able to deal with change was very apparent to me during my last season with the Minnesota Vikings. Because of the exceptional level of offensive prowess we possessed, the defensive looks we had prepared for were rarely the same schemes and alignments we would actually face in the game. Because many teams felt they could not hold up against our considerable offensive weapons, they often took drastic measures to try to stop us. As a result, we began to adopt an approach of "chasing ghosts." We spent a great deal of time projecting how a team might change its basic profile to face us, knowing full well that most of our preparation plans would probably never be used. Furthermore, we did not want to burden our players with too much information, particularly because we were not sure if the defensive adjustments we were developing contingency plans for would even occur. To this end, we created sub-game plans that the coaching staff used to identify possible adjustments in case the changing fronts and coverages we anticipated actually happened. Not only did these actions make us better prepared to handle each possible adjustment, they also enhanced the level of confidence that our players had in our coaching staff concerning whether we had adequately prepared them for any and all contingencies they might face in a game. As a result, this unique set of obstacles served as a catalyst to enable the Vikings to develop confidence in their ability to adjust to any situation.

This factor proved to be equally true in our championship season in Baltimore. Similar to the elite offense we had in

Minnesota, the 2000 Ravens' defense had the equivalent level of record-setting talent. Our opponents would change their offensive profile, feeling that they needed to show a different look to try and catch our defense off guard. Once again, the ability to anticipate the potential changes in the other team's attack gave our defense a great deal of confidence because they knew that they were properly prepared to face any and all circumstances. A couple of teams had moderate success against our defense by employing a four-wide receiver set and running a no-huddle offense. This was something we worked on every week, knowing that virtually every team we would face would try this tactic sooner or later in the game. It was interesting that our defense almost enjoyed waiting for an offense to try to change what they were doing so that our defense could put their contingency preparation efforts to the test.

SOLVING THE PROBLEM

"The most important thing to do in
solving a problem is to begin."

— Frank Tyger

Having decided that a problem exists that needs to be solved, the next step is to pursue a systematic process that will enable the problem to be solved. Not all problems are of equal size, complexity, and importance. Some problems are straightforward and can be addressed with a relatively simple solution; others are more involved and require more creativity and resources to solve. Regardless, in order to ensure that each problem receives the strategic consideration that it deserves, all problems should undergo the following six-step problem-solving process: define the problem; develop possible solutions to the problem; decide on a solution; implement the solution; and determine whether the problem has been solved.

Define the problem. Of the six stages in the problem-solving process, the most important step is defining the problem. Diagnosing and clarifying the problem is crucial. If the problem is misdiagnosed, deriving a solution is unlikely, if not impossible. Defining a problem accurately with the appropriate level of focus and sufficient detail is also necessary if available resources (e.g., time, energy, etc.) are to be allocated to the process wisely.

To a point, defining the problem may be the most difficult step in the problem-solving process, as well as the most important. Too often, individuals don't like to spend too much time on this aspect because they feel the problem is obvious. In reality, looking beyond the obvious can involve hard work and considerable effort.

Such effort can be well worth the travail given the fact that most situations involve a multiplicity of problems, rather than a single problem. When multiple problems are identified, they must be prioritized and attention given to the most important one first.

Lin Bothwell, in his book *The Art of Leadership*, described this issue as like being a deck-chair straightener on a sinking Titanic. That person has two problems: how to straighten the deck chairs that are sliding and the fact that the ship is going down. An individual who is not crystal clear about which problem is urgent and which is relatively irrelevant is about to undergo a very enlightening lesson on the need for prioritizing.

Determine the possible solutions to the problem. Once the problem has been defined and identified, the next step is to develop a list of possible options for solving the problem. In this regard, several factors should guide a leader's actions, including keeping an open mind; deciding what options are plausible; being imaginative; taking an aggressive—rather than a conservative—approach; being creative; if necessary, recasting the problem in a different way that would preclude any points that might be inhibiting the efforts to identify possible courses of action, etc.

Whatever criteria leaders establish to identify alternative solutions, the criteria should not discourage the desire to develop more, often better, alternatives. The point to keep in mind is that the process of discovery should not be bound or limited by unduly restrictive, preconceived notions of what should and should not be considered. In fact, to a degree, every option should receive fair consideration.

Decide on the solution. The third step in the problem-solving process is to make a choice concerning which solution is most appropriate for the organization. Depending upon how complex the problem is and how realistic the possible solutions are, choosing which solution to embrace can either be a relatively simple task or a time-consuming, complicated undertaking.

If the decision is not straightforward, then the viability and utility of the various options must be assessed. Ultimately, this information should be used to help rank the possible alternatives. For example, some of the proposed solutions may be clearly not doable. Some may require more resources than others. Still others may have a greater perceived upside or a potential downside. On the other hand, some may produce a greater cost/benefit result. The point to keep in mind is that someone must decide which criteria are the most important factors to consider.

Once all of the possible alternatives are prioritized according to whatever criteria the leader or the organization deems relevant, a decision must be made on which solution is "best." Since the leaders in an organization tend to be the individuals who are most able and capable of solving problems, they generally occupy the most influential positions within the workplace. As such, they usually have the responsibility of deciding which solution to pursue—particularly those decisions regarding "tough" choices. To a point, a number of parallels exist between the process involved in problem solving and effective decision making.

Develop a plan to implement the solution. Once a decision has been reached regarding which solution is best (given the alternatives), the next step is to develop an action plan for implementing the chosen solution. As a rule, such an action plan should address several factors, including a list of the specific objectives to be achieved by pursuing the solutions; a detailed overview of the actions involved in achieving each objective; a time line for performing each action; a schedule of the resources (e.g., material, personnel, etc.) that will be required to undertake each action; a system for monitoring the actions involved in implementing the plan; and a deadline for when the problem is to be solved.

Implement the solution. If the plan in the previous step is thoughtfully and strategically designed, the only factor that this step requires is sound leadership to ensure that the plan is well-executed. On the other hand, if the plan is ill-conceived, all the leadership in the world can't ensure that this step will be successful.

Determine whether the problem has been solved. At this, the final step in the problem-solving process, the leader must determine whether the problem has actually been solved. If the answer is affirmative, then the process has achieved its intended purpose. On the other hand, if the answer is negative, then the leader must revert to the first step of the process (i.e., define the problem) and start anew.

Like all organizations, NFL teams face serious problems from time to time, some much more serious than others. For example, when we were in the throes of a three-game losing streak in the middle of the 2000 season, we were standing at the edge of the abyss and everyone knew it. If all I had to offer my players at that time was a series of coaching cliches and a sense of false bravado, our players would have exposed my fraudulent efforts in a New York second. This was also not a time to use pseudo-psychology to trick players into believing they are somehow better than they actually are. At such a time, it is absolutely essential that your confidence as a leader comes through in a genuine fashion.

Oddly, a team on a losing streak and a team on a winning streak may have some of the same properties. For example, both will tend to focus too much on the pressures they are enduring or the final consequences that the season might bring. In the process, they lose the level of critical focus needed.

Most teams on a losing streak tend to dwell on the negative factors that losing will cause, thus making the situation look even bleaker than it really is. By keeping the focus on the immediate task at hand (i.e., win a game and stop the slide), you can help your players overcome any debilitating emotional reactions they might experience, such as self-pity and hopelessness. Similar to a batter in a hitting slump, it takes a great deal of experience and inner confidence to know that this situation will ultimately pass. You should focus on whatever positives have occurred and continually show examples of how close they are to getting back on the right track.

During our losing streak, I focused on three main themes. First, I was fully aware of the fact that virtually every team in the league was, is, or was going to go through this same type of difficulty. With the exception of the Oakland Raiders and the Tennessee Titans, every team in the league suffered through consecutive losses that could or did effectively end their season. I drew on my experiences with the Minnesota Vikings from 1992–1998 when we overcame three-, four-, and even five-game losing streaks to make the playoffs. To our players, I constantly emphasized the point that surviving this threat to our season would eventually be the key to whatever success we would be able to achieve in 2000. Fortunately, this team also had the experience of dealing with and the first-hand knowledge of having overcome a three-game losing streak the previous year, and of winning five of our last seven games after that point.

As the great John Wooden once asked, "Why do we fear adversity when we know it is the only way to truly get better?" One of the primary reasons that this team did get better was our knowledge that once we came out of our losing streak, we could survive. The key was showing them historical, tangible proof that we could get through this and that the experience would eventually make us better.

The three-game losing streak was not the only major problem I had to deal with in the 2000 season. In our divisional playoff game against Tennessee, the Titans took the opening drive 80 yards for a 7-0 lead. In a playoff atmosphere and while on the road, a drive like that would have sucked the life out of many teams. Previously, we had lost to the Titans at home 14-6, in the middle of our three-game losing streak. We then came back and beat them in dramatic fashion in Nashville. That game was the first that they had ever lost in their new stadium, Adelphia Coliseum—one of the toughest venues to play in the NFL.

Much was made of the fact that we were the only team to beat Tennessee at home in two years. Our players took this emotional edge with them into our playoff game against the Titans. Frankly, I was concerned we would lose that edge when they were able to drive the length of the field on their opening possession. But as I watched the players' reaction to the events that had unfolded, I saw a level of confidence in them that emanated from their having successfully faced the adversity we did during the season. The players responded by mounting our own 60-yard scoring drive that enabled us to regain our balance. I am not sure we would have had that same resolve if we had not been tested the way we were during the year.

My second focal point during our losing streak was the media. The minute adversity hits a team, the media swarms like buzzards to a carcass. All too often, the media can only apply abstract truths to real-life situations. They focus on "finger pointing," even when it doesn't exist. Even the most experienced beat man occasionally falls into this trap of assuming that a team can't help but give in to the natural impulse to blame someone else. To a point, it's hard to blame them, particularly when you see so many teams falling into the stereotype the media portrays.

I have been very fortunate to be around some very competent writers. While many of these individuals have a solid eye for the game and have a good perspective of players, I can honestly say I have never known a writer that truly understands the concept of "team." I guess they have just been exposed to too many examples to the contrary. This factor has proven to be an easy tool for me to use in challenging our players not to fall into a "finger-pointing" mode, if for no other reason than to just prove the self-proclaimed "experts" wrong. In reality, you have to be careful in portraying the media as the enemy too often. On the other hand, in many instances, they are the perfect example to support a team's perspective that those around them just don't understand or appreciate the real nature of the circumstances that they're facing.

The final theme I focused on during the streak was maintaining a consistent routine. Of all the things I have confidence in, the structure of our routine heads the list. Everything we do is with the idea of keeping our players fresh and healthy, all the while providing them with the information and guidance they need to do their job. Once our players are aware of that factor, they become very comfortable with the fact that I will not change our basic routine in response to our ever-changing circumstances.

Certainly, you should not become so recalcitrant that you don't leave room for adaptation. However, that too can be a part of our basic routine. The players can be taught that certain aspects of their preparation will be dictated as needed by the success or failure of a particular part of our situational offensive, defensive, or special teams. Indeed, that rare occasion may arise when you need to do something dramatic to get your players' attention.

After a particularly devastating loss to the Cincinnati Bengals, Mike Shanahan dramatically changed the routine of his Denver Broncos to adopt a more physical style of practice in an attempt to elicit a more physical style of play from his team. Like me, Mike was schooled in the Bill Walsh style of practicing, which dictates a diminishing level of physicality in your practice structure as the season progresses. Mike is one of the best coaches ever in the NFL, and I am sure that he felt this drastic change in his practice structure was the only way to right his team. I give Mike a lot of credit for taking such a bold step. I am quite sure he thought long and hard about it.

Mike obviously made the right move for the Broncos, who rebounded to make the playoffs. For us, however, I felt that maintaining our routine was the key to righting ourselves. I felt so strongly about it that in the middle of the losing streak, I gave the players the schedule for our bye week (still six weeks away), which included taking an entire week off. Some individuals thought that telling a team in the middle of a three-game losing streak that they were going to get a week off was, at the least, unduly ambitious. I felt that my action was the perfect way to underscore my philosophy to the players that we were going to dictate our schedule, regardless of the circumstances.

FORESEEING AND PREVENTING PROBLEMS BEFORE THEY OCCUR

"The only thing wrong with doing nothing is that you never know when you are finished."

— Anonymous

Quite obviously, the best way to deal with a problem is to take steps to prevent the problem from occurring in the first place. Not only is it less costly, but it also enables an organization to avoid negative circumstances that might otherwise be a by-product of the problem (e.g., disruption, time-consumption, low morale and confidence, distraction, etc.).

Preventing a problem, however, usually requires that a leader has (and employs) superior planning skills. In this regard, the leader must be able to foresee and evaluate the likelihood of a problem happening and then to develop a systematic plan for reducing or eliminating the possibility of such an occurrence. We devote a considerable amount of time and resources during our summer training camp to address issues that might become a problem during the season. Such issues involve personal, as well as professional, circumstances. Along with the structure of handling a losing streak or a prolonged period on the road, we address such personal issues as spousal abuse, drunken driving, and parental responsibilities. Handling these potential problems in a proactive way serves two purposes. First, it provides the players with a resource to draw on should the problems arise. Second, it gives the players a sense that management is well organized and has a plan for every contingency.

To the extent possible, effective leaders take a proactive approach to solving problems before they come to pass. The wisdom of such an approach is reflected in the words of the renowned author Robert Louis Stevenson, who once wrote: "It is the mark of a good action that it seems inevitable in retrospect."

PROBLEM SOLVING IN A CRISIS SITUATION

"The world is full of thorns and thistles. It's all in how you grasp them."

—Arnold Glasow
American humorist

Of all the circumstances that may require problem solving, perhaps none is more urgent and more dependent upon the skills of the leader than a crisis situation. Effective handling of such an unstable or crucial time requires a take-charge leader with specific attributes.

For example, leaders who can respond to crises in an appropriate manner have the ability to keep their cool under pressure. Not only does this demeanor enable them to inspire confidence in others (by—as the old saying goes—"their ability to keep their head while others around them are losing theirs"), it heightens the likelihood that they will be able to think clearly and rationally. Such an attribute is essential to sound crisis management.

In this instance, competent leaders also have the sense and insight to avoid pursuing any quick fix that might hurt the organization in the long run. They are able to handle the crisis in a way that thoughtfully considers and evaluates the potential solutions to the problem from a broadly based perspective. Furthermore, they're willing to modify their strategy as needed whenever the circumstances dictate such a change is justified.

Being able to handle crises effectively also requires that leaders possess the ability to act quickly and decisively. Given the urgent nature of a crisis, there is no time to conduct lengthy investigations into what possible solutions might ultimately help alleviate the crisis. Accordingly, leaders should learn to trust their intuition and to consider their gut feelings as one factor in developing and evaluating potential solutions.

Leaders should keep in mind that procrastination only deepens a crisis. Once the best strategy for dealing with the crisis has been identified, that strategy should be implemented decisively and promptly.

One final factor that should be considered in establishing an effective strategy for handling crises involves the structure of the organization. The best organizational structure for dealing with a crisis is one in which responsibility for leading the organization out of the crisis is assigned to one individual. Designating one center of authority to deal with such circumstances can help facilitate several desirable outcomes, including being able to devise, implement, and manage a suitable solution in a timely fashion.

Handling a crisis in an effective manner is the managerial skill that may well define your abilities as a leader. Certainly, I had a world-class opportunity this past season to practice my skills at handling a crisis with the circumstances surrounding Ray Lewis. The perspective I had standing on a podium in front of the nation's sports media the morning after winning Super Bowl XXXV was surreal on so many different levels. I couldn't help but think back to the sequence of events that had transformed and defined the personality of my organization, my team, and indeed the very fabric of my abilities as a head coach in the National Football League.

Ray Lewis, our starting middle linebacker and the heart and soul of my football team, was standing there with me. Exactly one year earlier, Ray was in jail, accused and indicted on two counts of murder following an altercation at a Buckhead, Georgia, nightclub just outside Atlanta following Super Bowl XXXIV. The sequence of events involving Ray has been well chronicled. Over the course of the next four months, Ray would go to trial only to have all counts dropped because the Atlanta district attorney was unable to prove any culpability on Ray's part.

While Ray was cleared of the murder charges against him, he did plead guilty to a misdemeanor obstruction of justice charge. Ray Lewis was not originally charged with obstruction of justice. The charge was added later when the prosecutors realized that there was no evidence that he was responsible in any way for loss of life in Atlanta. Subsequently, they said that Ray had been less than forthcoming in his first interview with the Atlanta police. Some people view the obstruction of justice charge as a face-saving step by the prosecution, which clearly had no case against Ray.

Certain facts involving the case are irrefutable. The court determined that Ray Lewis did not start a fight, did not participate in a fight, did not stab anybody, and clearly tried to prevent the incident from happening. He was obviously in the wrong place at the wrong time with the wrong people, and he was a victim of circumstance. The prosecutors recommended probation, not jail time, as the appropriate sanction for Ray's admission of obstructing justice. If the prosecutors had viewed this as a more serious violation, they would have recommended a harsher penalty.

I have no intention of rehashing the details of the case or making any kind of justification for Ray's right to continue as a member of the NFL and the Baltimore Ravens. The facts are clearly documented for any individual who is truly interested in assessing the truth. As a point of fact, Ray certainly needs no further vindication.

What is worth documenting is the sequence of events that had to be addressed by myself and the entire Baltimore Ravens organization and how that set of circumstances became such a tangible part of our journey to become world champions the next season. The circumstances surrounding this situation may indeed be the ultimate case study in organizational crisis management.

When I received the phone call notifying me that Ray Lewis had been arrested and charged with two counts of murder, it became painfully clear that we were going to enter new territory with regard to crisis management. There was no one to call, no manual to consult, because no coach or team in the NFL had ever had an active player charged with murder before. In response to these events, owner Art Modell, team President David Modell, Vice-President and Director of Public Relations Kevin Byrne, and I all met that next morning to decide on a course of action that would guide our organization's handling of this situation.

There are three perspectives that must be maintained in handling any crisis: dealing with the crisis itself, dealing with the effects on the organization, and finally, dealing with the ensuing media and its effect on the first two concerns. First and foremost, you must have a fundamental plan for addressing the crisis itself. For us, that meant determining what Ray's culpability was and what our ability to support him would be. Individually and collectively, we had a great deal of confidence in Ray as a person and could not believe he was capable of the accusations leveled toward him. Our team owner, Art Modell, was able to assist Ray in securing Ed Garland, one of the most prominent lawyers in Atlanta, to act as his counsel. Once Mr. Garland was able to meet with Ray and assess the situation, he too became convinced that Ray was innocent. From that point on, there was very little we could do with regard to the judicial process other than provide all the moral support for Ray that we could.

We then had to turn our attention to the effect this might have had on the organization and team. Although it may sound quite mercenary, our focus had to turn to the possibility that we might have to go into the ensuing season without our best player. From an organizational standpoint, this situation put us in a very difficult position. If we decided to pursue a top-flight linebacker in free agency, two things would or could have happened. First, it would have appeared that we did not truly believe Ray and were abandoning him at his time of need. Second, if we had expended the type of finances necessary to secure a top linebacker, and our faith in Ray was borne out and he did return for the season, we would have spent a huge amount of money on a backup. By the same token, if we did not have a contingency plan in place, we could be left very vulnerable should the situation not allow Ray to return for whatever reason. We decided to keep an eye on the existing linebacker market but do nothing to actively pursue one until such time that we had a better idea of what might happen. Although this would mean passing up on some potential replacements, we felt it was our only prudent course of action. In addition to these concerns, we needed to address the atmosphere that would be created within the organization, and ultimately for Ray, by the unfolding events.

While these two responses were being acted on, we also needed to develop a very specific and detailed plan for dealing with the media during this difficult time. This step needed to be undertaken not only to maintain a positive image for the organization but also to minimize any distractions and the negative effects this type of exposure would bring.

With regard to the actual form of communication you use to implement your plan, you should keep in mind that while there needs to be timely and informative internal communication, there must be cautious and limited external communication. We determined that due to the sensitive nature of the issues involved, there should be a single voice with a single message for the entire organization. This single voice strategy is vital because the media will approach as many different sources as possible. The primary goal of the media in such a situation is often to get whatever conflicting opinions or information they can in order to expand or to generate interest in the story. For the Baltimore Ravens' organization, it was deemed appropriate that the single voice would be mine.

In dealing with the media coverage surrounding any crisis, several key factors should be remembered. First, you have to determine the extent of coverage the matter will draw. It was obvious this was going to be an issue of national interest, and we would have to be as direct and forthcoming as the situation allowed. Next, you must appreciate the fluid nature of the events that may transpire. In each instance, there must be a speed assessment of the exposure and options available to you. This takes constant monitoring of the media and the focus points they are establishing. With regard to the initial event and any ancillary events that are generated, you should keep three perspectives in mind when formulating a response: fast is better than slow, slow is better that wrong, and proactive is better than reactive.

Once Ray was released on bail, he was recused by court order to remain in Baltimore while preparing for the trial. With the previous three axioms in mind, we arranged a new conference to "set the rules" for the ensuing months. The amassed media in our team room at our training facility was the most media assembled in the brief, five-year history of the franchise. After Ray made a short statement reaffirming his innocence, I outlined the parameters we would work under and delivered our single message. Throughout the ordeal we made certain to reiterate three main points of our message. First, we were sympathetic to the families involved in the incident and respectful of the loss of life. Second, we continued to reaffirm our faith in Ray. And finally, and the most difficult of the three, we reaffirmed our faith in the judicial process.

We needed to create a "safe harbor" of sorts where Ray could come to work out and get away from the pressures of the situation. We also needed to create a buffer for the organization as a whole, to prepare for the possibility of having to deal with free agency, the upcoming draft, and the ensuing season. To this end, we established the facility as off-limits to the media with regard to Ray or any other player concerning any of the issues involving the trial. Of course, we were all available to discuss regular Ravens business. I must say that the media acted very responsibly in this matter and respected our request to avoid Ray's trial.

In an odd way, the limitations placed on Ray proved to be an asset for the team and the organization. Ray has always been one to stay in condition and report to training camp in good shape. Given his history, he was not required to remain in Baltimore for offseason conditioning. This was the first time Ray was around his teammates for the entire offseason, and it proved to be a tremendous catalyst for the team on two fronts. First, it was great motivation for the other players to be around a player of Ray's caliber and to see firsthand the way he trained for the coming season. Second, his confidence in his innocence and his faith that the truth would eventually come to light buoyed the organization's faith in Ray.

One of our major concerns was that the trial might linger into the beginning of training camp and maybe into the season itself. Fortunately, Georgia law provided for very specific rules governing the rights to a quick and speedy trial. When the trial began in early April, it became increasingly clear with each witness that Ray was not involved in the killings and had actually tried to prevent the altercation altogether.

After all charges were dropped, Ray pled guilty to an ancillary charge of misdemeanor obstruction of justice. We were assured that this removed any grounds for suspension by the league. Earlier that year, the league had disciplined two players with the New York Jets, Jumbo Elliott and Matt O'Dwyer. Unlike those two individuals, who were suspended after pleading guilty to assault charges, Ray's violation of the law did not involve a physical assault on anyone. There was no testimony that he instigated or was involved in any fighting. The other player in the Jets' bar incident who was disciplined, Jason Fabini, accepted deferred adjudication to a disorderly conduct charge. Fabini was fined a game check but was not suspended.

When Ray returned to Baltimore, we held a final press conference. We invited the national press, most of whom came. Ray made a statement and answered questions. ESPN, CNN-SI, and Court TV carried the press conference live. For us, this conference ended the event. It was important to try to bring some finality to the issue for both the organization and Ray, even though we knew the media would carry this story for the rest of the year.

We began training camp with the same attitude. Because we felt that this issue was behind us, we did not engage in any dialogue concerning it. Since that incident in Buckhead the day after the Super Bowl until the beginning of training camp, not a single day went by that I did not have to deal with some issue concerning the tragic deaths in Buckhead and their consequences. To the extent possible, I refused to let this issue continue any longer, and the team backed me up. By keeping this perspective, it became less and less of an issue—until we went to the Super Bowl.

As we progressed through the playoffs and after we beat the Oakland Raiders, we recognized that this issue would resurface. It was not a major concern of mine because we had handled the specter of this throughout the entire season. There was no reason to believe the Super Bowl would be any different. We understood that although the Super Bowl atmosphere tends to magnify everything, our players had proven that they would be up to the task of dealing with anything that might come up concerning Ray's situation.

The first week of our preparation in Baltimore went very well. The local media had grown tired of the issue long before this and had no interest in reviving it. Even the national media seemed to be holding it at arms length. I had given the players an extra day off that Sunday before the Super Bowl, so we did not travel down to Tampa until Monday. Most teams had usually gone in on Sunday, but we had played two very arduous road games at Tennessee and Oakland just to earn the right to go to the Super Bowl. I wanted to do everything I could to rest our players. The first required event of the week was not until late Monday afternoon, and I knew that we would have no problem getting there in time.

I had mapped out the schedule we would follow for the entire playoffs, including the two weeks leading up to the Super Bowl. I had even given this schedule to the players the day after we beat San Diego to qualify for the playoffs, three weeks prior to the end of the season. The players appreciated this advanced planning about our routine, and they knew I would not deviate from it, as was my custom. Some members of the media labeled me "eccentric" and "arrogant" for changing what had been somewhat routine for other teams going to the Super Bowl. For me, it was just a matter of establishing a routine that was in the best interests of my players.

On the Sunday before we left for Tampa, a couple of national media ran reports regarding Ray that I thought were unprofessional and sensationalistic. It became clear to me that some individuals in the national media were intent on trying to revive this story. To a point, their intentions were somewhat understandable, given the unbelievable sequence of events that had transpired from one Super Bowl to the next. What were the odds of a player going from being jailed on murder charges following one Super Bowl to becoming the eventual MVP of the next? I understood this perspective, and as I had done on two previous occasions, I intended to simply reiterate our position regarding Ray. We understood the need to ask but, as we had done all season, we would not engage in the dialogue. In my opening press conference, I made this point clear. I then added a personal perspective concerning one of the national pieces on Ray that had been printed.

Jeremy Shaapp of ESPN had interviewed the families of the two victims. It would be unrealistic and unfair to think that the victims' families would have an objective view of the situation. Both the district attorney and the mayor of Atlanta stood in front of the national media a mere two days after the incident and declared that Ray Lewis was a murderer and that they would prove that without a shadow of doubt. (It continues to amaze me even to this day that these two gentlemen, who could not provide a single shred of evidence at the trial after three months of extensive investigation, had no difficulty in standing up in front of the world and declaring Ray Lewis guilty after just two days.)

To manipulate and capitalize on the frustration of the families in this way was in my opinion deplorable, smacking of yellow journalism, and was akin to ambulance chasing. And I said so. This seemed to upset several members of the almost 3,000 reporters covering the Super Bowl. Some reporters even suggested that Ray's situation was a nonissue with them until I brought it up. This viewpoint was either painfully naïve or blatantly ignorant.

I understand that part of my job is to let the media question, criticize, second-guess, and even denigrate my abilities. What some of them don't seem to understand is that I am allowed an opinion too. When you turn that bright, hot spotlight back on them, some of them tend to get a little nervous. Maybe even paranoid.

After my Super Bowl Monday press conference, the thrust of the media observations early in the week was that I had created a distraction for my team, and that it would be a problem for us as we prepared for the New York Giants. That was precisely the atmosphere I had hoped to create.

This team had rallied together all year long against the perceived attacks against us by the media, and this was just the catalyst I needed to sustain that edge going into the championship game with the Giants. By week's end, most members of the media began to see this was a nonissue for us, and that our preparation was unaffected. Our players had conducted themselves professionally all year long and continued to do so in Tampa as well. Our strength was our reliance on each other.

Some of the events that have provided either motivation or, at the least, a teaching environment for my team, are not ones that I would have chosen to put us through voluntarily. However, this team and this organization successfully faced every challenge put before them during the season and in the playoffs. Indeed, those challenges proved to be a significant catalyst and an integral part of the backbone that helped create our success.

BECOMING A BETTER PROBLEM SOLVER

*"The reward for being a good problem solver
is to be heaped with more and more
difficult problems to solve."*

—Buckminster Fuller
American engineer, poet, and philosopher

Even though they may be very adept at solving problems, skillful leaders understand that their ability to address problems in a suitable fashion is an ever-evolving skill that needs and can benefit from continual nurturing. Among the steps that leaders can take to improve their problem-solving skills are to be vigilant for troublesome circumstances that need attention; to study and learn from the problem-solving efforts of others in particular situations; to develop the ability to brainstorm effectively; to surround themselves with competent problem solvers who can not only provide valuable counsel, but also serve as exemplary role models of how to act and behave; etc. The point that leaders should keep in mind is that they should avoid complacency. New problems can and will arise—many of which will call for new solutions.

COMPETENT PROBLEM SOLVERS

*"In any moment of decision, the best thing you can do
is the right thing; the next best thing is the wrong
thing; and the worst thing you can do is nothing."*

—Theodore Roosevelt
26th president of the United States

According to John Maxwell in his book *The 21 Indispensable Qualities of a Leader*, there are three basic kinds of competent people in the world:

- those who can see what needs to happen
- those who can make it happen

- those who can make it happen when it really counts

Leaders who are really good at problem solving meet all of the qualifications for the third category of competent people. When a problem occurs, they know what to do, and they are able to do whatever it takes when it really matters.

Principle # 8:

Skillful leaders are able to recognize and solve problems in an effective and timely manner.

chapter 10

BE
A TEAM BUILDER

"Coming together is a beginning; keeping together is progress; working together is success."

—Henry Ford
American industrialist

What is a team and what is involved in building one? A team is another name for a group of two or more individuals who are interacting in pursuit of a common goal. Within the workplace, using the word "team" in place of "group" also implies an enhanced level of esprit de corps and a competitive attitude toward other teams (groups) in the organization.

Organizations utilize teams, as opposed to a command system where the top-down leader has responsibility for virtually everything, to achieve a number of specific purposes. For example, teams provide a more effective and efficient way to complete some tasks and projects—particularly those that are complicated. Because no one person can master all of the details of any undertaking that is relatively involved (no matter how smart or talented that individual is), employing a team can bring many minds, insights, skill sets, etc. to bear on the project. As a result, the primary role of the leader is to coordinate the efforts of all of the team members toward a single goal (getting the job done). In the football environment, you typically think of the team as strictly referring to the players and coaches. In fact, the Baltimore Ravens is an organization of sub-teams: coaches, personnel, training room, equipment room, public relations, stadium operations, suite sales, etc.

Not only can using teams enable an organization to get certain tasks and jobs done in a more productive manner, teams can also create benefits for team members. For example, working as a member of a team can instill a certain degree of parochial feelings toward the work in team members. These feelings make it more likely that individuals will accept responsibility for their efforts and take pride in the final outcome. Ultimately, this attitude of "ownership" of their work can lead to a greater level of productivity.

Becoming a member of a team enables an individual to be a part of a workplace environment that is much more "worker friendly," all factors considered. For example, because decision making often flows from the team members upward to the leaders, an atmosphere of "seeking permission," rather than merely "following orders," is established. This atmosphere serves to reinforce the parochial attitudes discussed in the previous paragraph.

Furthermore, because any failure of the team is also a failure of the leader, a broadened, two-way level of accountability tends to evolve. Not only are the team members accountable to the leader (the traditional practice), the leader also becomes accountable (to a degree) to the team members.

In addition, an aura of collective responsibility is ingrained. If the team succeeds, everyone succeeds. On the other hand, if the team fails, everyone fails. In a team-oriented situation, the focus tends to be on a corrective, rather than a disciplinary, approach (i.e., determining how to get the job done versus assigning blame).

Within the NFL, absolutely everything about this game, from the cap to free agency to the media, tears at the heart of the "team" concept. The vested self-interest that exists in almost every aspect of professional football supersedes the interests of the team. You would be ill-advised, as a head coach, to deny the existence of such self-interest or to be so naïve as to think that taking care of themselves isn't the primary motivation of most of the people with whom you're working.

Self-interest is as much a law of nature as is gravity. Keep in mind that you can't defy the laws of nature. You can, however, suspend them temporarily. Anyone who has flown in an airplane can attest to that. It is this suspension of self-interest that is at the heart of the ability of any coach to build a team structure and that defines his ability to lead.

In the NFL, teams deal with a "cap" (a salary structure that each team is allotted based on the gross revenues of the league as a whole, whereby the players are afforded somewhere between 64 and 65 percent of the profits). That structure gives each club a very clearly defined set of parameters concerning how much they can spend on their talent (players) and, to a point, how they choose to allocate those monies. For example, we have a 10,000-square-foot bubble next to our practice field that we use for our weight room. I have often thought it would be much easier for me to pick the 53-man roster, take the total money allowed under the cap (this year, it is $68 million), lock the players in the bubble, and let them figure out who gets what. Now that is something I would pay to see.

Obviously, that is not how the process works. Typically what happens is that eight or nine players on your roster will account for better than 50 percent of your team's cap. That distribution creates a huge diversity between the top players on a team and those at the other end of the spectrum. As you can see, because that dynamic is fraught with inequities for the players, it could lead to resentments that could affect a team's success.

Another issue teams deal with is incentives. A player's individual incentives may indeed be structured in a way to supersede a team's success. A defensive end could be used as an example. In his contract, that defender has incentives, upwards of $100,000 to $200,000 possibly, if he leads the league in sacks at the end of the year. Imagine that you're in the last game of the season, and this player is within striking distance of his individual incentive. He needs one sack to become the league leader in sacks. But your game plan calls for him to contain the quarterback. In other words, his primary responsibility is to keep the quarterback from breaking containment outside the pocket.

At this point, suppose you're playing a team like the Tennessee Titans, who have a very mobile quarterback. As such, our key to the game is to keep their quarterback, Steve McNair, in the pocket. The incentive for the team (that is, for the player but from the team perspective) is to win the game and go to the playoffs. A typical first-round playoff game pays $15,000. A player's total share for the three playoff games and winning the 2001 Super Bowl was $121,000. From a pragmatic standpoint, you can see the conflict a player goes through. In this last game of the season, his job is to contain the QB. On the other hand, if he's on rush, he might see an opportunity to go inside the tackle to get the sack. Does he go for the possible $200,000 payoff for leading the league in sacks or does he adhere to his responsibility of containing the quarterback? It's a classic example of a conflict between individual and team goals, and not an altogether easy choice.

It doesn't take a genius in math to recognize that there's a higher payoff for leading the league in sacks than there might be in going to the playoffs. What you have to do, as a coach, is develop a team dynamic where that player feels a greater responsibility to his team obligations than he might to his individual opportunities.

A key barometer for the 2000 Ravens was the willingness of Michael McCrary and Peter Bouleware to suppress their individual accomplishments and recognition for the sake of playing dominating "team" defense. Both Michael and Peter are repeat Pro Bowl performers who had healthy incentives for being selected to that team. In order for us to play record-setting defense, both of those individuals had to remain focused on their responsibilities and, at times, had to forgo the potential sack to maintain the integrity of our defense. These two players clearly displayed a willingness to "suspend" the laws of human nature and vested self-interest and place the team goals of breaking the all-time scoring defense record and going to and winning the Super Bowl above their personal agenda.

Given the positive impact that teams can have on the organization's ability to get things accomplished, it is not an overstatement to claim that building effective teams is one of the most important tasks that a leader can undertake. As a rule, such a task encompasses several steps, including determining the basic mission for each team, selecting team members, assigning duties to each team member, and creating a culture that enables the team to succeed.

How well a leader is able to tackle these steps is affected to some extent by how well the leader understands the basic characteristics of an effective work group. The greater the level of understanding, the better prepared the leader is to deal with the various factors involved in team building. For example, if a characteristic that is important for the group is absent or insufficient, the leader might develop an action plan to modify the team with respect to the deficiencies associated with that attribute.

A number of core features of an effective work team have been identified, including the following:

- a clearly defined and shared sense of purpose
- a list of mutually created and agreed-upon objectives

- a group structure that is compatible with the objectives to be achieved
- well-defined roles and role relationships
- an environment that encourages shared ideas and feelings
- a consensual decision-making process
- an atmosphere where power and leadership are shared as appropriate to the task assigned to the team

DETERMINING THE MISSION OF THE TEAM

"Individual commitment to a group effort—that is what makes a team work, a company work, a society work, and civilization work."

—Vince Lombardi
Hall of Fame football coach

A leader should define the team's mission and develop the systematic plan for achieving that mission. The team leader also sets the agenda for the group (i.e., the step-by-step process by which work should flow through the team). In this regard, the leader determines the basic focus of the group—for example, what is important; where resources (e.g., time, materials, effort) should be allocated; what opportunities exist; what opportunities should receive attention; etc.

As the head coach of the Ravens, I am integrally involved in setting the basic goals for the organization and deciding how we will address those goals. For example, going into the 2000 season, we had publicly stated that anything less than making the playoffs would be a failed season. Even though every team enters training camp with talk of a Super Bowl and winning a championship, I told our players that they first had to earn the right to go to the playoffs before they could talk about loftier goals. Certainly, everyone in the organization was aware of the fact that winning the championship was our ultimate goal and that setting our sights on the play-offs was just an intermediate step. On the other hand, I felt strongly that the organization needed to focus on the effort it would take just to make the playoffs and not overlook any challenge or underestimate any team.

As we approached the end of the season and it became apparent we would make the playoffs, I banned the use of the word "playoff" by anyone in the organization until we had actually earned the right to be in the playoffs. This policy made it somewhat difficult on the ticket office because the league office had notified them with about four weeks left in the season that they could go about selling playoff tickets. They were in a bit of a dilemma, because I had actually fined a couple of players for using the "P" word before we were officially in. In response, they creatively borrowed the term "Festivus" from a phony holiday created on the popular TV sitcom *Seinfeld*. They even began to use a euphemism for the Super Bowl, calling it "Festivus Maximus."

With two weeks left in the season we beat the San Diego Chargers and officially entered the playoffs. At this point, having earned a position in the playoffs, we quickly changed gears, and I challenged the players to talk publicly about winning it all. As I stood in front of our players in our locker room after the Chargers game in the euphoria of being in the playoffs for the first time in the history of the Ravens' franchise, I told them, "Men, it's time to go to a Super Bowl."

Regardless of the workplace setting—the NFL or corporate America, decisions ultimately have to be made concerning what tasks a team should undertake. As a rule, these decisions are either made by the leader or by the group for themselves under the watchful guidance of the leader. If possible, the tasks should be challenging. To a point, demanding tasks heighten the likelihood that team members will pull together and perform well. Assignments that are seen as unchallenging can "demotivate" team members who perceive the tasks as boring, insulting, unworthy of effort, etc.

To the extent feasible, the leader should solicit input from team members on an ongoing basis regarding how the team is addressing its mission, goals, and agenda. Whenever possible, team members should be actively encouraged to provide their feedback and feelings on any factor that might affect the team and its actions. Their feedback should receive serious consideration and should be used to identify any changes to the mission, goals, and agenda of the team that might be deemed appropriate.

SELECTING TEAM MEMBERS

"You are only as good as the people you hire."

—Ray Kroc
founder of the McDonald's restaurant chain

As a rule, it is usually the leader who selects the members of a team. This is an important responsibility that should be performed carefully, thoughtfully, and systematically. In this regard, the leader must be able to match the skills of potential team members with the jobs to which the team is assigned.

Over and above any particular skill set, knowledge, or experience that may be required, leaders should look for individuals who place their highest goals and aspirations in a team context. In other words, the people whom the leader is considering for selection should be "team players." In reality, not everyone who wants to be hired will like being a part of a team or will be good at assuming the role of a team player.

Team players in the workplace function much like the members of a football team—they work together and build on each other's strengths and achievements. They focus on a common goal. Within the context of competitive athletics, it is important to remember that individuals don't win football games, teams do. Similarly, in organizations that utilize work teams, individuals don't succeed (or fail), teams do.

One of the biggest challenges facing a head coach in the NFL is building a team dynamic when the "team" concept is constantly being challenged. The game itself hasn't changed dramatically since its inception. Kevin Byrne, the Ravens' vice president of public relations, recently gave me a book written by Knute Rockne in 1927. As I thumbed through the pages of this book, it became very clear to me that the fundamentals and approach to the game haven't changed a whole lot in the last 70 years or so. The basic concepts and the fact that this game is one of numbers and angles are timeless. As a coach, you try to bring superior numbers to the point of attack, and if you can't do that, you try to supply superior angles for your athletes in a one-on-one match-up.

Like most athletic endeavors, ultimately our success is going to come down to the personnel that we have. If we have personnel who are superior to our opponents, in most cases we will win. This doesn't mean, however, that you can simply absolve yourself of all responsibility for your team's performance simply because you aren't talented.

After the 1998 season in Minnesota, when we set the all-time NFL scoring record of 556 points in a single season, I was asked if my coaching was superfluous because of the overwhelming amount of talent we had on that 15-1 team with players like Cris Carter, Randy Moss, Robert Smith, and so many other skilled athletes. I wholeheartedly disagreed. Though I am the first to acknowledge that talent is a major key to a team's success, how could I continue in my profession if I didn't feel that my coaching could have a significant impact when I was surrounded by great talent?

ASSIGNING TASKS

"Never tell people how to do things. Tell them what to do, and they will surprise you with their ingenuity."

—George S. Patton, Jr.
general, United States Army

Once the members of the team have been selected, the next step in building an effective team is to assign specific tasks or roles to the individuals chosen. On occasion, the selection and assignment of team members is a concurrent process (i.e., a particular person is selected to fulfill a specific job). In other instances, the process is more open-ended. Individuals are chosen for the team because of their inclusive range of skills or their perceived ability to function as a productive member of a given team.

The latter approach requires that the leader prepare a detailed job description for each task to be undertaken by the group and develop a skills inventory of each member of the team. The leader then makes task assignments by matching the skills of each team member to the various job descriptions. The process is designed to make the best use of each team member's particular talents. Paul Brown, the legendary coach of the Cleveland Browns and Cincinnati Bengals, used to ask if "the job was too big for an athlete," when determining if a player was physically, mentally, or emotionally capable of doing a specific task.

As a head coach, you must also be able to recognize whether any member of your team is capable of doing a specific task but is being asked to fill a lesser role due to the talents of others on the team. For example, when I was on the staff in Minnesota, we drafted David Palmer in the second round out of the University of Alabama. Gene Stallings, the former head coach at Alabama and the longtime assistant coach to Tom Landry, head coach of the Dallas Cowboys, called Palmer "The best player I have ever coached." David played virtually every skill position in college, from running back wide receiver to quarterback. When David came to us with the Vikings, we had players like Cris Carter, Jake Reed, and Robert Smith. We eventually added all-world receiver Randy Moss. Needless to say, in spite of David's considerable talents, it was tough to find a place to get him in the game. David struggled with this diminished role at first, but when he learned he could create a special niche for himself as our punt returner and third-down back, he became one of the top specialists in the league and had a major impact on the Vikings in our 15–1 record-setting year.

CREATE A WORK CULTURE THAT FACILITATES TEAMWORK AND TEAM SPIRIT

"Ten strong horses could not pull an empty baby carriage if they worked independently of each other."

—John Wooden
Hall of Fame basketball coach

Skillful leaders understand the value of creating a work culture that fosters teamwork and enhances team spirit. The potential impact of both factors on the efficiency and productivity levels of a team is substantial.

The leader can cultivate teamwork (i.e., the ability of team members to work together effectively) in a number of ways. For example, the team leader can institute steps to facilitate the working relationship between team members. In this regard, mutual respect and trust are emphasized, and the need for candor and honest feedback is actively promoted.

Another step that can advance the level of teamwork in a group is to encourage the frequent use of terms and phrases that focus on the team, while avoiding expressions and language that emphasize the individual. Words like "teammates" and "team members" are used, rather than "employees" and "subordinates." Terms like "we," "us," and "our" are stressed, as opposed to "I," "me," and "mine." The point to remember is that language can shape attitudes and behavior. Speaking about a group as if it were a team can help make it a team.

The leader can also enhance teamwork in the group by making team members ever more dependent on each other. For example, individual and personal tasks, goals, feedback, and rewards can be linked to group performance. In other words, either everyone "wins" or no one "wins." This factor was at the crux of my policy of not assigning a bed check during the season. As part of the bed-check rule I instituted, any single violation of the curfew would have caused the reinstitution of bed check, and no one player wanted to be the one who made everybody else have to suffer.

Another factor that can affect teamwork is familiarity. In this instance, familiarity refers to how much knowledge team members have of their teammates, jobs, and the work environment. All factors considered, the more team members get to know each other and become familiar with the workplace, the more likely they are to be bound emotionally to the group. Such feelings (commonly referred to as "team spirit") can elevate team morale and improve team performance.

Within the workplace, team spirit is defined as the individual pursuit of excellence within the team concept. In the words of Vince Lombardi, Jr., "When individuals have team spirit, they want the team to succeed and will hold themselves—and every other member of the team—personally accountable for pursuing individual excellence."

We sometimes undertake specific steps to enhance team spirit. On Fridays, for example, our last real preparation day before a game, we have a special teams review whereby I arbitrarily rotate the different teams in and out, mainly checking for substitution. Each week when we get to the field-goal team, we have a volunteer offer to kick the field goal instead of Matt Stover, our Pro Bowl kicker. If he's successful, the volunteer gets varying amounts of money ranging from $100 to $500 based on the length of the kick. This amount is small potatoes compared to the betting that takes place on the sideline between the players. Most of the substitute kickers are so greedy they go right for the big money and miss. In addition to enhancing team spirit and morale, another point of this exercise is that the other players who attempt the kick get a better appreciation for how tough a kicker's job really is. All kicks are "chip shots," until you are the one who has to make the kick.

In reality, the leader of an organization has several possible courses of action that can be taken to foster team spirit. For example, one of the most common methods of enhancing team spirit is to rally the group against a real or imagined threat from the outside. Bashing the competition makes sense when the competition is external to the organization. This practice was a readily available tool for us in our championship season because so few people expected us to do well, even as we were working our way through the playoffs. At no point during our playoff run leading up to the Super Bowl were we favored. The players took up this perceived lack of respect by adopting the battle cry of "We don't get any respect."

Another step for cultivating team spirit is to emphasize the team's value to the organization over the individual's contribution. In this regard, team members can be recognized or rewarded on the basis of the group's identity or performance. The use of such devices as giving the group a nickname, placing the team logo on items such as T-shirts and coffee mugs, and posting information related to team activities on display walls or electronic bulletin boards is a common practice in many organizations.

Such a practice is a very familiar one in sports. The difficulty is coming up with just the right name. Furthermore, for it to really stick, it has to be given to you from some external source, like the media or the fans. The "Fearsome Foursome," "Wild Bunch," "Purple People Eaters," and "Orange Crush" are just a few of the more popular nicknames assigned to various teams over the years. The one I like the most for our championship defense was "Purple Reign." When I asked future Hall of Famer Rod Woodson what he thought we should be called, he quipped back, "How about just 'pretty damn good.'"

Other possible measures that can improve team spirit include fostering member interaction through physical proximity, encouraging individuals to share ideas, and promoting mutual accountability. When team members are located relatively close together, they tend to interact more frequently—a circumstance that can enhance feelings of camaraderie and belonging. Training camp proves to be invaluable in this regard. Many teams are deciding to have their summer training camps in their year-round facilities. Certainly, there is some efficiency to such a move. On the other hand, the bonding and camaraderie that occur when you go off to some college campus for five weeks and force the team to interact both on and off the field is hard to replace.

Sharing ideas is another step that can help develop teamwork because of the high level of cooperation that is involved. In addition, idea sharing can stimulate creative thinking (thereby further enhancing team members' positive attitudes toward their jobs) because of the intellectual and cognitive processes that are inherently required to generate ideas.

Developing a sense of mutual accountability is another step that can help cultivate team spirit. Team members should be given frequent feedback concerning how their behavior and actions are contributing to team goals and team productivity.

Making individuals adhere to rules—particularly if team members are involved in helping the leader set the rules—is one commonly employed step for establishing accountability. The practice of setting rules, however, can have its limitations. As Mike Krzyzewski, the great Duke basketball coach, once observed, "Too many rules get in the way of leadership. They just put you in a box and, sooner or later, a rule-happy leader will wind up in a situation where he wants to use some discretion but is forced to go along with some decree that he himself has concocted. People set rules to keep from making decisions."

When I took over the Ravens, I had two clear-cut premises that I wanted to establish: passion and accountability. When my predecessor Ted Marchiborda and his staff were fired after the 1998 season, I did not want the players to feel that their reason for losing had just walked out the door. In reality, our players had a part in both our 6-10 season in 1998 and the fact that the organization had never had a winning season in franchise history. In my opinion, until they faced their culpability in our lack of success, we had little chance of getting better. To that end, I wanted to establish as many ways for our players to be directly accountable for their own actions as I could.

As I have mentioned, one step I took to help players become accountable for themselves was to do away with bed checks during training camp and the night before games. We maintained curfews, but the players were expected to adhere to those curfews without having to be tucked in like children. I have always had a tough time with the concept of having to knock on the door of a grown man's room—an individual who is being paid an incredible amount of money to play—to make sure that he is where he is supposed to be. I promised my players at our first meeting that if they acted like men, I would treat them as such. Oddly enough, this policy did upset one particular player. Tony Siragusa, our playful, veteran defensive tackle, proclaimed that having no bed check would take the fun out of sneaking out after curfew. Siragusa dishearteningly announced, "I won't even enjoy my beer. I might as well stay in."

Interestingly enough, my policy of having no bed checks became an issue at the Super Bowl. The media felt that not having a bed check during the week leading up to the game was an extension of our supposedly bad-boy, bully image. The truth of the matter is that the players had acted professionally and like men for two years with regard to this policy, and I certainly was not going to disrespect them now simply because the stakes were higher.

In his book *Leading with the Heart*, Mike Krzyzewski states that he has one rule for his players: "Don't do anything detrimental to yourself." This rule is elegant in its simplicity. Like most people, players can conjure up any number of reasons to justify any given action. Some players even get indignant over any suggestion that their personal actions should be somehow modified because of their responsibility to the team. In this regard, the key is to get players to understand that they are affected by any negative impact on the image of the organization that results from their own or their teammates' actions. A good general guideline to try to get your players to understand is "If you're not sure whether a certain behavior is appropriate or not, it probably isn't."

It is my experience that most players truly want to do the right thing. The key is to take steps to ensure that they know what that right thing is. To that end, I have established a speakers bureau to address my team during the course of our training camp and the regular season. This group consists of a cross section of lawyers, law-enforcement professionals, and qualified counselors who have expertise in areas such as anger management, male-female issues, crisis intervention, and motivational speaking.

This bureau was not established to have someone stand up in front of our players and moralize about the dangers of drugs, alcohol, and women. It was intended to educate our players about the predatory environment in which high-profile athletes exist. If they can be schooled in the proper way to handle a compromising situation, they may be able to avoid a potentially precarious predicament. Educating our players on sensitive issues in a group setting also helps to foster a sense of team obligation, because these factors have been addressed as a team. Peer pressure is an excellent way to help "suspend" self-interest.

Finally, teamwork and team spirit are fostered when a leader takes specific steps to enable groups to lead themselves. In this regard, one of the most effective actions the leader can undertake is to empower the group to make decisions that affect the team. When decision-making authority and responsibility are delegated from the leader to the team members, a climate is created that encourages individual input, heightens group morale, and enhances team productivity.

WORKING AS A TEAM

"The secret of winning football games is working more as a team, less as individuals. I play not my 11 best, but my best 11."

—Knute Rockne
Notre Dame football coach

Skillful leaders are aware of the fact that well-organized teams with carefully selected members, a precisely defined mission, and goals that are appropriate to the circumstances can make a meaningful contribution to the organization. The scope and extent of this contribution will depend on how well the leader is able to deal with the inherent strengths and limitations of the team concept. Effective leaders have the knowledge, ability, and insight to handle this crucial responsibility.

While I am obviously biased, I firmly believe the championship won by the 2000 Baltimore Ravens was one of the premier examples of team play. Not only did individuals forego personal accomplishments to achieve the team's goals, but groups within the team structure committed themselves to a profile of winning even when they were criticized for it. Offensively, we went from being ranked 24th in the NFL in total offense

(1999) to 16th in the league in 2000. We finished the year ranked fifth in rushing, and only the Denver Broncos had more time of possession than we did. As our defensive dominance became obvious throughout the season, the offense knew that ball control and maintaining a lead would be our formula for winning a championship.

Once we were up by as few as 10 points, we knew that as long as we did not turn the ball over and literally "ran" the clock down, most teams would not be able to move the ball sufficiently against our defense to make a comeback to win the game. Although admittedly too conservative for my liking, this style of play was clearly our best option for achieving our goals. During the latter part of the season and into the playoffs, our critics were constantly berating our offense for this profile, even though it was winning. I give a great deal of credit to the players on the offensive side of the ball for not giving in to such criticism—most notably to Trent Dilfer.

Trent had been criticized throughout much of his NFL career in Tampa Bay for his lack of overall production. With the Buccaneers, he had been placed in a system that had demanded that the quarterback play a conservative "just-don't-screw-it-up" mentality. When he decided to come to Baltimore and play in my system (one that had previously featured a wide-open and explosive style of play), he had hoped that he would be allowed to be more assertive and open in his quarterbacking. And yet, when all was said and done, he was being asked to do the same things he had previously been asked to do in Tampa.

In our last game of the season against the New York Jets, we were in a unique situation in which the game meant nothing to our playoff position, but our opponent had to win or be eliminated from the postseason. The Jets moved the ball well in the first half against our top-rated defense and took a 14-0 lead. Fortunately, we created a number of turnovers, and Jermaine Lewis returned two punts for touchdowns on the way to an eventual 34-20 win.

Late in the game, with the outcome clearly determined, we had moved the ball into scoring range and were facing a third-and-long. Trent had come over to the sideline during a timeout where I was advocating taking a shot down the field to gain the first down. Trent looked me in the eye and asked, "Do we really need it?" Even though the extra numbers might have deflected some of the criticism he was facing about a lack of productivity, he had totally bought into the team mentality and was wholly unconcerned about his personal numbers or accolades. This was when I knew that we had developed a true, total team mentality that could take us to a championship.

Principle # 9:

Effective leaders are aware of the positive impact that a team can have on making the vision of an organization a reality and know how to maximize the contributions of the team to the organization.

chapter 11

BE
OPPORTUNISTIC

"The great secret of success in life is for a man to be ready when his opportunity comes."

—Benjamin Disraeli
British politician and author

Opportunities don't occur in life just because you want them to. More often than not, they take place because of planning and effort on someone's part. They arise because circumstances were created that enabled them to occur.

As such, effective leaders are opportunistic. In other words, they have both the ability to spot opportunities and the resolve to make full use of any that do transpire. An individual who is opportunistic should not be confused with someone who is an opportunist—i.e., a person who takes advantage of circumstances without regard for principles or consequences.

Opportunistic leaders want to succeed and grow professionally, but not at the cost of compromising their value system. They are fully aware of the fact that the efforts expended to search out and harness their opportunities can and will have a positive impact on the organization's vision and goals. Given the potential benefits of being opportunistic, leaders need to thoughtfully consider how best to deal with the ever-changing circumstances in their professional lives.

Accordingly, as a leader, you need to think strategically about what you can do to identify and take advantage of your opportunities. Such thinking should strengthen your judgment, expand your insight, and buttress your leadership skills.

As an opportunistic person, you need to realize that opportunities abound. They are everywhere if you can learn to recognize them for what they are. The more you create an environment in the workplace in which ideas and an atmosphere of open-mindedness thrive, the more likely it is that a situation where you will have an abundant number of opportunities will arise. By the same token, the more tolerant and receptive you are to new notions and conceptual links, the easier it will be for you to be opportunistic.

In their book *The Power of Focus*, bestselling authors Jack Canfield, Mark Victor Hansen, and Les Hewitt suggest that one of the most straightforward and meaningful approaches to creating opportunities in a person's life is to establish and adhere to a template of positive behavior. Such a template is characterized by a concerted effort to adopt certain desirable habits while working on (i.e., refraining from) any bad habits you might have.

In this regard, a list of the desirable habits that should help govern your behavior as a leader should include the following at a minimum: build on your strengths; see the big picture; develop exceptional relationships; act with confidence; ask for what you want and need; embrace success; act decisively; live purposefully; stay abreast of relevant technological advances; and embrace the potential of accepting challenges.

Denny Green, head coach of the Minnesota Vikings, often says that his grandmother taught him "When opportunity knocks on the door, you better have your bags packed." While it is one thing to have faith that things will work out for you, your faith must be accompanied by a vigilant effort to prepare yourself for when the time comes. This point is made more simply by the biblical phrase "Faith without works is not true faith."

This faith, coupled with your resolute commitment to be prepared, enables you to overcome the obstacles and failure that are the true conduit to opportunity. This factor is akin to the observations of a wealthy entrepeneur who remarked that "If the majority were right, the majority would be rich." In other words, if your opportunities were not validated by obstacles and failure, anyone and everyone would take advantage of them and, therefore, they would not exist.

Over the years, I have been fortunate to have a number of professional opportunities—a few that I've taken advantage of, some I passed on. For example, in 1978, after serving as a graduate assistant at Brigham Young University, I was looking for a full-time coaching job when Bill Walsh offered me an administrative position with the San Francisco 49ers. Although accepting this job would initially take my career in a decidedly different direction from what I had anticipated up to that point, it was clearly too good an opportunity to pass up. Working for the 49ers gave me a chance to interact with such exceptional individuals as Bill Walsh, Denny Green, George Siefert, Bruce Coslet, Ray Rhodes, Tony Dungy, Mike White, and Sam Wyche. In reality, I could not have orchestrated this type of good fortune on purpose if I had tried in a hundred professional lifetimes.

In 1997, I was approached about becoming the head coach at Fresno State University. I thought this might be an excellent opportunity to display my skills and aptitude as a head coach and a springboard that might eventually lead to other jobs. The president of the university accurately sized up the situation. Because he was concerned about how long I might stay in Fresno, he awarded the job to someone else.

The next year, Jerry Jones, the owner of the Dallas Cowboys, offered me the offensive coordinator job with the Cowboys at more than twice my salary at the time as offensive coordinator with the Minnesota Vikings. Normally, I would not have considered leaving Denny Green and the Vikings. It was a very volatile time for everyone in the Vikings' organization since Denny was not sure he would return as the Vikings' head coach for the 1998 season. Even though the Vikings' management was not sure they could firmly guarantee that I would have a job going into the 1998 season, the Vikings' ownership blocked my lateral move to the Cowboys.

Although both of these opportunities would have been excellent jobs, not getting them had a very noteworthy impact on my professional career. In 1998, for example, I had the responsibility of coordinating the Vikings' offense that set the all-time scoring record in the NFL. The 15-1 record and our record-setting offensive performance played a major role in the events that led to my being named the head coach of the Baltimore Ravens.

The point to keep in mind is that sooner or later, fate will take a hand. The question is will you be prepared when it does.

BUILD ON YOUR STRENGTHS

"The ladder of success doesn't care who climbs it."

—Frank Tyger

Opportunistic leaders focus on their strengths rather than their weaknesses. They are aware of their natural talents and employ them to their utmost ability. They devote most of their time to doing the things at which they are good (refer to the discussion in the previous chapter on the 80/20 principle of Italian economist Vilfredo Pareto). As such, they tend to get more accomplished. They are less likely to waste time on tasks they do not perform as well.

All factors considered, individuals who are opportunistic are better able to prioritize their time. Furthermore, when appropriate, they're willing to delegate or reschedule tasks they've been asked to do. If necessary, they're also willing to ask for help if they need it.

Early in my career, I recognized that I had a propensity for organization and the communicative aspects of teaching and coaching. Those strengths are what I built on as the foundation of my coaching abilities. As a result, I focused my attention on those aspects of the game that were more attributable to organization, planning, and teaching. I took the basic principles and fundamentals of practice and game-plan structures that I learned from Bill Walsh and Denny Green and augmented them in an effort to clarify and define the key aspects of this integral part of coaching. In this regard, my first published material was a book called, *Developing an Offensive Game Plan.* In great detail, this successful coaching manual outlined the parameters that should be employed when analyzing, formulating, and implementing a game plan. When developing the manuscript for that book, the process of articulating my ideas and concepts in written form helped me to formulate with more detail and definition those principles I have used successfully with the Vikings initially and the Ravens currently.

SEE THE BIG PICTURE

"Only he who can see the invisible
can do the impossible."

—Frank Gaines

Skillful leaders not only are able to attend to the important details that enable an organization to operate smoothly, they also have the ability to think big. As such, they are conscious goal-setters who are able to achieve a reasonable balance time-wise between their short-and long-range goals and the vision of the organization.

Because of their broad perspective, effective leaders are able to grasp how an action (e.g., a change in policy, procedure, personnel, etc.) in one part of the organization may elicit a particular response in other parts of the organization as well. This foresight can enhance their capacity to create, recognize, and take advantage of opportunities within the workplace.

By definition, individuals who are able to see the big picture are able to elevate their level of thinking. They have the aptitude to not only see things "as they are," but also "as they can be." They refuse to be channeled into a pattern of thinking small. Such a pattern may diminish their willingness to expend their energy and to make sacrifices to "expand their professional envelope." To paraphrase the malaprop musings of Yogi Berra, "If you don't know where you're going, you'll end up somewhere else."

This balancing of micro and macro management is not unlike appreciating a work of art. If you stand too close to the piece, you may be able to appreciate the fine detail and texture of the material, but you do so at the risk of being so close that you cannot keep the entire scope of the work in proper perspective. If you stand too far back, while you may have a better view of the "big picture," you risk losing the appreciation of the attention to detail and the quality of the work.

A position coach can and should "stand too close" to his work. It is his responsibility to keep his attention on the details and specific perspectives of the game plan as they pertain to his particular position. The coordinators, on the other hand, should step back a little further from the situation than a position coach should. They should be close enough to keep their attention to detail, but should focus on the larger perspective in order to make sure that the various components of their offensive or defensive unit are working well together and don't become too compartmentalized. It is also part of his responsibility to make sure the position coaches don't get so close to their perspectives that they lose sight of the overall main objective.

The head coach must pull back even a step further than his coordinators. He must have the broadest perspective of all. It is his responsibility to make sure that the offense, defense and special teams interact together in such a way that the balance that is needed to achieve any type of sustained success in the NFL is maintained. On occasion, he may have to constantly remind his coordinators that, in and of itself, finishing high in the league's statistical standings has little or no value except as it pertains to the overall organizational goal of winning and losing. The proper distance that a head coach needs from the day-to-day operations in order to accomplish this task is entirely subjective and very difficult to quantify.

On the other hand, when keeping this "big picture" in mind, you can tend to lose contact with the fundamental reasons you got into your profession. Many is the time that a school principal longs to return to the classroom, or the police desk sergeant craves the excitement of life on the beat, or the news editor misses chasing after a "scoop." For these individuals, the "void" in their lives must be adequately replaced with the challenges that having a higher level of position and responsibility brings.

DEVELOP EXCEPTIONAL RELATIONSHIPS

"The most important single ingredient in the formula of success is knowing how to get along with people."

—Theodore Roosevelt
26th president of the United States

You must have people skills to be a good leader. The ability to inspire trust, to interact well with all kinds of people, to understand how people feel and think, and to treat people as individuals are examples of people skills that can help create a strong foundation for building exceptional relationships. Opportunistic leaders understand that success in life is often derived more from who you know (relationships), than what you know (knowledge).

ACT WITH CONFIDENCE

"Experience tells you what to do; confidence allows you to do it."

—Stan Smith
tennis professional

Effective leaders have considerable confidence in their ability to perform their duties in a responsible manner, particularly their capacity to channel their energies and to pursue their priorities. The faith that they have in their professional capabilities tends to enhance their gift for leadership in at least two meaningful ways.

First, by acting with confidence, leaders tend to inspire their followers to believe in them. In other words, confidence begets trust and confidence from others. Second, confident individuals are more likely to exhibit certain desirable behavior patterns. For example, confident leaders are action-oriented. They confront issues head on. They resolve unfinished business. They don't procrastinate. They don't dwell on either grudges or the past. They don't let conflicts linger. They deal with their fears. They push themselves to achieve their goals.

ASK FOR WHAT YOU WANT AND NEED

"One who never asks either knows everything or nothing."

—Malcolm Forbes
American publisher and author

Almost everything in life is a choice. Effective leaders tend to make better choices. One of the primary reasons that skillful leaders are able to make better choices involves the fact that they often have more useful information available to reach and make decisions. They know what to ask for, how to ask for something, and whom to ask.

With regard to questioning, effective leaders tend to be very adept at the discovery process that attorneys often employ when attempting to obtain information (i.e., they ask questions that address the issues of who, what, why, when, where, and how). As a rule, they increase the likelihood of their questions being answered in a timely and accurate fashion by framing their questions with clarity, certainty, sincerity, and, if necessary, creativity.

Competent leaders are also aware of the fact that they should actively solicit feedback from their followers and seek advice from people who have knowledge that can help them. Ultimately, they are able to process and use whatever information they have on hand in an insightful and discerning manner.

EMBRACE SUCCESS

"Failure can be bought on easy terms; success must be paid for in advance."

—Cullen Hightower

Effective leaders embrace success by putting themselves in a position to be successful. Not only do they know what they want, they are able to focus their energies on getting it. In this regard, they do whatever is appropriate to add substance to their leadership skills and value to their existence. The cornerstones of their efforts are hard work, initiative, vision, and character. The precept to which they adhere is characterized by the maxim—*carpe occasionam* ("seize the opportunity").

ACT DECISIVELY

Effective leaders have both the ability and the courage to act decisively. They are able to understand the consequences of their actions and inactions. They tend to be thoughtful and insightful decision makers. They're neither impulsive nor dilatory. When a decision needs to be made, they make it. When a change is appropriate, they institute it. Whatever the circumstances, they take a proactive approach with regard to performing their responsibilities.

LIVE PURPOSEFULLY

Skillful leaders tend to have a very clear understanding of their role in the organization and act accordingly. Furthermore, they know what they expect from life and why. They have the ability to balance their perceived purpose in life with the organizational role they have chosen to undertake. They are aware of their skills and talents and employ them in a determined manner.

KEEP ABREAST OF TECHNOLOGY

Opportunistic leaders are acutely aware of the need to keep abreast of relevant technological advances. The technological explosion that has yielded innovative means to gather, process, manage, and utilize information and knowledge has provided leaders with an exceptional opportunity to achieve greater efficiency and effectiveness. Therefore leaders should not fear or be intimidated by technology.

Rather, leaders have an obligation to embrace technology for any number of reasons. At the least, technology can have a positive impact on the productivity level of everyone in the organization. In addition, not only can technology facilitate the task of sustaining and improving what is already known and what is already largely being done, technology can be an effective enabler of the new and the different. In other words, technology in this period of rapid change can create opportunities heretofore unforeseen or even unimaginable.

On a cautionary note, leaders should also keep in mind that technological advancement should not be an end unto itself. The use of technology should be kept in perspective. Technology should serve a worthwhile purpose in order to justify allocating resources (e.g., time, funds, etc.) to it. Too many organizations adopt a particular technological innovation in an attempt to be more efficient and then become bogged down in efforts to get the innovation to fulfill its intended function. For example, in some instances, whatever efficiencies that might have occurred are transcended by the time it takes to install or debug a technological advance. Such a situation would be a classic case of an organization being up to its neck in alligators while forgetting the ultimate goal of draining the swamp.

I enjoyed listening to George Lucas, of *Star Wars* fame, talk about the use of special effects. He commented that many film-makers make the mistake of developing a very unique special effect, then ruin it by overusing it in a film to justify the cost or just become very enamored with the effect itself, even though its use is not key to the story line.

I have had a similar experience with my efforts to employ technology to facilitate my efforts as a head coach. For example, my use of the computer has been instrumental in my abilities to teach. Yet I have to constantly remind myself not to trivialize the material with all the "bells and whistles" available via the internet. It is important to keep my focus on the purpose of the technology. When I first started working with computers to perform game analysis at San Diego University, I began with the individuals in the university's computer science department. The problem was that they were more interested in the me-chanics than the desired function of what I wanted. When I moved on to Utah State University, I found a young man named Everett Byington in the business office. He helped me develop a game-analysis program that is still being used by teams today. Everett, given his business perspective, was great at cutting to the chase and being able to develop a program that eliminated the "bells and whistles" and that focused on the information needed rather than on the apparatus to acquire it.

ACCEPT CHALLENGES

"What lies behind us and what lies before us are tiny matters compared with what lies within us."

—Oliver Wendell Holmes
American jurist and chief justice of the Supreme Court

Sooner or later, all leaders are faced with challenges. Per-haps no challenge is more daunting (and more prevalent) than the need to make tough decisions—regarding personnel, the allocation of resources, setting organizational priorities, planning for the future, etc. As such, skillful leaders are willing and able to confront challenges head on. They realize that they have an intractable duty to deal with challenges in a systematic and strategic manner.

Andy Grove, the CEO of Intel, defined this concept as well as any when he wrote: "I can't help but wonder why leaders are so often hesitant to lead. I guess it takes a lot of conviction and trusting your gut to get ahead of your peers, your staff, and your employees while they are still squabbling about which path to take, and set an unhesitating, unequivocal course whose rightness or wrongness will not be known for years. Such a decision really tests the mettle of the leader. By contrast, it doesn't take much self-confidence to downsize a company—after all, how can you go wrong by shutting factories down and laying people off if the benefits of such actions are going to show up in tomorrow's bottom line and will be applauded by the financial community?"

It is my experience that challenges tend to come at just the right time and in just the right proportion. When I took this job, the Ravens were in the bottom third of the league in both offense and defense, and had not had a winning season in franchise history. Yet it seemed like the perfect fit. Like the bottle of wine you receive as a gift, if it were any better they would not have given it to you and if it were any worse you would not have drunk it. In other words, if the Ravens' job had been any better, it would not have been available, and if it had been any worse, I would not have taken it.

Principle # 10:

Effective leaders search out and take advantage of their opportunities.

chapter 12

BE
SELF-ASSURED

"The man who believes he can do it is probably right, and so is the man who believes he can't."

—Lawrence J. Peter
author of *The Peter Principle*

Effective leaders project a strong leadership image that is grounded in a steadfast sense of self-assurance. They have confidence in themselves and their convictions. All factors considered, they like and are good at what they're doing as leaders. They pursue a can-do, rather than a make-do, approach to their responsibilities. They have high expectations of themselves. They set high standards of performance for themselves. Perhaps most importantly, they have a positive attitude toward the future of the organization.

Self-assurance can be very important to leaders for several reasons. To a point, self-confidence and leadership are interconnected. Self-assured leaders inspire confidence in others. As the level of confidence in the leaders rises, the likelihood that their followers will accept their leadership and act and behave as they want them to increases.

A substantial level of self-confidence can also enhance the faith that you, as a leader, have in your own capabilities to perform a particular task. Referred to as self-efficacy, this belief can lead to a heightened level of performance and a greater willingness for you to set high goals for yourself. Furthermore, to a point, the more you are convinced that you can perform the task at hand, the more you tend to be motivated to undertake the task.

Self-assured leaders also tend to be more willing to take responsibility for their actions. Driven by excellence and their expectation that excellence is reasonably within their grasp, self-confident leaders realize that if they want to lead, they have to produce. If, for whatever reason, they don't produce, they should be held accountable.

Finally, all factors considered, self-assured leaders are more likely to exhibit body language that reflects an image of being confident, friendly, and approachable. Such an image can facilitate your efforts, as the leader, to establish a positive relationship with your followers and help create a workplace climate where feedback is willingly given. Such feedback is often at the core of a successful organization.

Interestingly enough, a discussion of the general concepts of building a winning organization or a winning team should focus initially on how the individuals within the organization view leadership. Any hope of developing a winning organization has to begin with leadership exhibiting total self-confidence. Your very countenance must convey the strength of your convictions and a determined course of action. In the military, they call this factor "command presence."

I have never seen or been a part of any environment where false confidence is exposed and dismissed so quickly as in the NFL. When you stand up in front of a team of 53 professional football players, frankly, it is not for the timid or mild mannered. You must know what you're talking about, be in control of the situation, and exhibit self-assuredness at all times.

As the leader in any field, when you stand before your followers you do so knowing full well that at that very moment, you will be under constant and incessant scrutiny. Every one of your decisions will be questioned, criticized, and second-guessed. Some individuals will do this with a separate agenda in mind; others simply will not understand some factor involving one of your decisions and will want to know more.

When working in such an environment, you must be firm in your own heart. You must have the courage of your convictions; but first, you must have convictions. Before you can expect to be understood and followed, you must initially try to understand yourself. Convictions are more than strongly held opinions. They must be intrinsic to your nature. If they are loosely held on the periphery of your confidence, they will likely be ripped away by the torrent of events when facing any confrontation. Those critics who view me as arrogant, egotistical, and eccentric must at least give me credit for being *consistently* arrogant, egotistical, and eccentric.

Equally, self-assurance is not the conviction that things will always turn out the way we want or planned, but that there are reasons that make sense regardless of how it turns out. I have spent a lifetime attempting to craft my abilities as a coach. I have a great deal of confidence in those abilities because they have survived the test of battle time after time. I know I am a good coach. All that remains to be seen is how successful a coach I will be. Even how you determine that factor must become part of your mental and emotional convictions. To a point, the barometer you use in measuring your success will dictate your ability to sustain it.

If you let the critics, pundits, and experts act as the litmus test for your sense of self-worth, you are doomed to utter failure, for these individuals will never be satisfied. Because critics often know the price of everything and the value of nothing, they tend to be very limited in their perspective and abilities to understand. After each Super Bowl, the winning coach has a news conference the following morning with the national sports media. The first question posed to me, less than 10 hours after winning Super Bowl XXXV, was the same question I am sure was asked of the preceding 34 coaches whose teams won the Super Bowl: "Can you repeat?" I had not even been to bed yet, and I was being asked to outline my plans for repeating the following year. This is the ultimate in the concept of "What have you done for me lately?"

If you allow it to occur, there will always be countless others who will try to impose their will, or at the least their level of expectations, on you. As one leader observed, "You must never become the passive matrix upon which others impose their designs." You must constantly try to redefine whatever position you hold or you are destined to be nothing but the "quantitative manager" who simply and routinely implements the process. This does not, however, require you to reinvent the wheel. As Bill Walsh noted in our book *Finding the Winning Edge*, "Sometimes being innovative simply means doing something very common in a more efficient or productive way." In the previous Chapter, I discussed how I took the basic principles and fundamentals of practice and game plan structures I learned from Bill Walsh and Denny Green and augmented them in an effort to clarify and define the key aspects of this part of coaching.

I imagine that I am like most people, whose dreams of accomplishment are selfish dreams. When you envision yourself atop the podium holding the Super Bowl trophy, you dream of the accolades and adulation that people will shower on you because of your achievements. You think in terms of some validation of your self-image.

As I stood atop the podium at Super Bowl XXXV holding the Lombardi Trophy, which exemplifies excellence in my field, I took great satisfaction in knowing that my thoughts were not dominated by self-interest. The humbling experience of knowing how many people had to do their job competently, with passion and accountability, for us to be world champions was foremost in my mind.

Physical courage is courage in the face of personal danger, while moral courage is courage of responsibility to others or to a purpose. The latter is what will sustain you best in the face of never-ending expectations. If the result of your confidence and convictions is nothing more than self-aggrandizement, such a self-serving goal will eventually fail you. If, on the other hand, your resolve is based on your commitment to the team and the team's ultimate achievements, then you can hold up against the strongest of attacks because your motives and convictions are genuine. Above all else, that is the greatest gift I have received from winning a championship. People preach about this concept of team and unselfishness from the day they begin coaching. It is not until you stand atop the podium of success that you can truly quantify its validity.

On the other hand, I am not attempting to imply that a leader, in order to succeed, does not have to have a healthy ego. I am a firm believer in ego. However, I think the word "ego" gets a bad rap. Ego, by pure definition, is the need to distinguish ourselves from others. I do not see the negative connotation associated with this factor. There is a line in a Paul Simon song that says, "My life is so common it disappears." If I have one fear, it is living a life that is common. I want to distinguish myself from others. The key, like most things in life, is to not take it to excess. Most attributes, even positive ones, can be overdone ("generous to a fault" comes to mind). As such, I don't mind being egotistical as long as it doesn't lead to being self-centered, self-serving, and selfish. That critique must be left to my family and closest friends.

A great leader once wrote, "Curse ruthless time! Curse our mortality! How cruelly short is the allotted span for all we must cram into it! We are all worms. But I do believe that at the least, I am a glow worm." I hope that when all is said and done, that I too was a "glow worm."

RECOVER FROM SETBACKS

"They conquer who believe they can."

—Virgil
Roman poet

Self-confidence enhances the ability of leaders to conquer adversity, such as setbacks, disappointments, and embarrassments. Almost every leader will have to deal with at least one significant setback in their career. The more capable they are of handling negative circumstances, the better able they will be to bounce back from any such situation.

Self-confidence can help break the cycle of stress caused by adversity (i.e., adversity leads to stress that is followed by more adversity, followed by more stress, and so on). In this regard, self-confidence can enable leaders to effectively cope with the emotional elements attendant to negative circumstances by facilitating the ability to accept the reality of their problem, to avoid taking the setback personally, to minimize any feelings of panic, and to be willing to solicit assistance and support from others (e.g., professional colleagues, friends, family members, etc.).

The greatest lessons in confidence I have ever experienced in my life, quite naturally, came at a time of great stress and difficulty. In my first year as a head coach with the Baltimore Ravens, we suffered through a number of growing pains. After taking over an organization that had yet to experience a winning season in its history, we opened the season with a 2-5 record. In addition, much of our lack of success was due to our lack of production on the offensive side of the ball. This was particularly painful because I had been brought in as some sort of offensive "guru." Many assumed I had some sort of magic formula that could yield offensive productivity even in the face of a serious lack of talent.

As a result, I was coming under a great deal of criticism. At the worst of the losing was a three-game losing streak that included an exceptionally miserable performance that occurred in the national spotlight. This particular low point involved a Thursday night nationally televised game against the Kansas City Chiefs. To say we stunk could be accurately criticized as trying to put too positive a spin on the game. This type of performance not only brought into question my abilities with the Ravens, but also raised issues concerning my contributions to the offensive prowess we exhibited during my previous seasons with the Minnesota Vikings.

These circumstances constituted as severe an attack on my abilities and confidence as I have ever experienced. Since the Kansas City contest was a night game, I did not limp home until the early hours the following morning. My family had long since been in bed. When I pulled back the sheets, there was a letter sitting on my pillow from my oldest daughter, Aubree. At the time, she was a sophomore at an all-girls school. She had gone through her own trials and tribulations as the result of transferring schools when we moved from Minnesota, where she had lived for seven years and had built life-long friendships.

Aubree has always been very intuitive and has always been involved and attentive to whatever team I have been a part of. She wrote:

Dear Dad—

It was painful for me to see you go through what you did tonight. I know how disappointed you are with the way things are going. I have always gained strength from your confidence and your attitude about whatever circumstance we were facing as a family. This move has not been easy on me, but you have given me the confidence to know that the anxiety and frustration I am going through will eventually work itself out because you believe in my abilities.

You know you are a good coach and that you will get this thing turned around. You always do. So many people are counting on you to lead them out of this. Know I love you when I tell you this is not about you, so get over it.

Love, Aubree

Out of the mouths of babes! In all my readings and study, I don't believe I have ever come across a more meaningful and insightful passage. When you personalize whatever difficulties you will inevitably face, you complicate the issues in a way that has little chance of helping the situation. This organization had never overcome a three-game losing streak and had never experienced a winning season. They had no frame of reference from which to draw any other conclusion but that we were destined to fail. If the mindset was going to change, it was going to have to come from me. We were able to regroup that season, winning five of our last seven games to finish with the first non-losing season in franchise history—a modest accomplishment according to some, but a major step for this team and organization.

Our ability to effectively handle our difficulties in 1999 was instrumental in our overcoming a similar three-game losing streak the following year in our championship season. The lessons I learned as a leader and those internalized by my team gave us the experience and fortitude to get past the difficult times in 2000. My second Ravens' team did not fall into the familiar trap of self-pity and finger pointing because we recognized there was no future in it. By maintaining the basic principles of leadership (knowledge, passion, and energy), both individually and collectively, we were able to step back from the abyss and use the difficulty as a catalyst to draw strength from throughout the rest of the season. In other words, learn from the insightful observation of a teenager: it's not about you, so get over it.

PURSUE A CAN-DO, RATHER THAN A MAKE-DO, APPROACH

*"One can never consent to creep when
one feels an impulse to soar."*

— Helen Keller
American blind and deaf lecturer

Effective leaders are results-oriented. They discern what needs to be done to accomplish a given goal and they attempt to do it. Their sense of self-assuredness, bolstered by the fact that they have the courage of their convictions, will not permit them to willingly settle for less than their best effort. Self-confident leaders are task-oriented individuals. They have a passion for success and a desire to make the seemingly impossible possible.

One of my favorite stories in this regard was once told by Walt Disney. As a young man, Disney was enthralled with a marching band he had encountered. The pomp and circumstance of the band excited him, and he wanted to be a part of it. When an opening occurred in the band for a trumpet player, he immediately volunteered and jumped at the chance to be a part of it all. At the band's first practice, Disney grabbed hold of the instrument and blew it for all he was worth. What came out was described by Disney as, "the most horrendous noise ever produced by a human." When asked how long he had been playing, he replied that this was the first time he ever tried playing a musical instrument. The band director looked at him quizzically and asked why he volunteered for the band if he could not play. His response was, "I didn't know I couldn't until I tried." It is obvious that this type of energy and confidence was at the heart of what is today one of the most powerful multinational corporations in the world.

When I got the job with the Ravens one of the first people I knew I wanted to hire was Jim Colletto. Jim had been a longtime college coach at institutions like UCLA, Notre Dame, and Arizona State. He had also been the head coach at Purdue University. The fact that Jim had never coached in professional football was one of the reasons I wanted to hire him. Jim was one of the best offensive line coaches I had ever seen, and I wanted a line coach that had not been "pro-ized." Offensive line coaches in the NFL are a very tight-knit group. Of all the position coaches in the league, they communicate and interact more than any other. Although I admire this about them, it does tend to cause them to look at the league and their position with a group mentality. I had grown tired of line coaches whose answer to given suggestions about line play was always "That's not the way we do it in the NFL." To me, this begged the question "Why not?" By trying things that may be different from the established routine, even in failure, you are apt to learn something new and useful. The point to keep in mind is that as long as you stay true to the fundamentals of the task (job), it is always useful to stretch the boundaries of protocol.

SEE THE GLASS AS HALF FULL

*"A successful man is one who can lay
a firm foundation with the bricks others
have thrown at him."*

—David Brinkley
television journalist

Leaders who ascribe to the tenets of competitive leadership tend to see the positive side of things (i.e., they see the glass as half full, rather than half empty). Their vision enables them to frame issues in a constructive, rather than a negative, manner. This approach helps to create a positive atmosphere in the workplace—a climate that can enhance communication, morale, and productivity.

I owe a great deal to Denny Green, the head coach of the Minnesota Vikings. Of all the things I have learned from Denny over the years, none have been as meaningful or insightful as what happened on a drizzly, miserable night in Oakland in the 1996 season. The 1995 season was the only year that the Vikings have failed to make the playoffs during Denny Green's tenure. At the time, Denny had been under personal attack as well for some alleged off-field activities that eventually proved to be totally false. We had started the 1996 campaign with a solid 5–1 start before succumbing to a four-game losing streak. The worst of the losses was our fourth game—a contest that played in Seattle, where we were totally humiliated by the Seahawks 42–23. In addition, we lost our record-setting quarterback Warren Moon. The media was incessant in their attacks on Denny and were reporting that an agreement had been reached with Lou Holtz to replace Denny for the remainder of the season after what everyone assumed would be an impending loss to the Raiders in Oakland—a place known as the "Black Hole."

Denny had been hung out to dry by management who did not even offer the perfunctory "we-support-our-coach" statement that is usually a sure sign that a coach is about to be fired. Roger Hedrick, who was the president of the organization and headed up the 10-person group who owned the Vikings at the time, had gone to St. Thomas for a vacation and was unavailable for comment.

To add insult to injury, the game against the Raiders was a nationally televised contest on ESPN. The whole world was going to get to watch the destruction of a team and maybe a career. It was a rainy, miserable night in the Bay area, and we were facing one of the most physically talented defenses in the NFL with a new starting quarterback in Brad Johnson, who had only one previous start.

As I stood on the sideline just prior to kickoff, trying to keep my play-calling sheet dry, Denny flipped his headset over to the offensive side. As a head coach, Denny had the ability to switch back and forth between the offense and the defense. Denny was a great coach to work for because he was not one to intrude on your thought process to any great degree and only injected himself at certain times during the game. We were standing about 25 yards from each other on the sideline when he called for my attention. Denny and I had known each other for close to 20 years, and I had worked directly for him for 10 years. We had been through many previous battles and difficulties together—the kind when you truly learn about the character of a man. What he told me that night is something I will remember and draw on for the rest of my life.

At the apex of this absolute crisis, Denny told me, "Brian, I must really be sick because I absolutely love this. Everything we have worked for, everything we are about is on display right here and right now, with the whole world watching. No one believes we can do this, no one. God you have to love this game." Denny was right, he was sick. But I had caught the disease as well.

Most people compete to validate themselves and their sense of self-worth. What I learned from Denny Green was to compete for the sheer enjoyment of the competition. Regardless of the outcome, the mere testing of our abilities in these dire moments is the true measure of a man. I owe a great deal to Denny for giving me a chance to display my skills and subsequently earn a living far beyond my wildest imagination. But of all the things I owe Denny, what I appreciate most is the love of competition.

The rest, as they say, is history. We defeated the Raiders that night and went on to make the playoffs. Coach Green is still under fire in Minnesota, even though his teams have made the playoffs eight of the nine years he has been there. His is the only team to return to the conference championship game in two of the last three years. But even though Denny's achievements are largely ignored, I know that the perilous nature of his job situation is not an overriding concern for him because he still values the sheer competitiveness of the game. Regardless of what the future holds for him, those of ill-will and criticism will never defeat him, and will never understand why. As Denny is fond of saying, "This job is not who I am, it is just what I do."

Perhaps no better example exists of the value of taking a positive view of an issue than the immortal words of Martin Luther King, Jr.'s "I have a dream" speech. The fact that this distinguished civil rights leader framed his concerns in a positive manner, rather than a negative way, only served to enhance the significance and impact of his message. In reality, he could have just as easily said, "I have a problem with the state of civil rights in the United States" Instead, he made his point in a positive fashion. Over time, his words and his message have become an integral part of the fabric of our national conscience.

> *"I have a dream that one day this nation*
> *will rise up and live out the true meaning*
> *of the creed: we hold these truths to be*
> *self-evident—that all men are created equal."*
>
> —Martin Luther King, Jr.
> civil rights pioneer

Principle # 11:

Effective leaders have confidence in their ability to handle the demands and challenges of leadership.

chapter 13

BE COURAGEOUS

"One man with courage makes a majority."

—Andrew Jackson
seventh president of the United States

Courage is present in every great leader. For a leader, courage involves more than single, isolated acts of bravery or fortitude. Rather, courage is the personal strength that enables a leader to handle fear, make difficult decisions, take risks, confront change, accept responsibility, and be self-reliant. In other words, courage is the trait that empowers you to be yourself, follow your conscience (instincts), and pursue your vision. Keep in mind that as a leader, courage is not something you pursue; it's something you embody.

HANDLING FEAR

"Courage is the first of human qualities because it is the quality which guarantees all other."

—Winston Churchill
British prime minister and statesman

Courage is not the absence of fear; it's confronting your fears. Vince Lombardi Jr. says, "Courage means experiencing your fear, labeling it for what it is, acknowledging that you're afraid, and, if it's important enough to you, pushing ahead in spite of your fear."

The point to keep in mind is that all leaders experience fear. Fear comes with the territory of leadership. It's how you handle that fear that will impact on your ability to lead. While you can't avoid the stress and pressure that often accompany the demands of leadership, you can master your fears—whatever the circumstances.

One of the first steps you can take to deal with your fears as a leader is to recognize certain maxims about courage. In John Maxwell's book *The 21 Indispensable Qualities of a Leader*, he identifies four fundamental truths attendant to courage. The first truth involves the fact that every test you face as a leader begins with an inner battle. Dealing with your fear is an internal process that ultimately enables you to overcome your anxieties relating to either the unknown or the possibility of failing and to forge ahead into uncharted territory. Such courage is perhaps best reflected in the traditional firefighters' saying, "We run into buildings, while other people are running out."

The second truth refers to the fact that courage entails taking a stand when appropriate. In other words, courage involves having the conviction to do what's right, regardless of the circumstances. Although smoothing things over by attempting to appease someone else may be the path of least resistance (i.e., the most convenient way to go), you should never compromise your principles. The point is perhaps most clearly made by the words of civil rights advocate Martin Luther King, Jr., who asserted, "The ultimate measure of a man is not where he stands in moments of comfort and convenience, but where he stands in moments of challenge and controversy."

The third maxim attendant to courage is that courage tends to inspire commitment from others. One of the most admired characteristics in the world is courage—particularly moral courage. As such, a show of courage by you as a leader will enhance the desire of your followers to respond to your call for purposeful action.

The fourth truth involves the fact that fear can greatly limit a leader. More often than not, courage expands the parameters of your life. You are more willing to take risks, to engage in new experiences, and to stretch not only your comfort zone, but also your expectations. A courageous leader does not avoid the unpleasant or the unknown if dealing with such situations is the right thing to do.

For me, one such situation involved the playoffs after the 2000 season. Our initial playoff game in our ultimate road to the Super Bowl was the first in the history of our franchise. Our opponents, Mike Shanahan's Denver Broncos, had been picked by many people to make a Super Bowl run. Mike was 7-1 in playoff games going into our contest and along the way had led the Broncos to two Super Bowl titles. On the other hand, this was my first experience as a head coach in the playoffs. In all honesty, Mike's experience and proven abilities as a head coach caused me great concern, although I also knew that we had the talent and team chemistry to make a run at the championship and that our players had every opportunity to win. I did not want my lack of experience as a head coach in this situation to be the reason we were not successful.

As usual, the best antidote for anxiety is work. By throwing myself into the details of preparation, I did not allow myself to play the countless "what if" games that do nothing but heighten your sense of fear and panic.

Even though we were new to the playoff experience as a team, we did have a great deal of playoff experience individually among our players. Rod Woodson, Shannon Sharpe, Ben Coates, Harry Swayne, and Sam Gash were just a few of the players who had not only been to the playoffs, but had been to a Super Bowl. Their confidence and leadership, coupled with their heightened sense of preparation, infected both players and coaches alike. As the week progressed, everyone gained a sense of anticipation rather than fear of the impending task. It was what we had worked all year to achieve. We understood the fact that our efforts in the face of a somewhat increased risk of being humiliated by the playoff-tested Denver team would only enhance our sense of accomplishment when we were able to beat them. In the process, we would earn the first playoff win in the history of the organization and in my head coaching career.

MAKING DIFFICULT DECISIONS

"The difficulties and struggles today are but
the price we must pay for the accomplishments
and victories of tomorrow."

—Reverend William J.H. Boetcker
lecturer on industrial relations issues

As was pointed out in Chapter 10, decision making is not a mechanical undertaking. It involves risk taking and a challenge to your ability to make a sound judgment. All factors considered, the more difficult the decision, the greater the challenge. The key is to have the strength to address the various factors that can make a given decision particularly troublesome, such as time pressures, conflicting priorities, lack of a desired consensus, possible negative impact on those involved by the decision, etc., in a way that ultimately leads to a decision.

One dimension that is present in almost every decision—particularly difficult decisions—is time. As a rule, the more immediacy involved in a decision, the harder it is to reach a decision. Obviously, immediacy can preclude an in-depth analysis of the situation, thereby leading to a superficial, ineffective solution (decision). Some of the worst decisions leaders can make occur because they act before either they get all the relevant facts or before they are able to engage in a thoughtful, detailed review of the relevant information on hand.

Another aspect that can make some decisions particularly difficult occurs when a decision involves conflicting priorities, such as short-term versus long-range goals, employee morale versus "bottom-line" issues, productivity versus excellence, people issues versus maintaining competitive advantage, etc. Sound leadership requires the courage to resolve these conflicting priorities in a way that is consistent with the leader's sense of ethics and the organization's vision.

Making a hard decision can be further complicated for a leader when a consensus doesn't exist regarding the need for such decision or how such a decision should be reached. For example, as a leader, you may have to deal with a situation where your superiors don't attach any degree of urgency to reaching a particular decision, while your followers hold a diametrically different opinion. An additional dilemma may arise over whether a decision should be made in isolation or involve the active participation of others. It can take courage to make a thoughtful decision in such an ambivalent work environment.

One of the most difficult decisions that a leader will ever have to make is one that will have a demonstrably negative impact on one or more of your followers (e.g., layoffs, terminations, etc.). Although the decision may be integral to the responsibilities of the leader and consistent with the needs and interests of the organization, it can require courage when the results of that decision are potentially hurtful to a particular individual. As an NFL coach, for example, one of the toughest assignments I have all year is having to release a veteran player who is giving his best to the Baltimore Ravens' organization, but his best is simply not good enough.

One such player was Trent Dilfer. Trent performed magnificently for the Ravens in our championship season. He brought both passion and toughness to our offense and played unselfishly within the parameters we had set for him based on our overall team profile. To make the move of signing Elvis Grbac and letting Trent go and then to simply dismiss it as a business decision does not do Trent justice on a personal level. The fact remains that the organization and I, as the head coach, decided that in order for the Ravens to return to the Super Bowl, we would need an increased offensive presence. In reality, there was no easy way to do this.

In matters of this nature I can offer only one true bit of advice. It is the same advice I give to my players when they face the moment of truth in any given game: "Be right or be wrong, but be decisive in your actions."

TAKING RISKS

"Only those who risk going too far can possibly find out how far one can go."

—T. S. Eliot
American-born British poet

Responsible leaders must have the courage to take risks. Although risk is often inherent in making decisions, trying to eliminate any degree of the unknown by systematically forecasting what particular response a specific action will elicit is neither a worthwhile nor a precise undertaking. As renowned management consultant and author Peter F. Drucker points out in his book *Management: Tasks, Responsibilities, Practices*, "The attempt to eliminate risks, even the attempt to minimize them, can only make them more irrational and unbearable. It can only result in the greatest risk of all: rigidity." Leaders need to have the ability to identify the appropriate risks an organization should take and the proper procedures for undertaking those risks. This ability involves a measure of both skill and courage.

In reality, people too often mistake risk taking as being reckless. Much of this book has dealt with preparation. Taking a risk is no different. Anybody can take a risk. The key is to take a risk in an intelligent manner. For example, in game planning a specific play, there are times when, in order to put the quarterback at ease with his need to be decisive about his actions, I simply put the decision process back on myself as the head coach. Most vertical passing plays require the quarterback to look deep, and if the receiver is not open, to drop the ball off to a secondary receiver.

Throwing the ball deep is less a function of arm strength than it is a result of timing. Many times, this type of risk involves making the throw before you can actually see what has happened down the field. Most deep passes require the quarterback to be either anticipatory or just hopeful that the receiver will get to the designated point on the field. More often than not, however, he'll drop the ball off in a nice, safe action rather than taking the risk of going vertical. There are times when you have to tell the quarterback, "Look, regardless of the situation, go deep," in order to free him up from the need to make a decision about what pass to throw and to enable him to make a more decisive throw down the field.

CONFRONTING CHANGE

"The only thing constant in life is change."

—Francois de la Rochefoucould
17th century French classical author

Change is inevitable in almost all aspects of life. People change. Priorities change. Schedules change. Expectations change. Attitudes change. Procedures change. Organizational cultures change. The list of factors that might change with which a leader must be sensitive to within an organization is virtually endless.

For example, the final thing I asked the players to do in the locker room in Tampa before going on the field in Super Bowl

XXXV was to truly look each other in the eye and appreciate the fact that this would be the last time that all of them would be together on this team. Whatever form the team would take in the future would not necessarily be better or worse, just different. Furthermore, I told them that when you reach this level of success as a team, there are two fundamental beliefs that have made significant contributions to your success. First, you think of yourself as a team of destiny, right up to the point you lose. Secondly, you develop a sense of family. You believe that the relationships and bonding you go through as a team exceeds those of other teams. Hence, the change that the circumstances and conditions that this league dictate cuts at the heart of the two beliefs. Everything about this league dictates that change is inevitable. One of the keys to understanding and accepting that change is appreciating the moment for what it is. One of the biggest challenges I face, as a head coach of an NFL team, is the fact that we must recreate this sense of "team" each year.

The multiplicity of potential changes has important implications for you as a leader. In this regard, one of your biggest challenges is overcoming any fear of, and resistance to, change. Fear and resistance can prevent you from making the necessary adaptations to change.

Skillful leaders, on the other hand, have the courage and the candor to embrace change as an opportunity for growth and improvement. They tend to feel uncomfortable with the status quo. They don't rest on past accomplishments.

For example, after winning a Super Bowl, the easiest thing to do would have been to stand pat and simply try to repeat what we had already done. After the 2000 season and the subsequent Super Bowl win, we determined that we would need a greater offensive presence that we had had the previous year. It was unrealistic to expect our defense to again set the all-time scoring record for us to return to the Super Bowl. As a result, we pursued and signed both Elvis Grbac and Leon Searcey in order to increase our offensive presence. Whether it was the right or wrong decision is immaterial. What is important is that we had the courage to follow through with what we thought was the right course of action, fully aware of the fact that doing so would expose us to certain criticisms. How easy it would have been to keep everything at the status quo and simply place the blame for our lack of success in the future on our offensive personnel.

Effective leaders are often in fact the agents of change and transformation within an organization. Not only do they spearhead constructive change, they facilitate the acceptance of change by others in the organization by instilling a mission-oriented commitment to the organization by their followers, creating a shared vision (i.e., a "we-can-do-better attitude"), and providing a values-oriented standard to which others aspire (i.e., they lead by example).

ACCEPTING RESPONSIBILITY

"You can't escape the responsibility of tomorrow
by evading it today."

—Abraham Lincoln
16th president of the United States

Leadership not only involves a willingness to embrace responsibility, but also the courage to be answerable and accountable for your actions, obligations, and duties. You can't be a skillful leader if you're afraid of responsibility and accountability.

Effective leaders tend to exhibit a number of traits reflecting their eagerness to accept responsibility and their backbone to be held accountable. They are overachievers. They don't blame others when things go wrong. They search for a solution, not an excuse. They followthrough on their assignments. They don't try to just get by. They're motivated by excellence, rather than riches—by pride, rather than vanity.

Bill Walsh wrote in the book that we wrote together, *Finding the Winning Edge*, that "A system should never reduce the game to the point where it simply blames the players for failure because they did not physically overwhelm the opponent." Even if your opponent is physically overwhelming, to allow the players to take the fall for your failure leaves them with absolutely no hope of being better. As a result, they will forever give in to an attitude of defeatism that proclaims, "We are not good enough."

My first ever coaching job was at a small NAIA division school in Southern California, the University of Redlands. The Bulldogs' head coach was a hugely successful high school and small college coach named Frank Serao. When the 49ers cut me, I returned to my hometown and volunteered to work for Coach Serao in any capacity, for free. He was gracious enough to allow me to work with the wide receivers and tight ends. It turned out to be one of the most pleasant years in coaching I would ever have.

The players at the University of Redlands were not on scholarship and had no expectations of going on and playing professional football (even though Brian Deroo, one of our wide receivers, did get drafted in the fifth round and played in the NFL for a few years). These athletes played simply because they loved the game. The most amazing attribute about Coach Serao was that I never once heard him blame the players. He steadfastly believed that any deficiencies in our play were due to him or the coaching staff and that we had to accept responsibility for our success. His consistent belief in his players and his practice of taking on all responsibility for any failure fostered an incredible level of loyalty from both his players and his coaches. By accepting full responsibility, Frank knew that the players would do anything we asked and would give every ounce of effort to do it in a way that neither browbeating nor denigrating could have ever accomplished.

With regard to personal accountability, Bill Walsh had an interesting way of getting his players to accept responsibility— by criticizing their coaches in front of them to make a point about a player's lack of performance. For example, if Bill thought that the running backs were not taking on the pass rushers in their protection responsibilities as well as they should, he would approach his running backs coach in practice and question, "Billy, can you get these guys to pass protect better? They are not punching with their hands properly. Can you do that, do you think you can get them to do that?" Bill's unique way of critiquing a player forced the running backs to address their ability to execute their pass protection techniques in the intended manner. Rather than attacking the players and possibly diminishing their confidence in their abilities to do the job, Bill made them ramp up their efforts by getting them to perform better in defense of their coach. This practice could be tough on the coach, but Bill would usually follow up the process later in private with the coach in order to make sure that the coach knew what Bill was endeavoring to accomplish.

BEING SELF-RELIANT

"Self-reliance and self-respect are about as valuable commodities as we can carry in our pack through life."

—Luther Burbank
renowned horticulturist

Self-reliance is figuring out for yourself what the best course of action you can take is, and then taking it. It involves the ability to stand on your feet and solve your own problems despite relatively difficult circumstances. Instead of leaning on others, you have the courage to look out for yourself. Effective leaders have to be self-reliant because, for the most part, they simply have no one to lean on. In those situations when difficult decisions need to be made, they have the fortitude and the aptitude to rely on their own counsel.

I recently read about a young man named Nick Ackerman. Nick was nominated to carry the Olympic torch relay leading to the 2000 Winter Games in Salt Lake City. He was encouraged to do this after winning the NCAA Division III national wrestling title at 174 pounds. Nick commented that he plays basketball a lot and thought the run would be a great challenge for him. These accomplishments are noteworthy in and of themselves, but are more so given the fact that Nick had both legs amputated when he was less than two years old to halt a life-threatening bacterial infection.

He said he had been given a poem by a teacher when he was very young that stated, "You are the handicap you must face. You're the one that chooses your place." This to me exemplifies the utmost in self-reliance. This quality does not require any other skills or attributes other than self-confidence and a will to achieve. As Nick said, "If you don't believe you can do it, why should anybody else?" When a reporter referred to him in an interview as "disabled," Ackerman told him not to call him that. When asked what he should call him Nick replied, "How about national champion?"

THE COURAGE TO LEAD
Excellence can be attained if you . . .
care more than others think is wise.
risk more than others think is safe.
dream more than others think is practical.
expect more than others think is possible.

—unknown author

You can't be an effective leader without courage. Courage enables you to bring out the best in yourself and to inspire the best in your followers. Part of that courage is the ability to handle the criticism that comes with achievement. It is a hard precept to understand that even achievement is likely to be criticized. Albert Einstein wrote, "It is an odd occurrence to me that the more my abilities came to light, the more famous I became, the more those abilities were brought into question." There will always be those who will lack the courage and commitment of leadership, and therefore find it extremely difficult to understand how you possess those attributes. Because of their lack of a personal reference point, they are apt to label those attributes as arrogance, egotism, and eccentricity. There will even be those who take this criticism to a personal, rather than professional, level. I am always reminded of the words of my father: "When you are kicked by a jackass, you must consider the source."

Principle # 12:

Leadership must embody courage.

chapter 14

CRAFTING A MOSAIC OF EFFECTIVE LEADERSHIP

> "If a man is called to be a street sweeper, he should sweep streets even as Michelangelo painted or Beethoven composed music or Shakespeare wrote poetry. He should sweep streets so well that all the hosts of heaven and earth will pause to say, 'Here lived a great street sweeper who did his job well.'"
>
> —Martin Luther King, Jr.
> civil rights pioneer

Despite the proliferation of books and articles on leadership and a growing abundance of experts and consultants who are willing to share their opinions on leadership, no consensus exists concerning what it takes to be an effective leader. What one author or "expert" swears by, another warns against.

What is known, however, about being an effective leader is that leadership does not occur in a vacuum. By necessity, leaders have to react to their work environment and to the events and circumstances that occur in their environment.

Another point concerning leadership that is widely accepted is that skillful leadership does not occur by accident. While "experts" may not be able to agree on a single definition of what is involved in being an effective leader, most individuals who have spent any substantial amount of time studying leadership concur that skillful leadership emanates from the adherence to certain constructive habits, characteristics, and practices.

In reality, there is almost as much disagreement over what criteria should be on a list of essential leadership traits as there are individuals willing to share an opinion on the list. All of which served as the genesis for this book, *Competitive Leadership*.

I strongly believe that the "recipe" for effective leadership tends to vary from circumstance to circumstance. What remains constant in each situation, however, are certain attributes that are essential to sound leadership. These attributes are discussed in detail in *Competitive Leadership*.

In this regard, the point that you, as a leader, should keep in mind is that the degree of application and relative importance of each attribute varies form situation to situation. As a result, leadership should be viewed as a mosaic—not as a fixed recipe of particular traits. As the circumstances change, the mosaic of effective leadership evolves as needed.

One final factor that you should be aware of is that skillful leadership is a choice. In a world of infinite choices, you have the option of deciding the extent of your commitment to acquiring and putting into action the attributes that are integral to the leadership mosaic. If you want to be an effective leader, it is your responsibility to make the "right" choice.

To the extent possible, I have always tried to make the "right" professional choices in my life. Bill Walsh likes to refer to a "fully dimensional" offense as one that encompasses all the aspects of what it takes to be productive. I did not consider myself a "fully dimensional" coach until I recognized what it truly takes to be confident and self-actualized in my profession. I was fortunate to learn early in my career that I was not going to outwork anyone in the NFL or that I was not any smarter or more insightful than other coaches. This point was made even more vivid in my mind when I stood on the field at Raymond James Stadium in Tampa across from Jim Fassel, head coach of the New York Giants, prior to the start of the Super Bowl. Jim is probably the best friend I have in the coaching profession. Jim and his Giants were an outstanding team who had overcome considerable adversity to reach the Super Bowl. Furthermore, Jim is as hard working and capable a coach as I have ever known and was certainly just as deserving of winning a championship as I was. It really didn't matter if I was facing Jim or any other coach, I knew the situation would be the same. All the coaches in the NFL are hard working, competent, and deserving.

Having made this observation, what then is the difference between individual coaches and what truly distinguishes a leader? What distinguishes a successful career from one that is not quite as successful? It is confidence, born of the understanding that if you are looking for external validation for your success, you are doomed to failure. *You* are the only one who can validate and quantify *your* success. As I stood atop the podium in Tampa with the Lombardi Trophy firmly in hand, I recognized that I had reached the top of John Wooden's pyramid and realized the value of the top tier of "competitive greatness." I had self-actualized the line from the movie *The Legend of Bagger Vance* that for me said it all: "You can never win this game. All you can hope to do is play it."

DIARY OF A SUPER BOWL TEAM

Prior to the start of the 2000 season, I was asked by NFL.com to write a weekly column for their Internet site on my personal observations concerning the Ravens' weekly efforts to prepare for our upcoming opponent. Each entry on the site was made on the Tuesday following each game. The resultant 20 diary entries encompassed our 16 regular-season games, our bye week, and the three playoff games we played leading up to Super Bowl XXXV.

I decided to include my diary in *Competitive Leadership* as an Appendix because many of the relevant points made in the book are reinforced by the observations, impressions, and actions attendant to our Super Bowl–winning season. In that sense, the weekly diary entries offer an invaluable case study in leadership. The insights and skills that were applied during the week leading up to each game helped produce results when and where they counted—on the field on game day.

FIRST OPPONENT: PITTSBURGH

It is my hope that through this Internet access, NFL fans can get a better appreciation for the Baltimore Ravens, the NFL, and the game itself. This is an exciting time for this organization and this city. There is a great deal of anticipation and expectation about this year's team. Some might think that we are setting our sights too high and will leave ourselves at risk if we are unsuccessful. It is my philosophy that "If you can't talk about it, you certainly have no chance of doing it." The important thing to remember is that we created the expectations for ourselves. They were not forced on us by the fans or the media. We established them with a solid second half of the 1999 season, when we won five of our last seven games and four games in December. We created them by resigning 18 of our free agents last year and still adding the likes of Shannon Sharpe, Ben Coates, Sam Adams, and Sam Gash. These are the reasons the expectations are high for this team.

I was not satisfied with the players' focus the last two weeks. My concern is that it would have to be better this week, and it has been. This was our first chance to prepare for our challenge of five of our first seven games on the road to open the season. I believe that winning on the road in the NFL is the toughest task in all of professional team sports. A single loss in the NFL equates to a 10-game losing streak in baseball and a 6-game losing streak in the NBA.

Our focus and intensity are evident with each succeeding practice. I expect this team to be a serious playoff contender, and it starts with our focus in practice. It is not just a matter of effort. This team has always given good effort. But like the great basketball coach John Wooden used to say, "Don't mistake activity for production." Effort and desire are wasted if they're not focused and disciplined.

The media would have you think that Pittsburgh is not very good. I would never underestimate a Bill Cowher–coached team. Bill does a great job of motivating his team and getting his players to exert their best effort. Kent Graham is a big, strong, and smart quarterback who will get the opportunity to prove how capable he is. As long as Jerome Bettis is in the Steelers' backfield, our defense has to be ready for a physical game. With as good of a defense as we have against the run, the Steelers will definitely challenge us. The Steelers showed in the preseason that their defense is back to the swarming, aggressive attack style that they have been known for. Given their level of physical play, they will be a good challenge for our offensive line because of their blitzes and stunts.

I was a bit uneasy going into our last preseason game because, like most coaches, you really want to stay healthy, even to the point of overprotecting your players, a surefire way to get them hurt. I am feeling a little more settled because we are two days away from getting this show on the road, and with the exception of Kip Vicker, every man on the roster is cleared to play.

Our challenge this season is to be able to handle ourselves on the road early, and I can't think of a better test for us than to start on the road in a town like Pittsburgh. This first game allows us to get a real sense of what we're working with. After the opener, I will have a better idea of the personality of this team. What I have to guard against is letting the team overreact to whatever the outcome of our game is—good or bad. If we're unsuccessful in the first game, the team must have a sense that this is a marathon, not a sprint. If we win, I have to keep everyone from making flight arrangements for Tampa.

Game result: Baltimore 16–Pittsburgh 0

NEXT OPPONENT: JACKSONVILLE

Winning on the road, as I mentioned before, is the single most difficult thing to do in all of team sports, in my opinion, particularly opening the season on the road. It was very gratifying to go into Three Rivers Stadium, a place where this organization has always had a great deal of difficulty, and not only win and win a divisional game, but to "pitch a shutout," which was the only shutout of the weekend in the NFL.

Our opening-game win brought together all the elements that we have been focusing on as a team during training camp and our successful 4–0 preseason run. First, it takes extra focus and extra effort to win on the road. Indeed, this being our third road game in a row, the first two being in preseason, we've tried to use that as a format to duplicate the three-game road trip that we will have in October, when we have to play at Cleveland, at Jacksonville, and at Washington.

Second, the win involved backup players, who were called on to step up and contribute and play in unfamiliar roles. When Mike Flynn, our starting guard, had to move to center, a position at which he had only taken a half a dozen snaps during the week to replace the injured Jeff Mitchell, it put Mike in a difficult position. Flynn stepped up, as did Orlando Bobo, who then had to play right guard.

To run the ball for better than 100 yards with no turnovers and yet provide the level of protection that we did was very satisfying. Priest Holmes, who many had penciled out of a starting position for the Ravens due to the drafting of Jamal Lewis, was the workhorse of the day, running for 119 yards. Priest exhibited once again that he's a true professional; he gets done whatever he's called upon to do.

Finally, it is very difficult for a defense to shut out a team given the nature and rules of the game. To do so on the road is even more difficult. What I was impressed with was that during the game, the Steelers once had seven consecutive unsuccessful attempts to score inside our 5-yard line. Beginning with a first-and-goal on our 3-yard line and continuing on the third down, when they got a pass interference call that gave them another four shots, our defense was able to keep them from scoring a point under very difficult circumstances.

Now comes the challenge that faces us after playing three games on the road and the cumulative debilitating effects that such an arduous stretch can have on you. We come home to our stadium, in front of our fans, and play a team (Jacksonville Jaguars) that many think is a favorite to win the AFC Championship. This organization has never beaten Jacksonville. As such, this is a big game for us if we are truly going to take that next step to becoming a bonafide playoff team.

It has been close to a month since we've played a game at home. I know our fans are anxious for us to return to PSINet stadium. They're looking forward to seeing this team first hand in the regular season against a quality opponent such as Jacksonville.

I consider Mark Brunell to be one of the best quarterbacks in the NFL. He's one of those rare breed of guys who can beat you not only outside the pocket with his athleticism, but who has trained himself to be a bonafide pocket passer as well. The talent they have in Jacksonville will present a different style and a different type of play for our defense. In every regard, this game will be a real challenge for us. We need to eliminate the turnovers that cost us a seven-point loss during last year's game against the Jaguars at PSINet Stadium.

This week also marks the first time our players will be out actively in the community on Tuesday. This is an important priority we have created for ourselves. We work with different charities that we support individually and collectively. The players must be a viable part of the community because their presence can be a positive force, especially with the youth.

Game result: Baltimore 39–Jacksonville 36

NEXT OPPONENT: MIAMI

I had challenged the people of Baltimore to truly make PSINet Stadium a home-field advantage for us with the crowd noise. Their response was extraordinary. I have never been in a stadium where the fans were more into the game. There is no question in my mind of the debilitating effect that crowd noise had on Jacksonville, given the number of timeouts they had to use to get a play run. The crowd forced three timeouts. As a result, the Jaguars had none available for their last drive of the game. This, no doubt, made a tangible difference in the outcome of the game.

The win against Jacksonville was a big win on many different levels. Clearly, the fact that the Ravens had never beaten Jacksonville, a class organization that has set the benchmark for the AFC Central, made this a big win not only for this team but for the organization and the city as a whole. More so than just a win, it was the *way* that we won that was significant. In the first half, our players played very tight and tentatively. I probably underestimated the mindset that our players had about Jacksonville. We made several errors and basically looked terrible in the first half, falling behind by 17 points.

Halftime was not a time for ranting or raving. What I did tell the players was that "Win or lose, and truly winning or losing was insignificant, it was how we were going to conduct ourselves in the second half that was going to determine what kind of team we were." The players took the challenge immediately. The offense came out and drove the length of the field to score and went for and made a two-point conversion to make it a single possession game at 23–15.

At that point, possibly in honor of the approaching Olympics, it became a real track meet. Mark Brunell and Jimmy Smith may be the best quarterback/receiver combination in the game, and they certainly "schooled" some of our young secondary. Even with the productivity Mark Brunell had, our guys fought tooth and nail and forced some very key turnovers that gave us an opportunity to claw our way back into the game.

Offensively, Tony Banks, accepting the challenge, proved to be very efficient in the second half, not only hitting balls down the field but also dropping the balls underneath to keep the chains moving. I have been very upfront with our players about our expectations and how we look at ourselves this year. With respect to being a potential playoff team, this was a crucial test for us that measured exactly how far we have come.

With a 13-year absence of football in Baltimore and the lack of wins during the Ravens first four years, it has been a slow process for Ravens' fans to get back into the groove of life in the NFL. I think this game was clearly a milestone for us, given the fact that the town has embraced both what we represent and the challenges before us. I truly feel like our fans have accepted us to a point where they'll help us be a competitive part of the National Football League.

With as big a win as this was for us, our challenge now is to quickly refocus our energies and efforts for our next important contest, a Sunday night ESPN game that will be played in Miami. Furthermore, at the halftime of our game against the Dolphins, they are going to retire Dan Marino's number. Because there will be a great deal of emotion and most of the country will be watching, this contest gives us an opportunity to show people, on a national level, exactly how far we've come as a team and an organization. I know the players are looking forward to it. So am I!

Game result: Miami 19–Baltimore 6

NEXT OPPONENT: CINCINNATI

Handling a loss in the National Football League is among the most difficult things any coach has to deal with during the season. The scrutiny, the second-guessing, the individuals who jump off the bandwagon, the deafening silence from the fans, and the actions of the media, in some instances, can be overwhelming. They say that losing builds character, and I'm sure that at certain levels (Pop-Warner, Pee Wee, Junior, and Senior High School and even college to a degree), that has a certain amount of validity. Losing in the National Football League serves no purpose at all.

No matter how many wins you've had leading up to it, losing cuts at the heart of the level of confidence in your team and your organization. It opens up the door for players and coaches alike to second-guess themselves. At this particular part of the season, the key is to pull as many positives as we can from a difficult loss on the road against an excellent Miami team.

Offensively we had some outstanding play by some young players that we want to continue to develop, namely Jamal Lewis and Patrick Johnson. On special teams, Anthony Pointdextor got his first real taste of live action during the regular season in the NFL. The challenge now is to glean every opportunity we can from this situation to present our players with a learning environment.

One of the things I do on the Monday after a game is to put together clips of 10 to 15 plays where there was a schematic, mental, or physical error. Players need to learn from their mistakes, even if their mistakes are physical, which is the hardest thing to correct. The team needs to see these errors as a whole so we don't duplicate them.

What you don't want to dwell on with the players is someone just physically being beaten. That's the most difficult thing with which to help a player. If there's a technique (a proper step, a hand placement, alignment, etc.) that you can help them with, certainly there's value in that. But sometimes, players are just physically going to be overwhelmed by an opponent. That has to be understood and factored into the total equation of what you think your success is going to be. A coach has no business criticizing or correcting a player unless it's done in a constructive and instructive way.

Dealing with a loss is the biggest thing I've had to adjust to as a head coach. In my first year, I learned the hard way just how many people—not only the coaches and players, but also the entire organization, fans, and even the media—take their emotional tone from you. If you get too high after a big win or too low after a disappointing loss, they'll draw from you. It's at this time a coach has to be at his emotional best.

In dealing with the players you have to be as upbeat, positive and energetic as you can. The players don't need a cheerleader at this point (someone that's just clapping and urging them on), as much as they do someone who's giving them something tangible to improve themselves in an energetic and enthusiastic way.

The best medicine for any loss is to immediately absorb yourself with the next opponent, which will be easy for us to do. Cincinnati represents an important game for us in that it's a home game, it's a divisional opponent, it's a chance to end a (one-game) losing streak, and it gives us a chance to remain on top of the central division.

We've broken the season into four phases. This game vs. Cincinnati represents the last of our first phase. If we can rebound from the disappointing loss to Miami and use the home field advantage to beat a very talented Bengal's team, it will give us a 3–1 start in the first phase.

This would be an important stepping stone going into our second phase, which involves a very difficult three-game road trip including games at Cleveland, Jacksonville, and Washington. It's important that the fans treat this game against the Bengals with the same amount of attention and intensity that they gave the Jacksonville game. This game is as important for virtually all the same reasons. The challenge to our fans is to bring the same energy and noise to this game as they did to the Jacksonville game. This may be hard for them because they don't look at these two particular opponents in the same regard. Part of my job is to educate them so that they never devalue an opponent. They must take the same focused and enthusiastic approach into every game.

Game result: Baltimore 37–Cincinnati 0

NEXT OPPONENT: CLEVELAND

As we progress into the NFL season, each team has to deal with the effects of both winning and losing and the impact that either has on their players. Oddly, the team on a losing streak and the team on a winning streak may have some of the same properties. Both will tend to focus too much on the pressures and the final consequences of each game, thereby losing the important focus that they need to correct the latter and sustain the former.

A team on a losing streak will dwell on the negatives that losing generates, and tend to make the situation look bleaker than it really is. By keeping their focus on the immediate task at hand (i.e., to win a game and to stop the slide), coaches help their players overcome the debilitating emotions of self-pity and hopelessness. Similar to a batter in a slump, it takes a great deal of experience and inner confidence to know that, yes, this too will pass. As a coach, you must focus on the positives that have happened and continually show examples of how close the team is to getting back on the right track.

The team on a winning streak can suffer the same lack of focus, obviously for a different reason. For example, players will begin to ignore the attention to detail and execution that got them to this point in the season. Furthermore, they often feel that whatever success they may have achieved to that point signifies that they have already mastered certain fundamentals. As a result, they may feel that they no longer need to work on developing or refining these particular skills. Like a team on a slide, a team on a winning streak must be taught to realize that this too *could* pass.

Often, this is a time when the coach will tighten down on a team even more because his experience gives him the bigger perspective that if he does not "tighten the screws," so to speak, then the winning may get away from them. On the other hand, you have to be sure not to take this type of thinking too far. You must let the players and the organization as a whole enjoy the moment and euphoria that winning brings. Winning will usually energize and invigorate a team's preparation atmosphere. In your efforts to keep your players well grounded, you may indeed sap some of the energy that exists with a winning environment.

A proven method of dealing with this level of success is to allow the player to take the pats on the back on Monday and Tuesday and then make a conscious point to the players that Wednesday begins the new week and last week's success is ancient history. The players must be made aware of the pitfalls of becoming too receptive to all the accolades during the season, especially from the press. They must be made to understand that the media will many times pour it on in good times to give themselves more cannon fodder in the bad times. The difference between a pat on the back and a knife in the back is as subtle as an open or closed hand.

Game result: Baltimore 12–Cleveland 0

NEXT OPPONENT: JACKSONVILLE

Getting a shutout, particularly on the road, is a tough proposition in the NFL. The last time a team had three in a row was in 1976, when the Pittsburgh Steelers had five in a single season, including three consecutive. We've been presented with a unique opportunity to try and match the Steelers' feat. In today's game, that is going to be a major accomplishment. At this point in time, the rules are geared toward maximizing each team's level of offensive output because that's what the fans want. The league has progressively worked toward that goal, both offensively and through special teams. So to get a shutout, particularly in the modern era of this game, is extremely impressive.

For us to be sitting here with three shutouts in five games is noteworthy for this defensive football team. The nice thing about this particular record is that it's directly correlated to winning and losing.

Too often in this league, players and coaches are accused of trying to achieve individual goals, statistically speaking, and of overlooking the fact that it could indeed become detrimental to the outcome of the game. If a given receiver is working for a reception record or a running back is going for a yardage record or maybe a team is trying to achieve an offensive scoring record, they can be accused of putting themselves and a game at risk in hopes of achieving that record. In this particular instance, a defense earning a shutout is so directly correlated to winning and losing the game that no one could reasonably be accused of focusing on individual priorities. Shutouts are such a team-oriented goal—one that has a direct impact on the game in such a positive way.

When a goal like this exists for a team, it provides the coaches with an incredible learning environment; the players are incredibly receptive to the coaches' efforts due to the priorities and importance that they put on a goal of this nature. The idea of us shutting out Jacksonville is at a minimum ambitious and certainly a circumstance involving long odds. Jacksonville is still one of the best offensive teams in the league with Mark Brunell, Jimmy Smith, Keenan McCardell, Kyle Brady, and Fred Taylor who, collectively are one of the best skill groups in the NFL. On the other hand, the fact remains that with two previous shutouts, the goal of a third shutout exists regardless of who the opponent is.

Last year, our defense did a magnificent job in holding Jacksonville to only six points in a hard-fought, 6–3 loss in a game played at Jacksonville. Offensively, we just weren't able to produce the number of points needed to win that game. Certainly, our upcoming contest has the potential for our defense to play that kind of game, because we feel that we are a much better defensive team today than we were at that point last year.

Again, this is no reflection on our judgment about a high-caliber opponent such as Jacksonville. Tom Coughlin, one of the best coaches in the NFL, has an outstanding organization and has assembled an incredible group of talent in Jacksonville. Having lost the last two weeks, they are in a situation that puts them in a mindset where they will do absolutely everything they can to end their losing streak, thereby making our task even more difficult. The key will be for our players to respond to the circumstances if, indeed, the likely happens, and Jacksonville scores, particularly if they score early in the game. Regardless of how the game goes, however, it will provide a positive influence on our week's preparation and will allow our players and fans to dream of our team's potential.

Game result: Baltimore 15–Jacksonville 10

NEXT OPPONENT: WASHINGTON

As we sit atop the AFC Central, our players, coaches, and indeed the entire organization feels very good about itself, and they should. There is always a concern about being overconfident and losing sight of the fact that this is a long season and that we are not even halfway through it. By the same token, for an organization that has never had a winning season, has never been in the playoffs, or has never been 5–1, it is important to "stop and smell the roses" along the way.

I am reminded of John Wooden's *Pyramid of Success*. Wooden, the legendary coach of the UCLA basketball dynasty, created the pyramid not as a definition for success, or even as a guide for building a championship. Instead, he created the pyramid when he was a high school teacher to gauge personal development, rather than use some formula for societal success that is scrutinized and monitored in so much of what we do. As I reviewed the pyramid, I saw many of the individual and collective traits he mentioned in the makeup of this Ravens team:

COMPETITIVE GREATNESS
Be at your best when your best is needed. Enjoyment of a difficult challenge.

POISE
Just being yourself. Being at ease in any situation. Never fighting yourself.

CONFIDENCE
Respect without fear often comes from being prepared and keeping all things in proper perspective.

CONDITION
Mental-moral-physical. Rest, exercise and diet must be considered. Moderation must be practiced. Dissipation must be eliminated.

SKILL
A knowledge of and the ability to properly and quickly execute the fundamentals. Be prepared and cover every little detail.

TEAM SPIRIT
A genuine consideration for others. An eagerness to sacrifice personal interests of glory for the welfare of all.

SELF-CONTROL
Practice self-discipline and keep emotions under control. Good judgment and common sense are essential.

ALERTNESS
Be observing constantly. Stay open-minded. Be eager to learn and improve.

INITIATIVE
Cultivate the ability to make decisions and think alone. Do not be afraid of failure, but learn from it.

INTENTNESS
Set a realistic goal. Concentrate on its achievement by resisting all temptations and being determined and persistent.

INDUSTRIOUSNESS
There is no substitute for work. Worthwhile results come from hard work and careful planning.

FRIENDSHIP
Comes from mutual esteem, respect, and devotion. Like marriage, it must not be taken for granted; it requires a joint effort.

LOYALTY
To yourself and to all those depending upon you. Keep your self-respect.

COOPERATION
With all levels of your coworkers, listen if you want to be heard. Be interested in finding the best way, not in having your own way.

ENTHUSIASM
Brushes off upon those with whom you come in contact. You must truly enjoy what you are doing.

Game result: Washington 10–Baltimore 3

NEXT OPPONENT: TENNESSEE

Traditionally, most teams, fans, and media focus after the eighth game of the season—the midway point. This is a time to take stock and evaluate where you are. Enough games have been played where teams have, at the very least, determined the task ahead and the road they have to travel to make the play-off. Given our "journey" to this point in time (i.e., playing five of our first seven games on the road and just finishing a three-game road trip that concluded this tough early stretch), now seems a very appropriate time to raise our heads up above the crowd and see where we are.

As usual I like to begin with the positives. Our stated goal going into this season was to make the playoffs. This may be a modest goal by some people's standards, but for an organization that has never had a winning season, it is certainly an understandable one. As we approach the midway point of the season, we are 5-2 and are scheduled to play the Tennessee Titans Sunday, at PSINet Stadium for the lead in the AFC Central Division. We have beaten Jacksonville twice, a team this organization had never beaten previously. We are 5-1 in the AFC and undefeated in our division, having played everyone in the division except for the Titans. We have won all three of our division road games. We play six of the next nine games at home against teams with a combined record of 18-31 to this point in the 2000 season. This team has developed a strong bond on and off the field due to the challenges we have faced both at home and on the road. The chemistry is strong and the fans have been supportive.

We have a uniquely talented group on defense that has risen to the occasion game after game. In addition to the play of our defense, the fact that our special teams' play has been solid—particularly in not giving up the big plays and Matt Stover's consistency—have been the primary strengths for this team. Offensively, our line has been put through some very difficult situations, and our back-ups have stepped up and provided us with solid play. Our draft choices have played well and have shown that they can impact a game. Shannon Sharpe has been a great offseason acquisition with his play and leadership. Ben

Coates has not had an opportunity to make as many receptions as he would like, but has been a solid blocker and has given us a dimension that we did not have last year. Sam Adams has been a huge force inside to augment an outstanding front seven.

Offensively, we must begin to show the kind of production that the talent level we have represents. This is the one area in which we have not lived up to our potential. Its improvement has to be our highest priority coming into the next half of the season.

In spite of all this, there is a frustration and disappointment over the loss to Washington last week. This was a huge emotional game for the fans in the Mid-Atlantic region—one they will not get over quickly. We, on the other hand, must. We cannot allow the physically draining emotions attendant to the loss add to the already debilitating effects of playing the last three road games. The players must put this frustration behind them quickly and focus on the task at hand, which is take control of the AFC Central by beating the Titans. It is fitting that we are playing the Titans at this time because it is appropriate that our halfway mark reflect our play against the entire division.

Game result: Tennessee 14–Baltimore 6

NEXT OPPONENT: PITTSBURGH

Identifying the qualities needed to play quarterback in the NFL is one of the single most asked questions I get. Many times it is put in an indirect way: "Can this quarterback get you to the Super Bowl?" Similar to us, thus far in the season, many teams are dealing with varying levels of play by their quarterback, whether it is a longtime veteran or a relative rookie. Much of this position has to do with the mental and emotional state of the player, as it does with the physical.

In the book that I coauthored with Bill Walsh, *Finding the Winning Edge*, we isolated some of these qualities. We began with the quality of functional intelligence (i.e., the ability to organize and isolate different categories of tasks that you have to be able to perform). This step does not strictly involve looking at a player's IQ as the factor that is constantly being measured and quantified. It involves an individual's ability to break things down in a more simplistic manner and not overcomplicate the needed response. This ability is the key to quickly processing information while under severe stress.

The next quality involves whether the athlete has the instinctive intuition concerning the mechanics for playing quarterback. We say instinctive only in the sense that the athlete may not know that he possesses these attributes, and simply has to be exposed to them to know that they exist. If, however, after a period of time, this instinctive intuition does not begin to manifest itself, you cannot develop or manufacture it. If it is not there, you are wasting your time. Likewise, if a player shows a tendency to continually unravel or exhibits a level of anxiousness that removes his spontaneity and causes repeated mistakes, it is nearly impossible to change this.

A natural willingness to improve and learn from those he is working with is also vital to a quarterback's progression. Furthermore, a quarterback must have a certain level of compatibility with his teammates and coaches in the learning process.

Dealing with the quarterback's emotions is a key aspect in his development. The best approach in this instance is to educate him about the process of dealing with the stress and pressures that the position brings. You must find the threshold of any given quarterback concerning how he will handle the emotions of the position. As with the essential basic instincts for playing quarterback, he will either begin to show signs of being able to control and deal with his emotions within the framework of the game or he won't. In the latter case, you may be wasting your time.

The quarterback's leadership abilities must emanate from his performance. We have all seen a player who has a casual, easy way about him that naturally draws people to him. Even if this player exhibits skills that will naturally draw his teammates to him, if he cannot deliver the goods, so to speak, his teammates and coaches will eventually gravitate elsewhere.

Game result: Pittsburgh 9–Baltimore 6

NEXT OPPONENT: CINCINNATI

We're in a tough spot, one to which I think a lot of teams can relate. As when Tampa went through a four-game losing streak and even when Pittsburgh started out 0-3 at the beginning of the season, most teams go through something of this nature. In my seven years with the Vikings, Denny Green proved to be an absolute master of dealing with the types of adversity that challenge a team during a season. In 1994, after starting 7-2, we had a three-game losing streak. In 1996, we had a four-game losing streak after starting the next year at 5-1. In 1997, we struggled through a five-game losing stint after starting 8-2. In each instance, Denny was able to bring his team through the tough times and into the playoffs. What I learned from watching Denny handle those situations was pivotal in our being able to come back from a three-game losing streak last year and win five of our next seven games. I learned from him that you have to cherish the challenge that a losing streak presents, and I'm looking forward to this one as well.

The only way to work our way out of this slump is to focus solely on our next opponent. The tendency is to divert your attention by observing how the other teams are doing in the upper parts of their divisions. That's OK if you are in fact at the top of your division. On the other hand, I think that when you're where we are, 5-4 in the middle of the season, it becomes momentous that we stay focused on the task at hand.

The question we ask ourselves now is "What do we have to do to beat Cincinnati?" If we're lucky enough to reach the goal we've predetermined for ourselves, fighting our way through this anguish is going to be a big part of how we do in the playoffs. (The old notion of "What doesn't kill you only makes you stronger" comes to mind.)

To answer a question that has been asked a lot: Yes, there is frustration. But, our players are a close-knit bunch who support one another. I believe that they are handling these trying times with the best of them. They know that giving in to the potentially disruptive issues involving frustration and "offense vs. defense" or "one side vs. the other" holds no value. They look at our game film and know what's going on. It's difficult to look in the mirror that the game film provides and see the mistakes for which you were responsible. Part of this business is being accountable for your mistakes and exhausting every effort to correct them for the next game. We must not dwell on our blunders. Helping each other, in terms of preparation, is the only way to work through this.

There's a strong outlook here that once we finally reach the end zone, it will begin to flow for us. I liked the way Trent Dilfer played on Sunday. He did a lot of good things against the Steelers, and I have confidence in the talent we have to get the job done. We have to find an explosiveness in our passing game that I'm sure is there, but just hasn't emerged yet.

At this point in the season, the Bengals seem to be a completely different team than what we saw of them earlier this season. They are more self-assured, and they're obtaining more of a personality of what they want to do offensively. They are "showing up" in the second half of this season and beating their opponents. This, I'm sure, will be a hard-fought game, especially being that it will be played in their house.

Stress and frustration are a part of this business. You have to keep control of your priorities in understanding what's really important. I understand the pressures that come with the responsibilities of my job as a head coach. But the challenge that's in front of us, based on what we have been through, is what I love. I'm glad that I'll have the opportunity to look at film and help these guys out of this drought, and when we do get going again, it will be all the more satisfying. I am reminded of the quote by the great John Wooden: "Why do we dread adversity when we know that facing it is the only way to become stronger, smarter, and better?" Believe me when I say that I take the responsibility I have been given with this team, this organization, and our fans very seriously. What I try not to do is take myself too seriously.

Game result: Baltimore 27–Cincinnati 7

NEXT OPPONENT: TENNESSEE

Can you spell *touchdown*? Not scoring one these past few weeks has weighed heavily on us all emotionally. I think our players have done a great job at keeping things in perspective and not focusing on our scoring drought too much. Because everyone was tired of hearing and talking about it, there was clearly a great emotional release of tension once Brandon [Stokley] scored.

Our sole focus now is making a playoff run in November and December. Doing so takes the full team roster, and right now we are in good shape. It was great to have people like Brandon Stokley and Brad Jackson not only get to be activated, but have a meaningful impact on our game this past weekend. The roster rules prohibit using your entire 53-man roster during any given week. One of the most difficult things I have to do as a head coach is telling a player who has prepared and worked all week to play, that he will not suit up for this week's game. They have to have faith that their hard work will eventually pay off and, in this particular case, it came to fruition. The depth of a team becomes critical late in the season and can change the complexion of the entire season. Those players who have not had a chance to contribute a great deal must stay ready to do so when called upon. The overall success of the season may hang in the balance.

This week, we have the Titans. Both teams have a lot of respect for each other, and the statistics only tell us so much. The numbers only tell us what has happened and nothing of what is going to happen. Every week is a dogfight. Every team at the top of their division knows this. This is a great opportunity for us—a win would help to propel us closer to our goal, the playoffs.

Tennessee has never lost a game in their home stadium and has a great record in the division to this point. Those conditions give us a real taste of how things would be if, in fact, we had to go back there in the playoffs. Every team in the league is talented, wants to win, and works hard. In my opinion, it's games like this that make the NFL America's favorite game.

Game result: Baltimore 24–Tennessee 23

NEXT OPPONENT: DALLAS

Playing the Titans proved to be another tough battle fought by two teams who respect one another a great deal. The Titans are an outstanding team, and their fans make it one of the most difficult NFL stadiums to play in. I hope our fans were paying close attention to theirs because not only were they loud, but they also were well-orchestrated.

Those who saw the genuine display of emotion by Trent Dilfer had to appreciate what this win meant to him. I give Trent Dilfer a lot of credit for holding our guys together toward the end of the game. It takes a great deal of personal courage to come off the mistake he made in throwing an interception and getting back in there to pilot the game-winning drive.

We've come through a tough stretch with our second series of five of seven games being on the road. That being said, we've earned the right to be at home over the next month and a half, and we're counting on our fans to be a significant factor in the outcome of these upcoming games. I'm sure that our fans are capable of creating that same aggressive environment that we faced in Tennessee.

Our primary focus this week is our game against the Dallas Cowboys. It's essential for our players, coaches, and this organization to give the proper respect to our immediate opponent. From our perspective, everything about this game is going to be like the last one. It's going to be another challenging Sunday.

We've been through this streak of 28 games in which we've allowed no 100-yard rushers. In the process, we have faced several very talented running backs, including Jerome Bettis, Fred Taylor, Eddie George, and Steven Davis this year, and last year when we played against Marshal Faulk and Ricky Williams. In this game, our defense will encounter the challenge of facing a future Hall of Fame running back (Emmit Smith) who will take the hand-off from another future Hall of Famer (Troy Aikman), both of whom will be operating behind one of the best offensive lines in the NFL.

It has been 20 years since America's team has played in Baltimore, and it should be a great weekend for our fans. This was one of our first sellouts, because the Cowboys still have the mystique that comes from their longtime status as "America's team."

Game result: Baltimore 27–Dallas 0

NEXT OPPONENT: CLEVELAND

I think that Sunday was probably the best that I've seen this team play as a whole with the run, the pass, offense, defense, and special teams all proving successful for us. It was a great win for us. We are beginning to develop a personality on offense, and it's becoming the kind of "players offense" that it has to be for us to be good. We're getting great communication and input from guys like Trent Dilfer, Shannon Sharpe, Jonathan Ogden, and Jeff Mitchell, which is a good sign that things are coming together.

Our fans were great this week. They had a direct effect on the outcome of this game. One incident, where the crowd got the Dallas tackle to jump, turned it from a third-and-four, which typically has a 50 percent conversion rate, to a third-and-nine, which drops it to about a 20 percent chance of a conversion. This not only lowered their chances to get a first down, but also put them out of field-goal range. I give a lot of credit to them this week; they played a big part in our ability to shut-down the Dallas offense. I hope they'll keep the same focus for the Browns' game.

We achieved another goal this week (i.e., the defensive shut-out) on which we have a legitimate opportunity to expand. We are close to tying the 1976 Steelers' record of five shutouts in a season. Achieving this record is very important to both our defense and the team as a whole. Our guys know that it takes the entire team to accomplish a shutout, because there are a number of ways you can give up a score on good field position. Offensively, we are second in the NFL in time of possession, and our special teams have performed relatively well.

Good teams in the NFL don't take any other team for granted. We don't go into any game saying, "I don't think we need to do this particular thing this week because of who we're playing." It amuses me to hear members of the media comment that any given game will be "easy." While I have been in my share of games that have gone well, I have never been in any game that was "easy." We need to stay on course and make sure our guys are preparing for each opponent the same way. If we don't, we run the risk of leaving ourselves vulnerable.

We had a special opportunity Monday when Mike Singletary came in and spoke to our players. I told the guys on Sunday, in the locker room after the game, that Mike would be in to speak to them. When I see a player who is exhausted and fatigued from a game like we had just played sit up and take notice when I gave them the news, I knew I had garnered the response I wanted. The profound respect and admiration they have for a guy like Mike Singletary was evident. The message Mike delivered was direct and to the point: have passion for the game and be accountable to yourself and your teammates—both on and off the field. Words from which we can all learn.

Game result: Baltimore 44–Cleveland 7

BYE WEEK

The success we are experiencing this season has a lot to do with our personnel department—Ozzie Newsome, Phil Savage, James Harris, and staff. Our ability to draft well and our free-agent acquisitions are proving to be pivotal in the achievements that we are making. The longer I'm in this business, the more I recognize that it takes a joint effort by all departments to truly be a winning team in the NFL.

We are on pace right now to beat the all-time scoring-defense record. The record of a defense giving up the least amount of points goes back to a very good 1986 Chicago Bears team. This is a substantial goal for our defense—one that can provide a great deal of motivation. This type of production always leads to the debate of what is the greatest defense of all time (in a single season). Obviously, it is one of those questions that has no definitive answer. One of the great aspects of sports is that you can passionately debate one side or the other of a question of this nature, knowing there is no definitive answer.

Over the last few weeks, we have faced several different scenarios in our preparation. We've gone through a three-game progression of (1) beating a top opponent on the road; (2) handling that emotion, then coming back and dominating a challenging opponent in the national spotlight; and then, (3) defeating a struggling team, a scenario that gave us every reason and excuse to let up. Fortunately, the players have a lot of individual and team goals, which helps to snap them back into focusing on the task at hand.

Some of the things I try to make my players aware of are those factors that we can control and those that are completely out of our control. We are in a position to control whether or not we make the playoffs. We are in a position to control whether or not we have a home game in the playoffs. What is out of our hands is the ability to win our division. It will happen or it won't, depending on what Tennessee does. Accordingly, it's important for the players not to be distracted by those things we can't control.

With this being our bye week, it's going to give a lot of our guys a chance to heal from some of the injuries that have been bothering them. Everyone is looking forward to the break, a week off that has come at a pretty good time for us during the season. The key will be our ability to pick up where we left off and not lose the momentum that we have established.

NEXT OPPONENT: SAN DIEGO

We had workouts on Sunday and Monday with the players. They are very healthy right now and seem revived. It's really important for them to refocus on our next task (beating San Diego), especially now, after having this past week off. It is my understanding that the league has notified us that with a Ravens' win over San Diego this weekend we would qualify for the playoffs. This information will be a great motivating factor for our guys. From the end of last season, we have been very aggressive about our assertion that we felt we were a playoff-caliber team. With that goal in sight and two games still remaining in the season, reaching the playoffs would be quite gratifying for this team and indeed the organization as a whole.

The bye week gave me a little time to anticipate some of the factors that could prove to be a distraction to this team as we approach the end of the season and hopefully a playoff bid. These distractions include the upcoming Pro Bowl balloting, an increased level of media focus, and the holidays, just to name a few. At the top of this list are my concerns about those players who will be unrestricted free agents (UFA) at the conclusion of this season. Like every team in the league, the ability to succeed is based to a great degree on keeping the team together and focused. We have made it clear to the players that we want all of them back, but I think it would be unrealistic to feel that could happen.

Our plan is to begin discussions with all of our UFAs' representatives in order to alleviate any concern they might have about our intentions. My primary goal in this regard is to have our players understand that, yes, we want to keep the team intact, and we will proceed as best we can. But, our players are aware that we are somewhat limited because of the lack of data regarding what the "players' market" will be. In most cases, the players' representatives typically want to wait to negotiate anything until a player's market value has been established. It's important that we keep these discussions between our team's representatives and the players' representatives. It's my belief that discussions outside these boundaries become a distraction to everyone.

There is a time for *pay* and a time for *play*. In the offseason, you must address all the business aspects of the game and respect the player's right to better himself financially. We are, however, in the middle of a playoff run and it is clearly a time to *play*. The players and the organization must respect this if we have any hopes of achieving our goals this season.

Game result: Baltimore 24–San Diego 3

NEXT OPPONENT: ARIZONA

It's great that this team, this organization, and our fans can enjoy the first Baltimore playoff berth in 23 years. It has been a while, and it's great that the fans are having a good time with it. This idea of calling the playoffs "Festivus" and the Super Bowl "Festivus Maximus" is fun, and the fans should enjoy it. It has been a long time coming. It's my understanding that if we win these last two games, the least we'll have is one playoff game in Baltimore.

At practice, this team has shown me that they can enjoy what they do on a daily basis. They can have fun out at practice and be a little loose, but when it's time to step in and do their job during the course of practice, they can keep their focus. They are capable of understanding that this should be a fun time for them, this organization, and this city. They also know that at times, we have to hold such festivities at arms length. I think that a mistake a lot of teams make when they reach the playoffs for the first time is that they are too tight, and they put a little too much pressure on themselves for what making the playoffs represents. It's still just a game. It's the external things and how you handle them that determine success in the playoffs.

The fact that we'll more than likely have a playoff game on the road, and that our first week in the playoffs will probably involve a Saturday game is a scenario that this team needs to prepare for. Because the first week of the playoffs will, more than likely, be a short week, we'll need to adapt our preparation efforts and practice time. The fact that Monday was Pro Bowl balloting day is yet another example of a distraction. We are going to have some guys who are very deserving of going to the Pro Bowl who aren't going to be included for whatever reason. These guys are going to be very disappointed, and they are going to have to work through that individual disappointment to maintain what we have to get done this week (i.e., beat the Arizona Cardinals).

Being on the road in Arizona this week will be a great way for the players to remember what a "road show" has to be. For them to have the opportunity to face the mindset of playing another game on the road has come at a good time for our efforts to be properly prepared for the playoffs.

Our primary goal on Sunday is to win. If we have any other priorities that supersede that goal, we run the risk of getting a player hurt or not playing well as a team and losing the game. The players understand that they need to approach these last two games as we have every other game this season. This factor too can become a distraction for them, since they have a lot of people giving them advice and counsel at this point in the year, including their agent, the media, family, and friends. Everyone has a perspective about how he ought to approach these next two games, whether he should lay low and get healthy or save his efforts for the playoffs etc. It is my job to get this team ready for the playoffs, all the while keeping the primary object of the week in mind: beat Arizona.

Game result: Baltimore 13–Arizona 7

NEXT OPPONENT: THE NEW YORK JETS

For once, I agree with the headline that appeared in the *Baltimore Sun* after our game with Arizona: "Ravens Survive in the Desert." We had a lot of players who did not play their best game. There are a number of things we could have done better, but part of "the game" right now is surviving.

Jake Plummer proved to be very resourceful. He made some things happen for the Cardinals on Sunday, and it was the best I've seen him play. The thing we lacked the most in the game was explosive play downfield. Shockingly, however, we had 177 yards rushing, with Jamal Lewis rushing for 126 himself. For his performance, he received the offensive game ball. Jamie Sharper received the defensive game ball for what was probably the best single game he has had with the Ravens, while the special teams ball went to James Trapp.

As I said last week, being on the road in Arizona was a great way for our players to remember what a "road show" has to be. For our team to have the opportunity to face the mindset of playing another game on the road came at a good time for us in preparation for the playoffs. Regardless of how it looked out there, a number of teams (Oakland, Denver, Miami, and the Jets) would have loved to have a 13–7 win last weekend. I told the players that if they learn nothing more from me other than to appreciate every win, then my time with them will have been successful. So, we'll take this win; we are glad to have it. We'll make the corrections and move on.

We have the Jets this Sunday. I don't worry too much about the emotions our players bring on game day; our players come to play. My interest is the week leading up to the game. Trying to keep distractions to a minimum and making sure that the "value" of the game doesn't lessen for our players are the factors on which I focus. This game is going to be a great learning experience for our players. They are going to match up against a desperate team trying to make the playoffs, coming in with a lot of passion.

On another note, I'm glad to share that every member of this team will be out in the community (some on Monday and the others on Tuesday) visiting local hospitals, children and families, getting ready for the holidays. We've had a great response from the players and the community to our "NFL/Raven Tuesdays," and I think that speaks well of the character of the players we have here, and I congratulate them.

Game result: Baltimore 34–New York Jets 20

NEXT OPPONENT: DENVER

Sunday's game against the New York Jets was, in my opinion, as close to a playoff atmosphere as you can get without it actually being a playoff game. We overcame a lot; from a teaching perspective while going into the playoffs, we got a lot accomplished concerning the things that we had to face against the Jets. That game could be very typical of a playoff game, where you have two teams battling with turnovers and the emotional swing of being on top and losing the lead.

I've been asked about the "weaknesses in our defense exposed in the Jets game because of what they did down the field." In reality, if you throw the ball 69 times in the NFL, you're going to move the ball. With 69 passes, everything you are shows up, good and bad. The bottom line is that we won the game. The Jets did some really good things; they spread it out and made some good throws. But we responded, and I'm very proud of the way our guys came back. The Jets had a lot of turnovers, and we held them on some key third and fourth downs when we had to. Our players don't have anything to be ashamed of, and no, I don't think we revealed any weaknesses.

We are proud to be 12–4. We have the second best record in the NFL, and I hope that the players take some time to appreciate what we have done so far, especially the defensive players who broke NFL records for total points and total yards rushing allowed. Those are substantial accomplishments, and something they can be proud of for a long time. But there's an understanding around here that that's ancient history now that we are moving into a "second season" with the playoffs.

The emphasis we've put on special teams (i.e., changes that we've made in personnel and practice) was reflected in the play we saw on Sunday. Special teams should play a huge part in the outcome of the games we face in the playoffs. With great strides made by Jermaine Lewis, that entire group will enter the playoffs with some added confidence.

We had great energy from the fans on Sunday. I liked the intensity that our fans showed and the fact that they hung around until the end of the game. Although we had the Jets running a "no huddle offense," our fans were able to cause some problems for them with the noise that they made. I think if our fans can double our efforts (as we will with our players), their we'll have that much more of an advantage when facing Denver next week.

With what we've done in the past two weeks, while there are a number of things that we could do better, some factors aren't as bad as they seem. Trent knows there are some things that he has to do better, and the guys around him also need to improve. We are going to have to do better offensively. There is no doubt about that, so that'll be our focus this week.

With Denver this weekend, I feel we are facing the best offense in the league. Without question, they will move the ball. I think they have the most comprehensive balance in the league between running the ball (when they want to run the ball) and big receivers. In reality, we won't shut them down. They are going to make some big plays, but on the other hand, this is also a team that's second only to us in turnover ratio. In other words, they get turnovers and they turn the ball over at about the rate we do. With their offense facing this defense, it should prove to be an intriguing game.

Game result: Baltimore 21–Denver 3

NEXT OPPONENT: TENNESSEE

Sunday was a special day for this city and this organization. I had a chance to go home on Sunday night and celebrate New Year's Eve with my family. Watching the reports on the game gave me a better appreciation of how much this win meant to the city of Baltimore.

It's amazing: in 24 hours we went from being a team that had never been in the playoffs before to a team that now has playoff-win experience. There are a lot of organizations, during both this year and in previous years, where this kind of success in the playoffs takes a while. What you'll find is that there are typically stages a team will go through where they "take their lumps" (i.e., losing a game or two) before they learn what it takes to win at this level, particularly against a championship-caliber team like the Broncos.

We had a mandatory (weight) lift session on Monday and to give credit to Denver, our guys are as tired, sore, and beat-up as you can expect after a first-round playoff game. We are at a point right now where we're one game away from going to the AFC Championship game and that's an enticing thought. It feels good to go into this game with some momentum, but our players are tired and sore, and it's going to take every bit of effort this week to get things back underneath us.

Fortunately for us, our next game is against a team we are very familiar with (the Tennessee Titans) at a place we've played before. For some reason, we've always matched up well against Tennessee. Our teams respect each other a great deal, regardless of what's said or written throughout this week. Typically, with rivalries like this, you see some animosity manifest during the game, but I haven't seen that between these two teams. This type of respect is what playoff football is all about.

Since our two teams know each other so well, such familiarity makes our preparation efforts both easier and tougher at the same time. When you face an opponent that is not as familiar with your scheme, there are certain things you can do to counter your tendencies. Such an option is diminished when you play a team as familiar to us as are the Titans. They are familiar with the way we adjust from one game to the next over a span of time.

Having a game at home is a real advantage. I can't believe that Tennessee's crowd was louder than they were the last time we played them. They were incessant from the starting kickoff to the end of the game, reaffirming what it means to play on the road. Every team has a certain approach for handling crowd noise. What is difficult is the emotional and physical wear and tear on fighting a team the caliber of the Titans and their fans all day long.

Steve McNair has elevated his game. Before, it was "just keep him in the pocket," but now he's able to hurt teams down the field. As a result, we need to be cognizant of that fact. McNair, in my opinion, is one of the premier quarterbacks in the league and has been the biggest difference in the games we've played against the Titans.

This game is about the talent of the players. My value as a coach comes during the week. The battle I fight each week is that of keeping meetings timely (so we don't wear the guys out), keeping the players focused, and making sure our players have all the information they need to mentally prepare for the game. Both teams have talent and a very healthy respect for each other.

Game result: Baltimore 24–Tennessee 10

NEXT OPPONENT: OAKLAND

Coming home from Tennessee on Sunday night, we were greeted by several thousand people at Baltimore–Washington International Airport. The emotion they displayed leaves no question in my mind about how much this community appreciates this team and what we have accomplished. I want to thank them all for that, because it was an experience I'll never forget.

We played a hard fought game Sunday against a heck of an opponent, which is exactly what we expected. Our guys went in there against all the odds and with the utmost confidence in their abilities. This team has character and chemistry, and while some call us arrogant, it's my opinion that we need to have that kind of brash mentality during a road game when you advance to this level.

I'm very proud of Anthony Mitchell and the impact he had on the outcome of this game. With Anthony having had only limited playing time, he stepped up for us in the most dramatic of circumstances.

So much of the Titans' game plan is to dump the ball to Eddie George underneath, an action that isolated he and Ray Lewis for most of the game. Like a prizefighter, Eddie came into our locker room after the game to congratulate Ray and the team. His actions showed a lot of class and a strong character that's good for the game.

We are again on the road this weekend in what's called the "Black Hole." This is another business trip for us where we've got to maintain focus. To prepare for a cross-country trip to Oakland, we are going to cut back on practice slightly. This is a tired group of players, and I'd rather do too little than too much. Therefore, Thursday will be a regular practice, while Wednesday and Friday will consist of more mental preparation.

Of the remaining teams, I feel Oakland is the most balanced. I have a great deal of admiration for Rich Gannon. He's a tremendous athlete who has raised his level of play since the year I spent with him in 1992. I've said before that I don't feel there is any dominant quarterback play in the league right now, but I think Rich is as close to that as I've seen all year long.

We'll take a different approach with regard to game planning. Unlike the Titans (where we were more familiar with their game plan), this will be more of a challenge for us in trying to figure out what the Raiders' tendencies are.

Making it to the AFC Championship game in my second year as a head coach has been a humbling experience. It has made me realize just how many people it takes to reach this level. From ownership to the administration, all aspects have to unite. As I've said before, character and chemistry describe this team. This organization has it, and there is no denying it.

Game result: Baltimore 16–Oakland 3

NEXT OPPONENT: THE NEW YORK GIANTS IN SUPER BOWL XXXV

Volumes have been written that explain why a team's ability to handle the peripheral circumstances surrounding the Super Bowl are the key to success in the game itself. As we work our way through those circumstances and prepare for our encounter with the New York Giants in Super Bowl XXXV, I would certainly agree with that assessment. At the heart of it all remains the game. The preparation, the practice, and the implementation of the game plan on game day are all very familiar to the players and coaches who are participating in this extraordinary event.

The team that has the ability to maintain its focus and routine in its preparation and execution of the game plan has a clear-cut advantage in the game. Our two teams are very evenly matched without any obvious dominance by either team. Therefore, it only makes sense that we look for the intangibles as being a key factor in the game.

The way we have approached the two weeks leading up to the Super Bowl was decidedly different than that of the Giants. The Giants, being the number one seed in the NFC and being able to play two home games, could approach the two weeks differently than the Ravens. Because we were the fourth seed, we had to play three games, with the last two on the road. We had to travel across the country three times on a long flight for the AFC championship game. I feel that this team needed to rehab and recuperate physically and emotionally from the arduous schedule that got us here. As much as from a mental standpoint as from a physical one, we'll keep our practices short and specific. I chose to give the players last Sunday off, which was the first Sunday they've been able to spend with their families since August, as an additional way of allowing them to rest and recuperate.

We came down a day later than the Giants did because I wanted to keep our players as close as I could to the normal routine we followed during the regular season. We began the week with a weight workout on Monday morning, and after an amazing pep rally in downtown Baltimore, we departed for Tampa. Tuesday was a day off, not withstanding the incredible experience of participating in the NFL media day at the stadium. By Wednesday, we put the peripheral things involving any game behind us. This approach allowed the players and coaches to focus on the weekly routine of Wednesday, Thursday, and Friday preparation for a Sunday game. The only difference was that I've felt the need for my team to practice in shells on Wednesday to give the quarterbacks and the wide receivers the feel of performing in pads in order to enhance the timing that they are going to need for Sunday's game. I did so, not expecting to raise the physical level of practice (particularly in the front seven), but simply to enable them to get the feel of their pads again. Given the weather in Tampa, since it is so much warmer than it is in Baltimore, it was also beneficial to provide the players with an opportunity to get a good sweat and physical workout.

Experiencing the first two days at the Super Bowl has been a great learning experience for my team. In the college game, when a team earns the right to go to a bowl game, many coaches will tell you that a team's extra practice time is a great advantage for the next year's team. It gives the coaching staff additional chances to evaluate and enhance the abilities of their current players, thus leading to the observation that "success breeds success." Likewise in the NFL, the experience of going to the Super Bowl is like no other. When teams talk about there being an advantage associated with having playoff experience, they aren't talking about the actual game experience, but the experience of dealing with the circumstances that come up from one game to the next.

The experiences my players have had in preparing for the Super Bowl will be far reaching in years to come with regard to their understanding of what the dynamic of this league is and how and what you have to do to be successful in the long run. Now, when we talk about handling the pressures of the playoffs, dealing with the distractions of the media, family members, and all the other demands that are put on them—on top of the pressure of the game—the players will know first hand what we are talking about. They will more readily know how to prepare for these same circumstances in the future.

Game result: Baltimore 34–New York 7

index